Public Opinion
and the
Supreme Court

Public Opinion and the Supreme Court

THOMAS R. MARSHALL

University of Texas at Arlington

Boston
UNWIN HYMAN
London   Sydney   Wellington

Unwin Hyman, Inc.
8 Winchester Place, Winchester, MA 01890, USA

Published by the Academic Division of
Unwin Hyman, Ltd,
15/17 Broadwick Street, London W1V 1FP, UK

Allen & Unwin Australia Pty Ltd,
8 Napier Street, North Sydney, NSW 2060, Australia

Allen & Unwin (New Zealand) Ltd,
in association with the Port Nicholson Press Ltd,
60 Cambridge Terrace, Wellington, New Zealand

First published in 1989

Library of Congress Cataloging-in-Publication Data

Marshall, Thomas R., 1949–
  Public opinion and the Supreme Court / Thomas R. Marshall.
    p. cm.
Bibliography: p.
Includes index.
ISBN 0–04–497046–3. ISBN 0–04–497047–1 (pbk.)
1. United States. Supreme Court—Public opinion. 2. Judicial
process—United States—Public opinion. 3. Public opinion—United
States. I. Title.
KF8748.M287 1988
347.73'26—dc19
[347.30735]   88–5431
                                                                    CIP

British Library Cataloguing in Publication Data

Marshall, Thomas R., 1949–
Public Opinion and the Supreme Court.
1. United States Supreme Court. Decisions.
Formulation of role of public opinion
I. Title
347.307'26
ISBN 0–04–497046–3
0–04–497047–1 Pbk

Typeset in 10 on 12 point Palatino
and printed in Great Britain by
Billing and Sons Ltd, London and Worcester

Contents

List of Figures

List of Tables

Preface

Public Opinion and the Supreme Court asks two questions: first, how accurately has the modern Supreme Court reflected public opinion; and second, why? The results suggest that since the mid-1930s the Supreme Court has been an essentially majoritarian institution in American politics. Most modern Supreme Court rulings reflect public opinion, and overall, the modern Court has been roughly as majoritarian as other American policy makers.

The relatively high level of agreement between Supreme Court decisions and mass public opinion does not result from the Court's ability to influence (or "manipulate") American public opinion. Most Supreme Court decisions have little influence upon public opinion. Neither can the Court's majoritarian behavior be explained solely by political realignments, nor by patterns among the individual justices' backgrounds, tenure, or on-the-Court roles. Rather, the modern Court's pronounced tendency to reflect American public opinion results from a combination of factors — chiefly, judicial deference to federal laws and policies, the Court's deference to popular opinion during crisis times, and the greater stability of those Court rulings that reflect prevailing public opinion.

This research is based upon comparisons between specific Supreme Court rulings and nationwide public opinion polls from the mid-1930s through the final Burger Court term in 1986. I am greatly indebted to the polling organizations whose efforts during the last half century have made this research possible.

I am also indebted to many people for their suggestions, including Greg Caldeira, Richard Cole, Lee Epstein, Chris Harris, Beth Henschen, and Elliot Slotnick. I also express my appreciation to the National Endowment for the Humanities, the Roper Center at the University of Connecticut, and to the many authors upon whose work I have relied.

This book is for Aram, Erica, Deacon, and Sara.

CHAPTER ONE

Public Opinion, Judicial Review, and American Democracy

Judicial Review and Representation

The Debate over Judicial Review

Whether the United States Supreme Court does — or should — reflect majority public opinion has been a recurring controversy in American political thought. This issue has divided democratic theorists, practicing politicians, and Supreme Court justices themselves ever since the Constitution was first debated two centuries ago.

In his well-known essay, "Federalist 78," Alexander Hamilton wrote that the Supreme Court would be "an excellent barrier" against changing public opinion and against "the encroachments and oppressions of the representative body."[1] To Hamilton, the Supreme Court should not reflect popular opinion. Rather, the Court should serve "as an essential safeguard against the effects of occasional ill humors in the society."[2]

Hamilton argued that the Court should resist a political majority's "dangerous innovations" and its "serious oppressions of the minor party in the community." Manned by a well-educated elite, who enjoyed irreducible salaries and life tenure (during good behavior), the Supreme Court would be well positioned to resist shifts in popular opinion and to reject policies that ran counter to the Constitution's intent. When a law or policy was "incompatible with the provisions in the existing Constitution," Hamilton urged the Supreme Court to

1

exercise judicial review and "to declare all acts contrary to the manifest tenor of the Constitution void."[3]

Hamilton's view that the Supreme Court should restrain popular opinion might have been a result, in part, of the political and economic turmoil of the 1780s.[4] In part, Hamilton's views also reflected a then-widely-held "classical" view of public opinion. During the 1600s and 1700s most political writers viewed mass public opinion as based largely upon emotion, not reason; as unstable and easily changeable; as coercive of individuality; and, very frequently, as contrary to higher, principled views of law and rights. From this classical perspective, direct expressions of mass public opinion presented a serious threat to political and economic rights.[5]

During the late 1780s anti-federalist opponents of the proposed Constitution shared Hamilton's belief that the Supreme Court would curb popularly elected legislatures and public opinion. Unlike Hamilton, however, anti-federalists opposed the creation of an unelected (and, in their view, undemocratic), life-tenured national Court equipped with the power of judicial review. The prospect that the Supreme Court would exercise judicial review over congressional laws or presidential actions apparently played only a small role in the anti-federalists' complaints. The fear that the Court would review and overturn the actions of state assemblies, judges, and juries, however, was raised as a complaint against the proposed Constitution in virtually every state debate over ratification.[6]

Just as the debate over judicial review divided politicians during the 1780s, so, too, has it divided Americans over the last two centuries. Whenever the Supreme Court has been most active in striking down federal, state, or local laws, criticism of the Court has grown more vocal. During the late 1800s and early 1900s, the 1930s, and the 1950s and 1960s, for example, the Court's critics have argued that the Court should be more restrained in overturning the decisions of popularly elected officials.

At least three fundamental challenges have been raised to the Supreme Court's exercise of judicial review and its use of judicial activism. First, did the Constitution's authors actually intend the Court to exercise judicial review? Second, are judicial review and judicial activism compatible with democratic norms? Third, is the Supreme Court countermajoritarian —

2

does the Court, in fact, frustrate the will of popular majorities?

Whether or not the Constitution's authors intended the Supreme Court to exercise judicial review at all has frequently been debated. Alexander Hamilton's essay, "Federalist 78,"[7] or Articles III and VI and the *Judiciary Act* of 1787[8] are often cited as evidence that judicial review was originally intended. Other scholars have found early support for judicial review in the customs of the Colonial era,[9] pre-Constitutional practices in several states,[10] the constitutional debates,[11] debates of state ratifying conventions,[12] or reactions to the exercise of judicial review in early Congresses.[13]

Other scholars, however, have disputed whether judicial review was, in fact, originally intended. They have argued that many early political leaders explicitly opposed judicial review,[14] that the practice was neither common among states before the Constitution[15] nor particularly popular as a theory,[16] that judicial review was not originally intended to permit Supreme Court review over state laws on Bill of Rights issues,[17] that the Constitution's intent is unclear,[18] that the early Supreme Court seldom exercised judicial review,[19] or that the early Congress did not approve of the practice.[20] Yet other scholars have remained skeptical of both arguments, claiming either that the issue simply remains unsettled[21] or that the founders' intentions are essentially unknowable.[22]

The second question — whether the Supreme Court's use of judicial review is consistent with democratic norms — has also been widely debated. Critics who define democracy chiefly in terms of majority rule, popular suffrage, and political equality usually describe the Court as an undemocratic institution, one that is remote from popular control.[23] Still other critics have argued that the Court's status as a democratic institution cannot be defended on the grounds that the Court has historically promoted political equality,[24] that the Court's powers were expressly agreed to by the people,[25] or that Supreme Court justices have special knowledge of substantive democratic values.[26] Nor, these critics argue, can the Court and judicial review simply be defined as democratic because they are components of polities commonly described as democracies.

Those who have defended the Court and judicial review as consistent with democratic norms often reply that simple, unlimited majority rule has seldom, if ever, been the sole definition of a democracy.[28] Indeed, some authors have argued, American democratic theory is especially antimajoritarian.[29] Further, if civil rights and liberties are important democratic values,[30] then judges may be uniquely well-qualified to promote these values.[31] Some democratic theorists further contend that the Supreme Court frequently promotes political access and clears the channels of political change.[32] Finally, other scholars have argued that the Court and judicial review are democratic either because they are "ultimately" responsive to popular control,[33] because other policy makers in recognized democracies are equally remote from direct popular control,[34] or because the Supreme Court's role has been authorized by time and popular consent.[35]

In short, democratic theorists disagree on the questions of whether or not judicial review was originally intended, and also on whether or not judicial review can be described as democratic. Far less controversy, however, exists on the third issue. Almost all constitutional scholars and democratic theorists agree that the Supreme Court is, either in process or in substance, a countermajoritarian institution.[36]

In a formal or procedural sense, Supreme Court policy making is obviously and inevitably countermajoritarian. The Supreme Court may review, and, in many instances, strike down laws or policies enacted by legislatures and executives that are far more directly responsible to political majorities than is the Supreme Court itself.[37] Admittedly, the election and decision-making procedures of popularly elected legislatures and executives are by no means purely majoritarian, but the Supreme Court is even more remote from public opinion and majority control.[38] In this purely formal and procedural sense, judicial review and judicial activism are inevitably countermajoritarian.

Recasting the Argument: An Empirical Approach

This formal and procedural approach, however, cannot adequately address the question of whether or not judicial review is countermajoritarian. Comparing specific Supreme Court decisions with actual nationwide public opinion polls taken at the time when the Court's decisions are handed down is a different, more thorough approach. From this alternate viewpoint, a *majoritarian* Court ruling is one that, in substance, agrees with a contemporary public opinion majority (or at least, a plurality). By contrast, a *countermajoritarian* Court ruling is one that disagrees with a contemporary public opinion majority (or plurality).[39]

This alternate approach has several readily apparent advantages. It avoids the self-evident and largely uninteresting answer provided by the formal or procedural approach. At the same time, it avoids making an implicit, ipso facto assumption that the policies of the popularly elected branches necessarily represent a nationwide public opinion majority.[40] As Chapter Four argues, this ipso facto assumption is often unwarranted.

This alternate approach has several other advantages. By examining a relatively large and diverse sample of Supreme Court decisions, it is possible to analyze whether the Court's majoritarian behavior varies over time, between types of cases, between controversies originating at the federal versus state or local level, or between the Court's judicial restraint and activist rulings.[41] This methodology can also be extended to the individual justice, to examine whether some types of justices are more or less majoritarian than others.[42] Extending the methodology yet further makes it possible to test other commonly advanced hypotheses — for example, that Supreme Court decisions themselves influence mass public opinion,[43] or that the Court's countermajoritarian rulings less frequently withstand the test of time.[44]

A specific example may help to clarify this alternate approach. Assume, for example, that the Supreme Court chooses to review a (hypothetical) federal law that is itself consistent with a contemporary nationwide public opinion majority. If the Supreme Court exercises judicial restraint — in effect, upholding the law — it will also make a majoritarian ruling (that is, one that agrees with mass public opinion). By contrast, a judicial activist ruling that strikes down the law as unconstitutional will be a countermajoritarian decision.

Now, consider a second (and still hypothetical) federal law that is inconsistent with nationwide public opinion.[45] If the Court exercises judicial restraint and upholds this second law, the Court has disagreed with majority public opinion and made a decision that we must classify as countermajoritarian. By contrast, an activist decision to overturn this second law would be a majoritarian ruling (that is, one that agrees with nationwide public opinion). In short, the terms "judicial restraint" and "judicial activism" are not simply synonymous with "majoritarianism" or "countermajoritarianism" respectively.

To date, few discussions of the Supreme Court's majoritarian, versus countermajoritarian behavior have taken this more direct approach. True, several authors have argued that specific Court decisions did or did not agree with public opinion, but they do so without relying on any actual poll data.[46] Only a handful of published articles, however, have directly compared scientific, nationwide polls with specific Supreme Court rulings.[47]

In part, the infrequent attention to mass public opinion may be due to the relatively recent origin of scientific public opinion polls. Until the mid-1930s public opinion polling did not follow scientific, random-sampling methods. The few polls that were conducted were chiefly concerned with predicting election outcomes.[48] As a result, the present methodology cannot be applied for three-quarters of the Supreme Court's history. Even after the mid-1930s, scientific polls often have been unavailable.[49]

Many Court scholars also might have assumed that pollsters would have asked few questions that could be directly compared to Supreme Court decisions. Yet, in fact, reputable pollsters have often asked poll items that tap prominent Supreme Court cases. Indeed, this should not be surprising, since pollsters and their news media clients seek to survey public attitudes on prominent controversies.[50] And, as de Tocqueville observed (a full century before the advent of modern polling!), few major political controversies in America do not eventually become constitutional issues, as well.[51]

This book is based upon 146 instances in which part or all of a specific Supreme Court decision can be directly matched or compared to a specific poll item drawn from a scientific, nationwide poll. These 146 matches include a diverse sample of Supreme Court decisions from the mid-1930s through the 1985–1986 term.[52]

Together the 146 matches include a wide range of substantive issues and distributions of public opinion. The 146 matches include controversies from both the federal, state, and local levels; both judicial activist and judicial restraint decisions; and

6

both unanimous and nonunanimous decisions. The cases range from the Hughes Court's historic "switch in time" through the last Burger Court term. Taken together, these 146 matches permit a much broader analysis of the modern Court's majoritarian behavior than has been heretofore possible.

Summary of Chapters

Chapter Two moves from normative arguments to a more empirical focus, and specifies twelve possible linkages between mass public opinion and Supreme Court decisions. The twelve linkages vary considerably; some are simple and direct, and others assume several intermediary variables. Together, the linkages incorporate many different variables, among them, the state of mass public opinion, political socialization, the policy-making process, judicial appointments, on-the-Court roles, judicial norms, periodic realignments, a justice's length of tenure, short- or long-term opinion manipulation by the Court, the influence of interest groups, and the stability of Court decisions over time.

Chapter Three suggests that the modern Court has developed four major theories to explain what role public opinion should play in judicial policy making. Most Supreme Court references to mass public opinion refer only to normative or theoretical arguments and not to actual measures of public attitudes (such as specific polls). Indeed, the modern Court has seldom attached much weight to polls themselves. Perhaps surprisingly, each of the Court's four theories clearly predated the advent of scientific public opinion polling.

Chapter Four indicates that over three-fifths of the modern Court's decisions reflect public opinion majorities or pluralities. While precise comparisons are difficult to make, the modern Court appears to be as majoritarian as other American policy makers. The results provide little support for the argument that the Supreme Court is essentially a countermajoritarian institution in American democracy. Indeed, about half of even the Court's judicial activist rulings have reflected nationwide public opinion. The Court has been especially majoritarian both when faced by crisis times and when reviewing federal laws and policies.

Chapter Five shifts the analysis to the 36 individual justices who have served on the modern Court. While some justices may have been considerably more majoritarian than others, few of their background experiences or on-the-Court traits are strongly related to their majoritarian behavior. Justices from the most prestigious law schools, politically moderate justices, Chief Justices, and close presidential advisors all appear to be somewhat more majoritarian than other justices. Overall, however, the patterns among individual justices' traits are not especially strong.

Chapter Six provides evidence that the Supreme Court seldom influences (or "manipulates") mass public opinion, either in the short term or in the long term. Little empirical evidence exists to suggest that most Supreme Court decisions markedly affect mass public opinion. Few Court decisions are widely perceived, and the Court itself has enjoyed only moderate popularity in recent decades. There appears to be no evidence of strong pre- to post-decision opinion shifts toward the Court's announced positions, except in cases where the Court makes liberal, activist rulings.

Chapter Seven indicates that Supreme Court rulings that initially agree with mass public opinion endure longer than those that do not. Indeed, the Court's agreement with popular opinion is one of a bare handful of variables that significantly affects the stability of Supreme Court decisions.

Chapter Eight reconsiders the twelve linkages from Chapter Two, in light of the conclusions reached in Chapters Three through Seven. Since no empirical support could be found for seven of the twelve linkages that were originally proposed, this chapter offers a simplified linkage model. The five remaining linkages are substantially modified and the resulting linkage model better fits the available data.

References

1 Alexander Hamilton, "Federalist 78 — The Judges as Guardians of the Constitution," in Benjamin Wright, ed., *The Federalist*, (Cambridge, Mass.: Belknap, 1961), 489–496.
2 Public opinion has been defined in many different ways. Here, the term "public opinion" indicates attitudes held by the mass

public on issues of political interest. For a review, see Harwood Childs, *Public Opinion* (Princeton, N.J.: D. Van Nostrand, 1965), 14–26.

3 Judicial review refers to the Supreme Court's power to consider laws and policies of other branches of government and invalidate them if they violate the Constitution. Judicial activism refers to the Court's decision to strike down a disputed law (or policy) as unconstitutional. Judicial restraint refers to the Court's decision not to strike down a law (or policy) as unconstitutional.

4 Jacob Cooke, *Alexander Hamilton* (New York: Charles Scribner's Sons, 1982), 31–57.

5 For a discussion of the classical view of public opinion, see Elizabeth Noelle Neumann, "Public Opinion and the Classical Tradition: A Reevaluation," *Public Opinion Quarterly* 43 (Summer 1977): 143–156; Hans Spier, "Historical Development of Public Opinion," *American Journal of Sociology* 55 (January 1950): 378–388; Paul A. Palmer, "The Concept of Public Opinion in Political Theory," in *Essays in History and Political Theory in Honor of Charles H. McIlwain* (Cambridge, Mass.: Harvard University Press, 1936), 230–257; Ernst Vollrath, "That all governments rest on opinion," *Social Research* 43 (Spring 1976): 46–61; and Hannah Arendt, *On Revolution* (New York: Viking, 1963), 86–90. For a discussion of the classical tradition in public opinion, as applied in modern Supreme Court decisions, see Chapter Three, at notes 147–174.

6 For a review of the anti-federalists' positions, see Jackson Turner Main, *The Antifederalists: Critics of the Constitution* (Chapel Hill: University of North Carolina Press, 1961), 124–127, 155–160; John Lewis, *Anti-Federalists Versus Federalists* (San Francisco: Chandler, 1967), 10, 184, 288; Cecelia Kenyon, ed., *The AntiFederalists* (Indianapolis: Bobbs-Merrill, 1966), 9–14, 51–52, 398, 413–414; and Alpheus T. Mason, *The States Rights Debate: Antifederalism and the Constitution* (Englewood Cliffs, N.J.: Prentice-Hall, 1964), 4–13, 104–110.

7 Alexander Bickel, *The Least Dangerous Branch*, 2nd ed., (New Haven, Conn.: Yale University Press, 1968), 16; and George Mace, "The Antidemocratic Character of Judicial Review," *California Law Review* 60 (June 1972): 1140–1149.

8 Charles Black, *The People and the Court* (New York: Macmillan, 1960), 6–25, 178, 183; Jesse Choper, *Judicial Review and the National Political Process — A Functional Reconsideration of the Role of the Supreme Court* (Chicago: University of Chicago Press, 1980), 64; William Bishin, "Judicial Review in Democratic Theory," *Southern California Law Review* 50 (September 1977): 1099; *West Virginia State Board of Education v. Barnette* (1943), 638; and Herbert Wechsler, "Toward Neutral Principles of Constitutional Law," *Harvard Law Review* 73 (November 1959): 4.

9 James Bradley Thayer, "The Origin and Scope of the American Doctrine of Constitutional Law," *Harvard Law Review* 7 (October 1893): 129–156.

10 Geoffrey Hazard, Jr. "The Supreme Court as a Legislature," *Cornell Law Review* 64 (November 1978): 1–27; Eugene Rostow, "The Democratic Character of Judicial Review," *Harvard Law Review* 66 (December 1952): 195–196; and Mason, *The States Rights Debate*, 11.

11 Rostow, "The Democratic Character of Judicial Review," 195–196; Henry Abraham, *The Judicial Process*, 4th ed., (New York: Oxford University Press, 1980), 322–332; Thomas Grey, "Do We Have An Unwritten Constitution?" *Stanford Law Review* 27 (February 1975): 715–718; Main, *The AntiFederalists*, 125–126, 155–160; Mason, *The States Rights Debate*, 104–110; Lewis, *AntiFederalists Versus Federalists*, 184; and Kenyon, *The AntiFederalists*, 45–52, 414.

12 Rostow, "The Democratic Character of Judicial Review," 195–196.

13 Bickel, *The Least Dangerous Branch*, 21; Charles Warren, *The Supreme Court in United States History*, vol. 1, 2nd ed., (Boston: Little, Brown, 1937), 62–69, 82–83.

14 Mace, "The Antidemocratic Character of Judicial Review," 1143–1145;Raoul Berger, *Government by Judiciary — The Transformation of the Fourteenth Amendment* (Cambridge, Mass.: Harvard University Press, 1977), 283–299, 351–396; Philip Kurland, *Politics, the Constitution, and the Warren Court* (Chicago, University of Chicago Press, 1970), 18–25.

15 Thayer, "The Origin and Scope."

16 Thayer, "The Origin and Scope."

17 Michael Perry, *The Constitution, the Courts, and Human Rights* (New Haven, Conn.: Yale University Press, 1982), 61–75.

18 Bickel, *The Least Dangerous Branch*, 1–33.

19 Hazard, "The Supréme Court as a Legislature"; Berger, *Government by Judiciary*, 252–258, 355.

20 Bickel, *The Least Dangerous Branch*, 21.

21 Leonard Levy, *Judgments: Essays in American Constitutional History* (Chicago: Quadrangle Books, 1972), 24–63; Perry, *The Constitution, the Courts, and Human Rights*, 32.

22 Paul Brest, "The Misconceived Quest for the Original Understanding," *Boston University Law Review* 60 (March 1980): 104–238; and "The Fundamental Rights Controversy: The Essential Contradictions of Normative Constitutional Scholarship," *Yale Law Journal* 90 (April 1981): 1063–1109; Ronald Dworkin, "The Forum of Principle," *New York University Law Review* 56 (May/June 1981): 469–518; and Perry, *The Constitution, the Courts, and Human Rights*, 32.

23 Bickel, *The Least Dangerous Branch*, 18–21; Clifton McClesky, "Judicial Review in a Democracy: A Dissenting Opinion," *Houston Law Review* 3 (Winter 1966): 354–366; Kurland, *Politics, the Constitution, and the Warren Court*, 18, 201–204; Wallace Mendelson, "Learned Hand: Patient Democrat," *Harvard Law Review*, 76 (December 1962): 322–335; Ward Elliot, *The Rise of Guardian Democracy: The Supreme Court's Role in Voting Rights Disputes, 1845–1969* (Cambridge, Mass.: Harvard University Press, 1974), 3–8; Mace, "The

Antidemocratic Character of Judicial Review," 1145; Robert Bork, "Neutral Principles and Some First Amendment Problems" *Indiana Law Journal* 47 (Fall 1971): 2; Jesse Choper, "The Supreme Court and the Political Branches: Democratic Theory and Practice," *University of Pennsylvania Law Review* 122 (April 1974): 811, 848–855; John Hart Ely, *Democracy and Distrust: A Theory of Judicial Review* (Cambridge, Mass.: Harvard University Press, 1980), 67; and Wallace Mendelson, "Mr. Justice Frankfurter and the Process of Judicial Review," *University of Pennsylvania Law Review* 1003 (December 1954): 300–301, 318–320.

24 Henry Steele Commager, "Judicial Review and Democracy," *Virginia Quarterly Review* 19 (Summer 1943): 422–428; and Robert Dahl, *A Preface to Democratic Theory* (Chicago: University of Chicago Press, 1956), 58–59.

25 Choper, "The Supreme Court and the Political Branches," 854–855.

26 Alexander Bickel, *The Supreme Court and the Idea of Progress*, 2nd ed., (New Haven, Conn.: Yale University Press, 1978), 10–43; and McClesky, "Judicial Review in a Democracy."

27 Mace, "The Antidemocratic Character of Judicial Review," 1143; and Hazard, "The Supreme Court as a Legislature," 9–10.

28 Dahl, *A Preface to Democratic Theory*, 36–37; Bishin, "Judicial Review in Democratic Theory," 1109–1117, 1129–1133; Choper, "The Supreme Court and the Political Branches," 812–813, 858; and Ronald Dworkin, *Taking Rights Seriously* (Cambridge, Mass.: Harvard University Press, 1977), 137–142.

29 Jesse Choper, "On the Warren Court and Judicial Review," *Catholic University Law Review* 17 (1967): 20–43; "The Supreme Court and the Political Branches"; and *Judicial Review and the National Political Process*, 60–122; Ely, *Democracy and Distrust*, 84–94; Grey, "Do We Have An Unwritten Constitution?"; Dworkin, *Taking Rights Seriously*, 142; Harry Wellington, "The Nature of Judicial Review," *Yale Law Journal*, 91 (January 1982): 487–488; and Brest, "The Fundamental Rights Controversy," 1096–1104.

For two related views, see Laurence Tribe, *American Constitutional Law* (Mineola, N.Y.: Foundation Press, 1978), 51; and Martin Shapiro, *Freedom of Speech: The Supreme Court and Judicial Review* (Englewood Cliffs, N.J.: Prentice-Hall, 1966), 5–45.

30 Rostow, "The Democratic Character of Judicial Review"; Choper, *Judicial Review and the National Political Process*, 9, 79–122; David A. J. Richards, "Sexual Autonomy and the Constitutional Right to Privacy," *Hastings Law Journal* 30 (March 1979). For discussions of natural rights, reserved rights, and fundamental rights in American political thought, see Clinton Rossiter, *Seedtime of the Republic* (New York: Harcourt, Brace, 1953), 362–401; Henry Steele Commager, "Constitutional History and the Higher Law," in Conyers Read, ed., *The Constitution Reconsidered* (New York: Columbia University Press, 1938), 225–245; Bishin, "Judicial Review in Democratic Theory," 1107, 1130; Wellington, "The

Nature of Judicial Review," 706–707, 715–717; Rostow, "The Democratic Character of Judicial Review," 195–197, 210; and Choper, "The Supreme Court and the Political Branches," 812.

31 Black, *The People and the Court*, 46, 176; Bishin, "Judicial Review in Democratic Theory," 1129–1134; Perry, *The Constitution, the Courts, and Human Rights*, 97, 102–111; Dahl, *A Preface to Democratic Theory*, 6–7, 22–23; Wellington, "The Nature of Judicial Review," 493; and "Common Law Rules and Constitutional Double Standards," *Yale Law Journal* 83 (December 1973): 244, 267, 284.

32 Bishin, "Judicial Review in Democratic Theory," 1135; Rostow, "The Democratic Character of Judicial Review," 196–198, 208; Karl Llewellyn, "The American Common Law Tradition and American Democracy," *Journal of Legal and Political Sociology* 1 (October 1942): 14–45; and Ely, *Democracy and Distrust*, 73–134. See also Justice Stone's opinion in *U.S. v. Carolene Products Co.*, 304 U.S. 144 (1938), 152, n.4.

33 Rostow, "The Democratic Character of Judicial Review," 197; and Wellington, "The Nature of Judicial Review," 506–516.

34 Rostow, "The Democratic Character of Judicial Review"; Choper, *Judicial Review and the National Political Process*, 12–28; and Wellington, "The Nature of Judicial Review," 487–491.

35 Rostow, "The Democratic Character of Judicial Review."

36 Richards, "Sexual Autonomy," 958, 992; Choper, "On the Warren Court and Judicial Review," 37–38; and "The Supreme Court and the Political Branches"; Wellington, "The Nature of Judicial Review"; Kurland, *Politics, the Constitution, and the Warren Court*, 18, 182, 204; and Bickel, *The Least Dangerous Branch*, 16, 18, 21.

A few authors have described the Supreme Court as "majoritarian," but in the sense of applying majority-oriented standards against local customs or traditions. See, for example, Bickel, *The Supreme Court and the Idea of Progress*, 108–115, for a discussion of voting rights cases.

37 The case is more problematic for decisions made by administrative agencies. See Eugene Rostow, *The Sovereign Prerogative: The Supreme Court and the Quest for Law* (New Haven, Conn.: Yale University Press, 1962), 15; and Charles Black, *The People and the Court*, 179–180. Even so, critics such as Clifton McClesky would concede that even independent regulatory agencies are more directly responsive to popular majorities than is the federal judiciary; see "Judicial Review in a Democracy," 361–362; and Bickel, *The Least Dangerous Branch*, 19.

38 For discussions, see Choper, "The Supreme Court and the Political Branches," 810–811, 815, 848–858, 821–822; and *Judicial Review and the National Political Process*, 4–59; Wellington, "The Nature of Judicial Review," 490–498; Kurland, *Politics, the Constitution, and the Warren Court*, 18, 182, 201–204; Bickel, *The Least Dangerous Branch*, 16–21, 45; and Mace, "The Antidemocratic Character of Judicial Review," 1147–1148.

39 For a similar view, see Ely, *Democracy and Distrust*, 11–12.

40 Bickel, *The Least Dangerous Branch*, 18, 33; and Kurland, *Politics, the Constitution, and the Warren Court*, 18.

41 See Chapter Four.

42 See Chapter Five.

43 Bickel, *The Least Dangerous Branch*, 30–31.

44 Wellington, "The Nature of Judicial Review," 514–520.

45 This could occur in a variety of ways. A well-organized interest group, representing a numerical minority, might prevail over a less well-organized public opinion majority. Or, a law might initially have been consistent with nationwide public opinion, but due to later opinion shifts, may no longer represent majority attitudes. Many other circumstances can also be supposed.

46 See, for example, Bickel, *The Least Dangerous Branch*, 45.

47 This research is reviewed in Chapter Four.

48 See Mervin Field, "Political Opinion Polling in the United States of America," in Robert Worcester, ed., *Political Opinion Polling — An International Review* (New York: St. Martin's Press, 1983), 198–228; and Charles Roll and Albert Cantril, *Polls — Their Use and Misuse in Politics* (Cabin John, Md.: Seven Locks Press, 1972), 5–11.

49 The Gallup (or AIPO) Poll, the Survey Research Center (SRC) and the National Opinion Research Center (NORC) polls all publish summary results. Other major polls are available through the Roper Center at the University of Connecticut, Storrs, Connecticut.

50 Except for the SRC and NORC Polls, the major nationwide polling organizations are all sponsored or supported by news-gathering organizations, major newspapers, or networks. See Field, "Political Opinion Polling."

51 "There is hardly a political question in the United States which does not sooner or later turn into a judicial one." Alexis de Tocqueville, *Democracy in America*, trans. George Lawrence (New York: Harper & Row, 1966), 248.

52 Sample procedures and results are further described in Chapter Four. The specific Supreme Court cases used are listed in Appendix One.

CHAPTER TWO

Public Opinion and the Supreme Court: An Empirical Approach

The relationship between mass public opinion and Supreme Court decision making can be considered from either a normative or an empirical viewpoint. As Chapter One suggested, the normative approach reflects a long-standing tradition. By contrast, empirical studies of mass public opinion and the Supreme Court are of a much more recent vintage, dating back a bare two or three decades.

This chapter identifies twelve possible linkages between mass public opinion and Supreme Court decision making, each based upon previous research. The twelve individual linkage models are evaluated in Chapters Three through Seven, and then reconsidered in Chapter Eight.

The Utility of Empirical Models

One way to describe and explain a political relationship is to construct and test an empirical model. An empirical model is a simplified version of reality that specifies two or more important elements (or variables), as well as the interrelationships (or linkages) between or among the elements.[1] Empirical models of public opinion and judicial policy making have been based upon a variety of underlying theoretical frameworks,

14

particularly the systems analysis framework.[2] A large number of linkages between public opinion and Supreme Court policy making have been described.[3]

Model building offers several advantages over purely descriptive, biographical, case study, polemic, or anecdotal studies. At a minimum, model building encourages a clear description of the important variables involved in a process, and the relationship between the variables.[4] Even models that are not actually tested empirically ("heuristic models") may usefully organize the existing literature.[5]

Empirical models also encourage systematic data gathering and permit hypothesis testing. In turn, testing a model may suggest that the model should be revised. Models that generate inaccurate predictions, or that contain wrongly specified linkages may thereby be revised or rejected,[6] and more accurate and complex models can be constructed.[7]

Most empirical models also purport to be causal. Strictly speaking, it may not be possible to prove causality, even in experimental settings.[8] Nor does co-variation among the variables, per se, establish a causal relationship. A causal relationship may be inferred, however, even if it cannot be proven, provided that four conditions exist. First, causally related variables should co-vary together. Second, a causal (or independent) variable should bear an asymmetric or "forcing" relationship to its effect (or dependent) variables.[9] Third, a substantial relationship between the independent and dependent variables should persist even after controls are imposed.[10] Fourth, a good causal model should include all those independent variables that are strongly related to the dependent variables.[11]

In many circumstances all these conditions are not met, and causality cannot be firmly established. Even so, a study may still examine evidence of causality, such as making a comparison of otherwise similar groups exposed to different treatments, or an analysis of the time sequence among the variables.[12] Analysis based upon a well-specified model may still be an improvement over unsystematic descriptions, or the post hoc interpretation of statistical results that is not tied in with an underlying model.[13] Even these weaker tests may suggest that some linkages or variables should be discarded from a model, that the linkages should be respecified, or that new variables should be considered.[14]

Building and testing linkage models is seldom simple. It is often difficult to include all the key variables within a model,[15] and many empirical models appear to be grossly oversimplified. The actual variables measured may only inadequately reflect the underlying concepts; over-time data are often unavailable; and if sampling procedures are used, the sample itself may be limited or biased.[16] Some variables or linkages may be measured at an aggregate or group level while others are measured at the individual level.[17] Not infrequently, descriptive accounts — from which the empirical models are derived — are vague, incomplete, or even self-contradictory.

Still other problems exist in the standard of proof used to evaluate an empirical model. Quite often a linkage is evaluated through an arbitrary statistical cutoff level (most frequently, the .05 probability level). These cutoff levels exclude weak linkages, but they also introduce both a bias toward rejecting significant linkages and a bias toward oversimplified models.[18] Key variables (such as a justice's votes) may be dichotomous or categoric, making it difficult to apply more powerful statistical techniques.[19] Nonlinear, nonadditive, or multicollinear relationships may also exist among the variables, or serious measurement errors may occur. In practice, all these conditions make it difficult to choose among competing models or to specify the correct relationship among the variables.[20]

These problems exist in this study, as elsewhere, but do not imply that empirical model building should be abandoned. Rather, the results of empirical modeling — here and elsewhere — should be interpreted cautiously and, where possible, the models should be revised and refined.

The Twelve Linkage Models

The available literature describes a variety of linkages between public opinion and Supreme Court policy making. Some linkages are simple and direct; others involve intermediate or multiple variables. Some linkages are well-developed in the literature; others must be extended from case studies, biographies, or even normative accounts. The twelve linkages described here do not exhaust all the possible linkages, but they do include the most frequently described linkages.[21]

(1) The State of Public Opinion

The first linkage assumes that public opinion itself directly affects Supreme Court decision making. This model may easily be misunderstood. It does not necessarily assume that justices make a particular effort to seek out public opinion polls, or even that they give much weight to available polls.[22] Indeed, in many instances, poll results would not be easily available to the justices or to the general public at the time the Court's decision was reached. Rather, it assumes that justices "sense" and share widely held attitudes, and that the Court defers to public opinion particularly often when mass public opinion itself is unusually one-sided or closely focused upon an issue.

This model makes three assumptions. First, a significant (positive) relationship should exist between public opinion and Court decisions; that is, Supreme Court decisions should reflect public opinion significantly more often than a random-choice model would predict.[23] Further, although justices may often be uncertain (or indifferent) about popular attitudes, their "mandate uncertainty" should be less pronounced when public opinion is relatively united or when an issue closely engages public attention. A second assumption, then, is that the Court should be more majoritarian when public opinion is unusually one-sided.[24] Third, the Court should be especially majoritarian during crisis times — when public opinion is closely focused upon an issue.[25] Figure 2.1 depicts this linkage, and the model is examined at the aggregate (or decision) level in Chapters Three and Four.

(2) Political Socialization

In the second linkage, political socialization is conceptualized as those experiences that foster values shared by public opinion majorities and the dominant political culture.[26] Political socialization may occur from childhood through adult life — up until the point at which a justice joins the Court.[27] Indicators of majority-oriented socialization experiences here

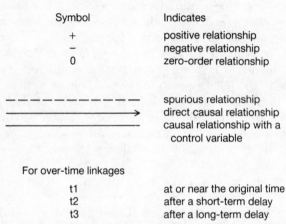

Figure 2.1 State of Public Opinion

include a justice's home region, religious beliefs, sex or racial status, political party, education, career patterns, and ideology.

Conceptualized in this way, the impact of political socialization can be examined empirically. Justices with majority-oriented socializing experiences are predicted to be more majoritarian than other justices. This linkage is tested at the individual (justice) level by examining the voting patterns of the 36 justices who have served on the modern Court. Figure 2.2 depicts this linkage, and the results of this linkage model are reported in Chapter Five. In Figure 2.2 the positive relationship between contemporary public opinion and a justice's votes is assumed to result from a justice's prior socialization experiences.

(3) The Federal Policy Process

The first two models may seem oversimplified because neither includes any intermediary variables between public opinion and either an individual justice's votes or the Court's collective

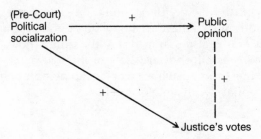

Figure 2.2 Political Socialization Model

decisions. In reality, however, the Supreme Court is quite insulated from mass public opinion; justices sit for life ("with good behavior") and reversing Court decisions is seldom simple. The next three linkages recognize the intervening policy-making and appointment processes.[28]

The third linkage makes two assumptions: first, that public opinion strongly influences federal policy making; and second, that the Court typically exercises judicial restraint toward federal laws and policies. As a result, a strong, positive, if not perfect relationship exists between mass public opinion and Court decisions. This linkage, however, is entirely mediated by federal-level policy making. While there are several intermediate steps (such as presidential or congressional elections) between mass public opinion and federal-level policy outputs, these variables cannot be tested here, and are not indicated in Figures 2.3–2.5.[29]

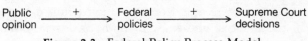

Figure 2.3 Federal Policy Process Model

(4) The State/Local Policy Process

The fourth model is, to some extent, a "non-model" since it assumes that state/local laws or policies carry no particular weight in Supreme Court decision making. When nationwide polls disagree with state or local laws, the Court usually prefers nationwide public opinion. Both the third and the fourth linkage models are tested at the aggregate (or decision) level in Chapter Four.

In the fourth linkage, the assumption is that state and local policies do not reflect nationwide public opinion very accurately.[30] It is also assumed that the Court shows very little deference or restraint toward state or local laws and policies,[31] and that the Court usually favors nationwide public opinion when it conflicts with state or local laws.

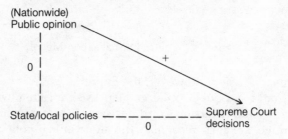

Figure 2.4 State/Local Policy Process Model

(5) The Appointment Process

The fifth linkage assumes that the appointment process mediates the linkage between public opinion and Supreme Court decision making. Presidents seldom nominate unpopular justices, and the Senate will not confirm nominees who arouse public hostility.[32] Nominees with a broader popular appeal are predicted to be more majoritarian during their service on the Court.[33]

The most majoritarian Supreme Court justices are predicted to be justices with a bipartisan appeal (that is, "crossover" appointees who are not from the president's own political party), and justices who enjoy unanimous or near-unanimous Senate confirmation margins. This linkage is tested at the level of the individual justice in Chapter Five.

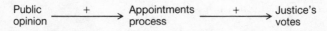

Figure 2.5 Appointment Process Model

(6) Judicial Roles

On-the-Court roles may also affect a justice's tendency to reflect public opinion. Justices who view their role as that of a "delegate," rather than as that of a "trustee" may be more majoritarian.[34] Unfortunately, a justice's values and votes cannot be measured separately in this study.[35] Nevertheless, three on-the-Court roles can be measured: chief justice status, political "ambition," and reputation (or prestige). The hypothesis is that each of the three roles encourages majority-oriented voting by sensitizing a justice to public opinion.[36] Chief justices, ambitious justices, and well-regarded justices more frequently hand down rulings that reflect the polls. Roles are treated as intervening (or control) variables between public opinion and a justice's votes. Chapter Five tests this linkage at the level of the individual justice.

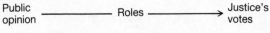

Figure 2.6   Judicial Roles Model

(7) Length of Tenure

The length-of-tenure linkage assumes that justices grow increasingly isolated from public opinion during their Court tenure because as they age they become more conservative. Older, conservative justices with a long tenure are less representative of public opinion.[37] This model is tested in Chapter Five.

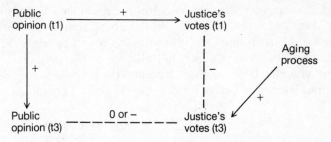

Figure 2.7   Length-of-Tenure Model

(8) Realignment

The realignment linkage differs from the length-of-tenure model. In the realignment model, "exogenous" shocks to the political system are predicted to affect public opinion much more rapidly than the values or votes of individual justices. As a result, in the realignment model, justices grow less majoritarian whenever a realignment occurs during their Court tenure. This model is examined, somewhat indirectly, at the level of the individual justice in Chapter Five.[38]

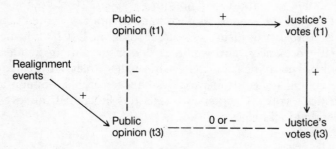

Figure 2.8 Realignment Model

(9) Short-term Manipulation

The next two linkages recognize that Supreme Court decisions themselves may influence public opinion, either in the short term or in the long term. The short-term "manipulation" model assumes that public opinion does not strongly influence Supreme Court decisions; rather, the Court's decisions themselves have an immediate, direct effect on public opinion. As a result, Supreme Court decisions are more strongly related to public opinion after the decision is announced than before the decision is announced. While post-decision agreement between Court rulings and public opinion will be high, this is a result of the Court's ability to influence public opinion.

Individually, both the short-term and the long-term manipulation models are recursive (or one-directional). If combined with

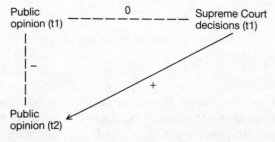

Figure 2.9 Short-term Manipulation Model

other linkages, however, they add a nonrecursive (or feedback) element to the full model. The short-term manipulation model is tested in (Chapter Six), by examining pre- to post-decision poll shifts.[39]

(10) Long-term Manipulation

The long-term "manipulation" model assumes that the Court does not respond to public opinion; instead it shapes public opinion — by influencing the context of American politics over a long period of time. In this model, Court rulings reshape American society and the socialization experiences of future generations — thereby affecting future public opinion.[40] Chapter Six tests this model in a very limited way.

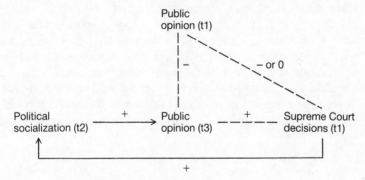

Figure 2.10 Long-term Manipulation Model

(11) Interest Groups

Interest groups often play an important role in initiating, financing, and organizing lawsuits; in filing amicus curiae briefs; or in otherwise aiding lawsuits as they progress to the Supreme Court level. In recent decades, the activity of such groups has clearly grown.[41] Apparently, litigation-oriented groups that seek to influence Supreme Court decisions seldom try to influence mass public opinion directly.[42] In the interest groups linkage, interest groups and mass public opinion are not themselves closely or causally related; rather, each has an independent effect upon Court decisions. This linkage is tested at the aggregate level in Chapter Four.

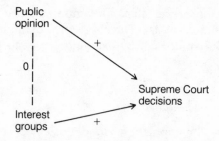

Figure 2.11 Interest Groups Model

(12) The Test of Time

A final linkage recognizes that Supreme Court decisions are not necessarily final decisions. In the test-of-time linkage, public opinion affects Court rulings in two ways: first, during the Court's initial decision making; and second, after the Court's decision is announced. This model assumes that the Court's more popular rulings persist, but its unpopular rulings are usually overturned through statutory revision, through constitutional amendments, or by the Court itself.[43] In the test-of-time model, Court rulings do not in themselves greatly influence public opinion. This model is evaluated in Chapter Seven.

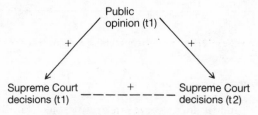

Figure 2.12 Test-of-Time Model

While the twelve individual linkages do not exhaust all the possible linkages between American public opinion and Supreme Court policy making, they do include most of the variables and processes typically found in descriptions, diagrams, or models of public opinion and Supreme Court policy making. Individually, each linkage is simple and recursive (one-directional), and all the models can be examined empirically, at least in part. The addendum to this chapter presents each

24

model, expressed as a formal set of assumptions. Chapters Three through Seven evaluate each linkage. Chapter Eight then reevaluates the evidence and presents a reduced, empirically based full model.

Addendum

The twelve linkages can also be expressed formally:

(1) The State of Public Opinion
If 1 = public opinion and 2 = Court decisions, then:
$$r12>0$$

(2) Political Socialization
If 1 = political socialization; 2 = public opinion; and 3 = a justice's votes, then:
$$r12>0;\ r13>0;\ r23>0;\ but\ r23.1=0$$

(3) The Federal Policy Process
If 1 = public opinion; 2 = federal laws and policies; and 3 = Court decisions, then in federal-level disputes:
$$r12>0;\ r23>0;\ r13>0;\ but\ r13.2=0$$

(4) The State/Local Policy Process
If 1 = (nationwide) public opinion; 2 = state/local laws or policies; and 3 = Court decisions, then in cases from the state/local level:
$$r12 = 0;\ r23=0;\ r13>0;\ and\ r13.2=r13$$

(5) The Appointment Process
If 1 = public opinion; 2 = appointment process; and 3 = an individual justice's votes, then:
$$r12>0;\ r23>0;\ r13>0;\ but\ r13.2 = 0$$

(6) Judicial Roles
If 1 = public opinion; 2 = judicial roles; and 3 = an individual justice's votes, then:
$$r3.1,2> r13$$

(7) Length of Tenure, and (8) Realignment
If public opinion (t1) = 1; a justice's votes (t1) = 2; public opinion (t3) = 3; and a justice's votes (t3) = 4, then:
in the length-of-tenure model:
$$r12>0; r13>0;\ r24<0;\ and\ r12>r34$$
and in the realignment model:
$$r12>0;\ r13<0;\ r24>0;\ r12>r34;\ and\ r14>r34$$

(9) Short-Term Manipulation
If public opinion (t1) = 1; Court decisions (t1) = 2; and public opinion (t2) = 3, then:
$$r23>0;\ and\ r23>r12$$

(10) Long-Term Manipulation
If public opinion (t1) = 1; Court decisions (t1) = 2; political socialization (t2) = 3; and public opinion (t3) = 4, then:
$$r23>0;\ r34>0;\ r24>0;\ and\ r24>r12$$

(11) Interest Groups
      If public opinion = 1; interest groups = 2; and Court decisions = 3,
      then:
          $r12=0$; $r13>0$; $r23>0$; and $r3.1,2>$ either $r13$ or $r12$ alone
(12) The Test of Time
      If public opinion = 1; Court decisions (t1) = 2; and Court decisions
      (t2) = 3, then:
          $r12>0$; $r13>0$; $r13>r12$; and $r23.1=0$

References

1 May Brodbeck, "Models, Meanings, and Theories," in May Brodbeck, ed., *Readings in the Philosophy of the Social Sciences* (New York:
   Macmillan, 1968), 579–600; Abraham Kaplan, *The Conduct of Inquiry*
   (San Francisco: Chandler, 1964), 263–265.
2 David Easton, *A Systems Analysis of Political Life* (New York: John
   Wiley & Sons, 1965). For a review of models in the judicial
   process, see Charles Sheldon, *The American Judicial Process: Models
   and Approaches* (New York: Dodd, Mead, 1974). For a review of
   models linking public opinion to public policy making, see
   Norman Luttbeg, ed., *Public Opinion and Public Policy* (Homewood,
   Ill.: Dorsey, 1974), 6–10; and John Sullivan, "Linkage Models of
   the Political System," in Allen R. Wilcox, ed., *Public Opinion and
   Political Attitudes* (New York: John Wiley, 1974), 637–659.
3 This literature is reviewed only briefly in this chapter, with
   citations given in later chapters; see also note 21, below. For
   a general discussion of linkage models, see Sullivan, "Linkage
   Models"; Luttbeg, *Public Opinion and Public Policy*; and Robert
   Weissberg, *Public Opinion and Popular Government* (Englewood
   Cliffs, N.J.: Prentice-Hall, 1976).
4 Hubert Blalock, Jr., *Theory Construction — From Verbal to Mathematical Formulations* (Englewood Cliffs, N.J.: Prentice-Hall, 1969),
   1–7, 24–47; and Kenneth Arrow, "Mathematical Models in the
   Social Sciences," in Brodbeck, ed., *Readings*, 635–667. Most social
   science models specify only positive or negative relationships
   between the variables, rather than the strength or precise form
   of the linkage; see Paul Meehl, "Theory Testing in Psychology
   and Physics: A Methodological Paradox," *Philosophy of Science* 34
   (June 1967): 103–115.
5 See Charles A. Johnson, "The Implementation and Impact of
   Judicial Policies: A Heuristic Model," in John A. Gardiner, ed.,
   Public Law and Public Policy (New York: Praeger: 1977), 107–126.
6 Robert Merton, in Brodbeck, ed., *Readings*, 465–496. For examples
   of this approach, see Sullivan, "Linkage Models"; and Arthur S.
   Goldberg, "Discerning a Causal Pattern Among Data on Voting
   Behavior," *American Political Science Review* 60 (December 1966):
   913–922.

7   Hubert Blalock, Jr., *Causal Inferences in Nonexperimental Research* (Chapel Hill: University of North Carolina Press, 1964), 62; *Theory Construction*, 46–47, 71–75.

8   Blalock, *Causal Inferences*, 11–14, 21–26.

9   Blalock, *Causal Inferences*, 10; and Herbert Simon, *Models of Man* (New York: John Wiley & Sons, 1957), 10–13 focus on the asymmetric relationship between causal and effects variables, rather than the time sequence. In practice, the time sequence involved is often an important indicator of a causal relationship; see Herb Asher, *Causal Modeling*, 2nd ed. (Beverly Hills, CA: Sage, 1983), 12–17.

10 Blalock, *Causal Inferences*, 63–68; Simon, *Models of Man*, 127–128, 162–163.

11 Simon, *Models of Man*, 10–27, 37–43, 59–61; Blalock, *Causal Inferences*, 45–49; and *Theory Construction*, 12–25. In practice, the assumption of uncorrelated error terms presents particular difficulty.

12 Claire Selltiz, et. al., *Research Methods in Social Relations* (New York: Holt, Rinehart and Winston, 1959), 80–88, 127–136.

13 Meehl, "Theory Testing," 103, 134; Merton, in Brodbeck, ed., *Readings*, 465–481.

14 Blalock, *Causal Inferences*, 20–21, 64–68; *Theory Construction*, 20–25, 75, 142.

15 Here, justices' votes are taken as an indicator of their values. It was not possible to test the hypothesis that the Court is more responsive to the politically attentive public than to the mass public; see Donald J. Devine, *The Attentive Public: Polyarchial Democracy* (Chicago: Rand-McNally, 1970). Nor was it possible to examine the hypothesis that strategic considerations on the Court affect the quality of representation; see C. Neal Tate, "Personal Attribute Models of the Voting Behavior of U.S. Supreme Court Justices," *American Political Science Review* 75 (June 1981): 361–367.

16 Simon, *Models of Man*, 50–61. This problem is more severe when the variables are also dichotomous, as they often are here, since it is not always possible to test all possible outcomes of the independent (or causal) variables. See also Stuart Nagel and Marian Neef, *The Legal Process — Modeling the System* (Beverly Hills, Calif: Sage, 1977); H. T. Reynolds, *Analysis of Nominal Data*, 2nd ed. (Beverly Hill, CA: Sage, 1984).

17 May Brodbeck, "Methodological Individualism: Definition and Reduction," in Brodbeck, ed., *Readings*, 280–303.

18 See Meehl, "Theory Testing," for a discussion of the bias that operates in the opposite direction in most social science research. See also Nagel and Neef, *The Legal Process — Modeling the System*; and Denton Morrison and Ramon Henkel, eds., *The Significance Test Controversy* (Chicago: Aldine, 1970), particularly 79–80, 150–152, 155–171, 194–195.

19 Blalock, *Causal Inferences*, 119–124, 184–188; Nagel and Neef, *The Legal Process — Modeling the System*, 42–65.

20 Simon, *Models of Man*, 38–39; Blalock, *Causal Inferences*, 71–91, 147–149.

21 Compare, for example, Glendon Schubert, *Judicial Policy Making* (Chicago: Scott, Foresman, 1965), 105–107; Walter Murphy, *Elements of Judicial Strategy* (Chicago: University of Chicago Press, 1964), 32; Sheldon Goldman and Thomas Jahnige, *The Federal Courts as a Political System* (New York: Harper & Row, 1971), 199; Charles Johnson, "A Heuristic Model," 109; Joel Grossman, "Social Backgrounds and Judicial Decisions: Notes for a Theory," *Journal of Politics* 29 (May 1967): 337–343; and "A Model for Judicial Policy Analysis," in Joel Grossman and Joseph Tanenhaus, ed., *Frontiers of Judicial Research* (New York: John Wiley & Sons, 1969), 410.

22 See Chapter Three, at notes 9–16.

23 More precisely, this model assumes that the percent of Court decisions that reflect public opinion will significantly exceed a random-choice base-rate level — here, 50 percent when instances of inconsistent and closely divided polls are excluded. This higher-than-random-choice level of agreement between court decisions and nationwide public opinion should persist even after controls are imposed. For a discussion of this standard, see William Klecka, *Discriminant Analysis* (Beverly Hills, Calif: Sage, 1980), 50–51.

24 See Chapter Four, at notes 42–44.

25 Close public attention and one-sided opinion distributions approximate a condition of high citizen participation, which has been reported to facilitate both elite-mass issue agreement and more accurate elite perceptions of mass attitudes. See Susan Hansen, "Participation, Political Structures, and Concurrence," *American Political Science Review* 69 (December 1975): 1181–1199; and "Linkage Models, Issues, and Community Politics," *American Politics Quarterly* 6 (January 1978): 3–28; and Sidney Verba and Norman Nie, *Participation in America: Political Democracy and Social Equality* (New York: Harper & Row, 1972). See also Chapter Four at notes 42–47.

26 Political socialization has been described in several different ways, some of which are too vague to permit empirical testing here. For a general review, see Richard Dawson, Kenneth Prewitt, and Karen Dawson, *Political Socialization*, 2nd ed., (Boston: Little, Brown, 1977). The hypotheses are reviewed in Chapter Five, at notes 3–16. For an argument that shared values may lead to issue representation even if formal linkage mechanisms are weak or absent, see R. W. Cobb and C. D. Elder, *Participation in American Politics* (Boston: Little, Brown, 1972), 12; and Robert Weissberg, *Public Opinion and Popular Government*, 206–221.

27 In fact, later socializing experiences could also affect a justice's majoritarian tendencies. A few justices have changed their voting patterns during their Court tenure. For a prominent example, see Stephen L. Wasby, "Justice Harry A. Blackmun: Transformation

from 'Minnesota Twin' to Independent Voice," paper delivered at the 1986 Annual Meeting of the American Political Science Association, Washington, D.C.

28 These three models also assume that the political process is an intervening, not an independent variable; see R. Kenneth Godwin and W. Bruce Shepard, "Political Process and Public Expenditures," *American Political Science Review* 70 (December 1976): 1127–1135.

29 Variables or linkages that cannot be tested separately, and that are not of primary interest here, have been omitted from the diagrams. Admittedly, this may result in oversimplified models.

Examples of intervening variables might include voters' party preferences or candidate perceptions, candidate perceptions of mass public opinion, or officeholders' own preferences. The literature on linkages between mass public opinion and federal policy making is extensive; for a brief review, see Luttbeg, *Public Opinion and Public Policy*; and Sullivan, "Linkage Models."

30 The available literature does not indicate how well state-level policies reflect nationwide public opinion. In most instances, state-level policies have been compared to actual or simulated state-level public opinion. For evidence that only a weak relationship exists between nationwide public opinion and state-level policies, see Weissberg, *Public Opinion and Popular Government*, 126–136; and Benjamin Page and Robert Shapiro, "Effects of Public Opinion on Policy," *American Political Science Review* 77 (March 1983): 183. For evidence that a much stronger linkage exists between statewide public opinion and policies in that same state, see Gerald Wright, Jr., Robert Erikson, and John McIver, "Public Opinion and Policy Liberalism in the American States," *American Journal of Political Science* 31 (November 1987): 980–1001.

31 For evidence that the Supreme Court is more deferential toward federal, rather than state or local policies, see Stephen Wasby, *The Supreme Court in the Federal Judicial System*, 2nd ed., (New York: Holt, Rinehart and Winston, 1984), 228–229, 240–244, 267; and Henry Abraham, *The Judicial Process*, 4th ed., (New York: Oxford, 1980), 296–297.

32 This hypothesis cannot be tested very adequately. Some supportive evidence appears in the failed nomination of Judge Robert Bork; see *Congressional Quarterly Weekly Report*, October 17, 1987, 2511. Polling evidence on the other five failed nominations since the 1930s (Abe Fortas for Chief Justice in 1968; Homer Thornberry in 1968; Clement Haynsworth, Jr., in 1969; G. Harrold Carswell in 1970; and Benjamin Ginzberg in 1987) is not available. For anecdotal evidence that presidents may not nominate unpopular candidates at all, see Henry Abraham, *Justices and Presidents*, 2nd ed., (New York: Oxford University Press 1985), 274. An alternative (but untestable) hypothesis is that failed nominees would have been less majoritarian than confirmed nominees. For an overview of the appointment process, see Jeffrey Segal, "Senate

Confirmation of Supreme Court Justices: Partisan and Institutional Politics," *Journal of Politics* 49 (November 1987): 998–1015.

33 An intervening step of presidential and Senate candidate choice might be diagrammed between mass public opinion and the appointment process. For evidence that Supreme Court justices usually reflect the key values of their appointing presidents, see Robert Scigliano, *The Supreme Court and the Presidency* (New York: Free Press, 1971), 125–148; John P. Frank, "The Appointment of Supreme Court Justices: Prestige, Principles, and Politics," *Wisconsin Law Review* 16 (July 1941): at 488; and John Gates and Jeffrey Cohen, "Presidents, Justices, and Racial Equality Cases, 1954–1984," Paper presented at the 1986 Annual Meeting of the Midwest Political Science Association, Chicago, Ill.

34 For a discussion, see Chapter Five at notes 19–23.

35 For a discussion of this problem for justices on the modern Supreme Court, most of whom are now dead, see C. Neal Tate, "Personal Attribute Models," at 365.

36 This relationship represents a causal and a control variable; see Stuart Nagel and Marian Neef, *The Legal Process — Modeling the System*, 42–68. Figure 2.6 has been simplified for convenience.

37 See Chapter Five, at notes 24–25.

38 This model can only be examined somewhat indirectly, since poll data are not available before the New Deal realignment. See Chapter Five, at notes 26–27.

39 See Chapter Six, particularly at notes 50–67.

40 This thesis is often argued. See, for example, James Willard Hurst, *Law and Social Progress in United States History* (Madison, Wisc.: University of Wisconsin Press, 1960), 14, 17; Chapter Three, at note 175; and Chapter Six, at note 68. The available evidence on long-term poll shifts is limited and largely negative; see Chapter Six.

41 The literature on interest group involvement in Supreme Court decision making is extensive; see Chapter Four at notes 59–63.

42 Some exceptions occur: see Lee Epstein, *Conservatives In Court* (Knoxville, Tenn: University of Tennessee Press, 1985), 45–56, 74–75, 94–104, 113–114, 141–145.

43 As well, unpopular rulings may be more often evaded. This linkage also assumes that Court rulings do not affect mass public opinion.

CHAPTER THREE

Public Opinion
and Constitutional Law

Since the mid-1930s many Supreme Court rulings have referred, either directly or indirectly, to mass public opinion. The modern Court has also developed four major doctrines to explain the role that public opinion should play in judicial policy making.

This chapter addresses several questions. First, how do justices recognize mass public opinion? Second, in what types of decisions does the Supreme Court consider public opinion? Third, has the Supreme Court's usage of public opinion varied over time? Finally, what judicial theories or doctrines has the Court employed to consider the proper role of public opinion?

Supreme Court Decisions and Public Opinion

Since the New Deal period numerous Supreme Court opinions have directly mentioned mass public opinion. From 1934 through the 1985–1986 term, some 142 majority, concurring, dissenting, or per curiam opinions have directly mentioned "public opinion" — an average of nearly three direct mentions per Court term.

In fact, these 142 direct mentions of public opinion represent only a conservative estimate of the modern Court's attention to public opinion. In many other instances a Court opinion has used a closely related synonym that clearly denotes mass attitudes. Examples of such close synonyms include "the prevailing sentiment,"[1] "an enraged community" or "great and well-justified public indignation,"[2] "the consensus of society's opinions,"[3] "great excitement and indignation" or "so huge a wave of public passion,"[4] "an ugly public temper,"[5] "an environment so permeated with hostility,"[6] or "the dominant communal sentiment."[7] Because so many synonyms for public opinion have appeared in Court opinions, it is impossible to compute any precise count of decisions that indirectly refer to public opinion. Overall, close synonyms appear to greatly outnumber direct mentions of "public opinion."[8]

Direct and Indirect Evidence of Public Attitudes

If the modern Court frequently considers public opinion, what evidence of attitudes does the Court actually use? In referring to public opinion, a justice may consider either direct evidence (such as published polls) or indirect evidence (such as election results, media coverage and editorials, community or group actions, specialized or elite opinions, legislation, or even lower court decisions). On the other hand, a justice may simply use the term "public opinion" in a normative, theoretical, or abstract sense, and make no reference to actual attitudes.

Table 3.1 separates the modern Court's direct references to public opinion into the various types of evidence used in citing public opinion. For comparison, direct mentions of public opinion are also reported for two earlier periods, 1792–1859, and 1860–1933.[9]

While these results should be interpreted cautiously,[10] they suggest that the modern Supreme Court seldom refers to specific public opinion polls. Of the few decisions that have referred to specific polls, about half occurred in death penalty cases, in which both pro- and anti-death penalty opinions frequently involved a review of nationwide polls.[11] Other decisions that cited specific (often local, or privately sponsored) polls fall in widely scattered areas. Examples of poll topics include admission to practice before the Supreme Court, paddling for school children, postal privileges, jury instructions, and even radio broadcasts on public buses.[12]

Even Court rulings that cite specific polls do not necessarily give poll results a great deal of weight. Often poll results, along with other evidence of public attitudes are simply noted in passing. In several instances, justices who cited specific polls also

Table 3.1
Evidence used in direct mentions of public opinion,
three historical periods

	1792–1859	1860–1933	1934–1986
Direct evidence of attitudes	—	—	9%
(Specific poll results cited)	—	—	(8%)
(Poll results mentioned, but no specific polls cited)	—	—	(1%)
Indirect evidence of attitudes	73%	81%	39%
(Referendum results cited)	—	—	(2%)
(Community actions cited, including rumors, word-of-mouth media coverage and editorials or mob actions)	(9%)	(14%)	(4%)
(Elite or specialized opinion cited)	(3%)	(14%)	(2%)
(General knowledge: no specific source cited)	(32%)	(48%)	(17%)
(Statutes or lower court decisions cited)	(29%)	(5%)	(14%)
Normative, theoretical, or abstract (non-empirical) discussions	44%	19%	70%

Note: Percentages sum down, by column, and may exceed 100% due to multiple sources indicated.

wrote to suggest the limited importance of polls. In *Furman v. Georgia* (1972), for example, Justice Marshall wrote that "while a public opinion poll obviously is of some assistance in indicating public acceptance or rejection of a specific penalty, its utility cannot be very great."[13] Instead Justice Marshall proposed a test based on the opinions of a hypothetical, well-informed citizen.[14] Dissenting in *Furman*, Justice Powell argued that "(p)ublic opinion polls (have) little probative relevance."[15] Justice Burger, also dissenting, wrote that recent legislation was a better indicator of contemporary attitudes.[16]

More frequent than decisions that report specific polls are decisions that cite indirect evidence of public attitudes, such as referendum results,[17] news coverage,[18] juror attitudes,[19] mob actions,[20] or elite attitudes.[21] In other decisions, mass attitudes have been inferred from legislation,[22] lower court decisions,[23] or officeholders' actions.[24] Other Court decisions offer no particular evidence of public attitudes at all, and simply assume that public opinion was so well-recognized as to require no specific evidence.[25]

Most of the modern Court's direct mentions of public opinion have not referred to existing attitudes — whether these attitudes have been directly or indirectly measured. Instead, the term "public opinion" was used in a normative or theoretical sense to describe the role that mass public opinion should properly play.

For example, in many First Amendment rulings, the modern Court has argued that media coverage, public protest, or labor picketing might inform and influence public opinion and therefore each deserved constitutional protection. Or, in judicial restraint decisions, the Court has argued that some controversy should be left to the interplay of legislatures and public opinion.

Substantive Types of Cases

A second way to view the modern Court's use of public opinion is to examine the substantive types of cases in which references to public opinion appear. In Table 3.2, the modern Court's 142 direct mentions of public opinion are classified by the substantive types of case involved; results for the period 1792–1859 and 1860–1933 are also listed.

Since the mid-1930s direct mentions of public opinion have most often occurred in disputes concerning the criminal process, press coverage, freedom of speech or dissent, and labor-related cases. Direct mentions of public opinion occurring in cases involving business regulation, or foreign or military policy, were more common before the 1930s, and occurred less frequently in the modern Court.

Over-time Trends

A third way to examine the modern Court's concept of public opinion is through an over-time analysis. Table 3.3 reports the average number of direct mentions of public opinion per year within the three time periods.

Perhaps surprisingly, the Court's direct mentions of public opinion have occurred at a relatively steady rate during the last half century. While scientific, published polls were more

Table 3.2
Type of case involved in direct mentions of public opinion,
three historical periods

Type of case	1792–1859	1860–1933	1934–1986
Criminal process – trials, prisoners, trial rights	19%	24%	35%
Press, media	—	6%	21%
Dissent – political, free speech, religious	—	—	18%
Labor unions – strikes, bargaining, picketing	—	6%	14%
Elections – campaigning, spending	—	6%	8%
Business regulations	48%	50%	8%
Foreign, military policy	33%	9%	5%
Civil rights, race	5%	12%	4%
Privacy, sex, obscenity	—	—	3%
All others	—	3%	6%

Note: Percentages sum down, by column, and may exceed 100% due to multiple issues raised in a single decision.

Table 3.3
Over-time frequency of direct mentions of public opinion

Time period	Average number of direct mentions, per year
1792–1859	.3
1860–1933	.5
1934–1986	2.7
The modern period, further broken down:	
1934–1959	2.4
1960–1986	3.1

readily available after the 1950s, the Court was only slightly more likely to refer to public opinion during the 1960–1986 period.[26] By contrast, "public opinion" was mentioned less often before the mid-1930s. From 1792 to 1859, Court opinions mentioned "public opinion" only .3 times per year, on the average. From 1860 through 1933 the Court directly mentioned public opinion, on the average, only .5 times a year.

Table 3.4
Direct mentions of public opinion, by type of opinion

	1792–1859	1860–1933	1934–1986
Direct mention occurs in:			
majority opinion	76%	79%	52%
concurring opinion	5%	0%	13%
dissenting opinion	19%	21%	35%
	100%	100%	100%

Types of Opinions

Some evidence indicates that the Court's direct mentions of public opinion have not been simply a tactic of dissenters who sought to appeal to public opinion when unable to muster a majority on the Court. Throughout the Court's history, direct mentions of public opinion have appeared predominantly in majority or concurring opinions, and not in dissents. Before the mid-1930s (when dissents were less common) over three-quarters of direct mentions of public opinion appeared in majority opinions. Even after the mid-1930s (when dissents grew more common) over half of all direct mentions appeared in majority opinions. Over two-thirds (65 percent) of all direct mentions of public opinion appeared in either a concurring or a majority opinion. See Table 3.4.

The Four Judicial Theories on Public Opinion

The remainder of Chapter Three further explores those rulings that rely, at least in part, upon the concept of public opinion. Nearly all of the modern Supreme Court's references to public opinion can be classified into one of four judicial theories, each described at greater length below:

- first, that some forms of speech (or action) inform and influence public opinion, and therefore merit constitutional protection;
- second, that elected officials and public opinion, alone, adequately protect constitutional rights, and judicial review is not necessary;

● third, that law and policy should reflect changing public opinion;

● and fourth, that in some instances, public opinion poses a threat to constitutional rights.

As Table 3.5 indicates, virtually all the direct mentions of public opinion reflect one of these four theories. From 1934 to 1986, the first theory — that speech (or action) influences or informs public opinion and merits protection — appeared in about two-fifths of all explicit mentions of public opinion. The remaining theories each appeared in about one-fifth of direct references to public opinion during this time period. Only a small fraction of direct mentions of public opinion could not be classified into any of the four categories. Before 1934, however, virtually no mentions of the first theory appeared.

Ensuring an Informed Public Opinion

The theory that speech informs and influences public opinion, and should be protected, appeared in nearly two-fifths (41 percent) of modern Court opinions that directly mention public opinion. Many of these decisions cited a particular benefit, either to public opinion itself or to a democratic society, that results from free speech.

This theory was developed as a constitutional doctrine during the early 1900s, most notably by Justices Oliver Wendell Holmes and Louis Brandeis.[27] In *Schenck v. U.S.* (1919), Justice Holmes argued that most, although not all speech or dissent was constitutionally protected by the First Amendment. Limiting free speech required showing that "the words used are used in such circumstances and are of such a nature as to create a clear and present danger that they will bring about the substantive evils which Congress has a right to prevent."[28] Almost a decade later, in *Whitney v. California* (1927), Justice Brandeis added a stronger test — that the "serious evil" occur almost immediately, even before public debate and discussion could ensue.[29]

In the *Schenck* and *Whitney* tests, then, suppressing speech required three elements. There must be "reasonable grounds" to believe that a "serious evil" (such as interference with the conduct of a war, or widespread and violent industrial strife) will result almost immediately after the speech, and before

Table 3.5
Frequency of four judicial theories in direct mentions of
public opinion, over time

Judicial theory	1792–1859	1860–1933	1934–1986
I Speech or action influences or informs public opinion, merits protection:	—	6%	41%
in press cases	—	(6)	(17)
in dissent cases	—	—	(16)
all others	—	—	(8)
II Public opinion is an adequate check on policy:	24%	50%	21%
for government policies	(14)	(44)	(11)
for non-government groups	(10)	(6)	(10)
III Law and policy should reflect evolving public opinion	43%	29%	21%
IV Public Opinion is a threat to rights, should be restrained	29%	18%	19%
in fair trial rights	—	(6)	(8)
in speech and dissent	—	(3)	(8)
in economic rights	(29)	(9)	(3)
All other usages	5%	3%	6%
government influences opinion	—	—	(3)
miscellaneous	(5)	(3)	(3)

Note: Percentages may exceed 100 percent since multiple usages appear in some decisions.

public debate and discussion can occur. Thus, "(o)nly an emergency can justify repression."[30]

Under other circumstances, argued Holmes and Brandeis, even if the vast majority of citizens believe the particular views expressed to be false, even dangerous, political viewpoints should be tested in the "marketplace of ideas."[31] In Holmes and Brandeis's view, free speech and the airing of unpopular views benefited public opinion and democratic society by ensuring "the discovery and spread of political truth"[32] or the correction of false beliefs.[33]

In later rulings other justices added to the list of benefits that might result from controversial or unpopular views. The list of presumed benefits to public opinion or to a democratic society is, by now, lengthy.

Various rulings have held that free speech makes the government more responsive to popular views and promotes peaceful change.[34] Exposure to controversies "will ultimately produce a more capable citizenry."[35] It might "strike at prejudices and preconceptions."[36] Open discussion of controversies "keeps a society from becoming stagnant and unprepared for the stresses and strains that work to tear all civilizations apart."[37] Protecting controversial speech might be "in the long run essential to enlightened opinion and right conduct on the part of the citizens of a democracy."[38] Among children, exposure to controversy might promote the development of "independence and vigor" later in adult life, which is useful training in a "relatively permissive, often disputatious, society."[39] Exposure to dissent might also help children to understand first hand "the important principles of our government."[40]

Free speech, through press coverage of open trials, might be "an effective restraint on possible abuse of judicial power." It might also encourage "key witnesses unknown to the parties" to step forth, and it might inform the public about judicial remedies and their government in general.[41] It might dispel "ignorance and distrust of courts,...and contribute to public understanding of the rule of law and to comprehension of the functioning of the entire criminal judicial system, as well as improve the quality of that system by subjecting it to the cleansing effect of exposure and public accountability."[42]

Election-day news coverage and editorials might provide voters with timely information.[43] In labor disputes, picketing, as a form of speech, might be "essential to the securing of an informed and educated public opinion" in the arena of economic disputes.[44] Even purely commercial speech (such as advertising) has been protected on the grounds that it provides information on important issues, improves resource allocation in a free enterprise system, helps assure informed decision making, and affects attitudes on how the economy should be regulated.[45] Finally, protecting the media's freedom of speech might allow media to point out and restrain government abuses.[46]

The modern Court, however, has not protected all forms of speech. Several alternative tests for judging free speech afford less protection for unpopular speech than the clear, present, and imminent danger test.[47] Further, even proponents of the clear, present, and imminent danger test may approve limits on speech that is libelous,[48] provocative,[49] obscene,[50] or purely commercial;[51] speech occurring within a conspiracy,[52] speech that also involves action,[53] or speech that occurs in an inappropriate place, manner, or time.[54]

Arguments favoring the protection of speech, on the grounds that it informs public opinion and benefits a democratic society, may be found in many Court rulings over the last half century. This theory has most often been applied in media, trial rights, or dissent cases, although other instances occur in labor, election or commercial speech controversies, discussed below.

MEDIA CASES

The theory that informed public opinion relies heavily upon press coverage underpins many Court rulings that protect newspapers (and later, films, as well) from government-imposed restrictions.[55] Among the early landmark cases that advance this theory are *Near v. Minnesota* (1931), and *Grosjean v. American Press Company* (1936). In *Near*, a narrow 5-to-4 majority struck down a state law permitting prior restraint. For the majority, Chief Justice Hughes, quoting Blackstone, held that by informing public opinion about government abuse, "(t)he liberty of the press is indeed essential to the nature of a free state."[56] In *Grosjean*, Justice Sutherland, for a unanimous Court, struck down a Louisiana tax levied only against newspapers with large circulations. Wrote Sutherland, the tax was, in reality "a deliberate and calculated device in the guise of a tax to limit the circulation of information to which the public is entitled."[57]

Many later Court decisions have used this logic to extend greater protection to the media. In *Joseph Burstyn, Inc. v. Wilson* (1952), the Court used this theory to extend First and Fourteenth Amendment protection to motion pictures.[58] A year later, the Court prevented a congressional committee from using a lobby regulation statute to demand information on dissenters' efforts to influence general public opinion through books and periodicals.[59] In *Miami Herald Publishing Co. v. Tornillo* (1974), a unanimous Court struck down a Florida right-of-access law requiring a newspaper to print rebuttals to editorials critical of a candidate. While recognizing the increasing concentration of media ownership, the Court held that right-of-access laws for newspapers would effectively limit news coverage and reduce the vigor of public debate.[60]

Those Court opinions that argue that media coverage informs public opinion, however, do not always strike down restrictions on the press. In restricting the media, the Court frequently has reconciled limits on the press with this first theory in one of two ways. First, the Court may hold that the particular restriction does not meaningfully limit the press's role in informing public opinion. Second, the Court may argue that other values are, on balance, more critical.

The Supreme Court has frequently acknowledged the role of the press in informing public opinion, yet held that a given regulation does not significantly impede the press. In 1973 a divided Court upheld a local ban on sex-designated "help wanted" ads, ruling that the ban involved only "purely commercial advertising" not covered by the First Amendment.[61] In *Pell v. Procunier* (1974) and *Houchins, Sheriff, v. KQED* (1978), the Court upheld limits on face-to-face contacts between prisoners and reporters, and limits on media visits to jails. Since other means existed for inmates to communicate with reporters, the Court reasoned, the public's right to be informed was not unreasonably limited.[62]

In still other rulings the Court acknowledged the role of the press in informing public opinion, yet held that its role was outweighed by other important values. These decisions, balancing the First Amendment against other claims, may be found in a wide variety of areas. In *New York Times Co. v. Sullivan* (1964), for example, the Court balanced free speech, press, and public right-to-know claims against a public official's right to be protected from libel.[63] The Court devised the test that a public official must prove "actual malice" — knowledge of false statements and reckless disregard for the truth — before libel damages could be awarded.[64] In *Branzburg v. Hayes* (1972) the Court balanced a reporter's need for confidentiality (which might better inform the public about future crimes) against the public's present interest in prosecuting crimes.[65] In some instances the Court has also permitted pre-trial or suppression hearings to be closed.[66]

COURT PROCEDURES

The argument that speech, action and news coverage inform public opinion, and merit protection, has also been advanced in many other controversies. Open trials, for example, have frequently been held to restrain judicial abuse. As Justice Black wrote in *In re: Oliver* (1948), "(t)he knowledge that every criminal trial is subject to contemporaneous review in the forum of public opinion is an effective restraint on possible abuse of judicial power."[67] While some pre-trial or suppression hearings may be closed,[68] criminal trials themselves cannot be closed to the media or to the public. In 1978 and 1980 the Court held that media coverage and public attendance at trials inform the public, and are therefore protected.[69]

In a related area, judge-issued punishments for contempt, the Supreme Court has shown increased tolerance for criticism of judges by newspaper editors and litigants. In the early 1900s the Court often upheld judge-issued contempt punishments against newspapers or litigants for criticism made during a trial or as a court carried out its orders. In *Patterson v. Colorado* (1907), *Toledo Newspaper Co. v. U.S.* (1918), and *Craig v. Hecht* (1923), the Supreme Court upheld contempt punishments for criticism well outside the courthouse, because the criticism was found to be intended to influence public opinion during a pending case.[70]

By the 1940s, however, the Court had begun to restrict far-reaching contempt punishments, expressly overruling *Toledo Newspaper Co.* in *Nye v. U.S.* (1942).[71] In a long line of decisions the Court held that criticism of a court, when intended to influence public opinion alone, could not be punished by contempt unless the criticism also constituted a clear, present, and imminent danger to a fair trial. In 1941, the Court held that out-of-court newspaper editorials, which might influence public attitudes and cause disrespect for the courts, did not sufficiently interfere with a pending case to justify a contempt punishment.[72] In *Pennekamp v. Florida* (1946) a judge's desire to "retain public esteem and secure reelection" was held insufficient to punish a publisher and associate editor for cartoon and editorial criticism of a judge in a pending, nonjury proceeding.[73] In *Craig v. Harney, Sheriff* (1947), the Court held that "the law of contempt is not made for protection of judges who may be sensitive to the winds of public opinion." Even extreme newspaper criticism usually did not constitute a clear and present danger to a court proceeding.[74] Years later the Supreme Court also overturned contempt citations for a defendant's criticism of the court during summation,[75] and for criticism of a grand jury investigation by a public official's press release during a political campaign.[76]

DISSENT CASES

The clear, present, and imminent danger tests were developed in the cases involving accused anarchists and communists. Throughout the last half century, the Supreme Court has often questioned whether unpopular or controversial speech merits constitutional protection. Except in cases involving accused Communists (especially during the 1950s and 1960s) the Court has often protected dissent, partly on the grounds that dissent influences and informs public opinion.[77]

In several decisions during the Cold War era the Court acknowledged that dissent might inform or influence public opinion, but could, nonetheless, be overbalanced by security interests. In *Dennis v. U.S.* (1951), Chief Justice Vinson, for the Court, interpreted the clear and present danger test more narrowly than had Justices Holmes and Brandeis. Vinson argued that in the case of high-ranking Communist party officials, the test should ascertain "whether the gravity of the 'evil,' discounted by its probability, justifies such invasion of free speech as is necessary to avoid the danger."[78] In a foreign-dominated, "highly organized conspiracy with rigidly disciplined members," where speech advocates action, dissent by top Communist party leaders might be suppressed. In *Scales v. U.S.* (1961) the Court again sustained a conviction for a "knowing" and "active" Communist party member and denied First Amendment protection to advocacy intended to influence public attitudes.[79] In *Wilkinson v. U.S.* (1961), a five-member Court majority held that attempts to influence public opinion (by an alleged Communist organizer) did not preclude a congressional committee's investigation of Communist infiltration.[80]

In other rulings, however, the Court has been more sympathetic toward arguments that dissent informed public opinion, and deserved protection. In *Weiman v. Updegraff* (1952) the Court struck down an Oklahoma loyalty oath for college professors that barred employment for teachers who had merely held membership in a subversive-designated group.[81] The Court held that an unknowing or innocent member, who lacked knowledge of the group's subversive purpose, could not be penalized. The Court held that the Oklahoma law, as applied to college professors, stifled "the flow of democratic expression and controversy at one of its chief sources."[82] In *Yates v. U.S.* (1957) the Court limited prosecution of low-ranking, unknowing, or inactive Communist party members, and held that mere advocacy of the forcible overthrow of the government, as an abstract argument only, was a protected form of speech.[83] Still later, in 1965, the Court struck down a regulation requiring an addressee to return a postcard to receive unsealed foreign mailings of "Communist political propaganda"; the postal regulation was held to inhibit an informed public.[84]

In non-Communist dissent cases the Court has been far more protective of free speech, often arguing that exposure to dissent informs public opinion. In *Terminiello v. Chicago* (1949) Justice Douglas, for the Court, held that "the vitality of civil and political institutions in our society depends on free discussion." "(P)rovocative and challenging," even offensive speech, has been protected unless the speech was likely to produce "a clear and present danger of a serious substantive evil that rises far above public inconvenience, annoyance or unrest." Even speech that "stirred people to anger, invited public dispute, or brought about a condition of unrest should be protected."[85]

Still later in *Edwards v. South Carolina* (1963), a civil rights case, the Court acknowledged that speech "may strike at prejudices and preconceptions...as it presses for acceptance of an idea."[86] In 1969, the Court upheld the passive, nondisruptive wearing of black armbands in public schools as a Vietnam War protest, partly on grounds that students' exposure to dissent encouraged "independence and vigor" in later adult life.[87] And, in 1971, the Court held that even vulgar or offensive words (in this case, sewn on a jacket) might be protected as promoting "a more capable citizenry and more perfect polity."[88] Indeed, even a mailed pamphlet appealing to racial prejudices, libeling the president, and criticizing the war effort during World War

Two was held to be a protected method of influencing public opinion.[89]

RELATED DECISIONS

In decisions concerning picketing by strikers at the site of a labor dispute, the Court expanded Justices Holmes and Brandeis's logic. In *Thornhill v. Alabama* (1940) the Court held that, barring a clear, present, and imminent danger, picketing was a protected means of informing and influencing public opinion about economic disputes.[90] Peaceful picketing was held to "enlighten the public on the nature and causes of a labor dispute" and was "essential to the securing of an informed and educated public opinion."[91] Picketing could be restricted, but not simply because it might cause economic damage to the picketed firm.[92]

While early Supreme Court decisions refused First Amendment protection to purely commercial speech,[93] during the 1970s the Court extended protection to truthful commercial speech — largely on the grounds that truthful commercial speech informs and influences public opinion. In 1975, 1976, and 1977, Justice Blackmun, for the Court, held that commercial advertising might provide information on services and programs available in other states or communities, bring about more intelligent and better informed economic decision making, improve the free enterprise system, shape attitudes on how the economic system should be regulated, and provide information on significant public issues.[94]

The argument that speech informs or influences public opinion and merits protection has also occurred in several campaign spending decisions. A lengthy per curiam in *Buckley v. Valeo* (1976) acknowledged that limits on campaign spending, donations, and disclosure requirements might limit speech.[95] Even so, the Court upheld campaign spending limits, contribution limits, and disclosure requirements,[96] but struck down limits on independent spending (judging it to be only indirectly connected with candidate campaigns), disclosure requirements for some minor parties or independent candidates (because these requirements could threaten the speech of dissenters), spending by candidates themselves or their own families, and spending limits for Congress (when not matched by federal funds). In *First National Bank of Boston v. Bellotti* (1978) the Court further permitted campaign spending by upholding referendum spending by corporations — partly on the grounds that corporations, too, enjoyed free speech rights, and partly on the grounds that the public was entitled to a full range of information.[97]

Judicial Restraint

A second major theory of public opinion argues that the Court should defer to elected officials and to public opinion. This theory holds that public opinion is itself an adequate check on government action and, hence, judicial review and judicial activism are unnecessary. About one-fifth (21 percent) of the modern Court's direct mentions of public opinion reflected this view.

This theory is one of several doctrines, rules, principles, or tests which the Court may apply to refuse judicial review or to invoke judicial restraint.[98] Some "threshold" tests are procedural. For example, a real case or controversy must exist; the suit must be ripe (but not yet moot); no advisory opinions must be issued; the litigants must have standing to sue, and "political questions" must be avoided. If at least four justices believe that an appeal meets the threshold standards, the Supreme Court may consider whether to uphold or overturn a challenged law or policy. At this point justices who prefer judicial restraint may cite the second theory — that the Court should defer to the interplay of public opinion and elected officials.

Because so many other grounds for judicial restraint exist, many restraint decisions do not explicitly discuss deference to public opinion at all. Judicial restraint opinions may focus entirely on other grounds, such as the Court's inability to formulate a manageable policy, or deference to precedent or original intent. A few justices (most notably Justices Holmes and Frankfurter) have developed explicit arguments in favor of the use of mass public opinion to support judicial restraint.

In *Tyson and Brother v. Banton* (1927), Justice Holmes criticized the Court's conservative, activist theories in economic regulation cases. Argued Holmes, with regard to government-regulated business owners or corporations, "subject to compensation when compensation is due, the legislature may forbid or restrict any business when it has a sufficient force of public opinion behind it."[99] Dissenting in *U.S. v. Butler* (1936), Justice Stone argued that in economic cases "for removal of unwise laws, appeal lies in...the ballot and...the processes of democratic government."[100] In *Minersville School District v. Gobitis* (1940), a flag salute case, Justice Frankfurter, for the Court, wrote that "(t)o fight out the wise use of legislative authority in the forum of public opinion and before legislative assemblies rather than to transfer such a contest to the judicial arena, serves to vindicate the self-confidence of a free people."[101] Concurring in a 1949 ruling that upheld local restrictions on the use of sound trucks, Frankfurter wrote that "(t)hese are matters for legislative judgement controlled by public opinion."[102] And, in a 1955 court-martial dispute, Justice Reed, in dissent, argued that "the methods for maintenance of Army discipline should be subject to public opinion as expressed through Congress."[103]

Other decisions have also held that public opinion itself will protect basic rights, and hence, that further judicial review is unnecessary. In *Wolf v. Colorado* (1949), Justice Frankfurter declined to apply the exclusionary rule to state-level courts, arguing that defendants were adequately protected by "the remedies of private action and such protection as the internal discipline of the police, under the eyes of an alert public opinion, may afford."[104] In *Frank v. Maryland* (1959), Frankfurter declined to review warrantless residential code inspections, on the grounds that "experience (has not) revealed any abuse or inroad on freedom in meeting this need by means that history and dominant public opinion have sanctioned."[105]

A few opinions go further to argue that excessive judicial activism causes public opinion to grow complacent on political issues. Justice Frankfurter is best known for such arguments. In *West Virginia Board of Education v. Barnette* (1943), Frankfurter, in dissent, argued that judicial review may "dwarf the political capacity of the people and...deaden its sense of moral responsibility."[106] In *Baker v. Carr* (1962), again in dissent, Frankfurter wrote that appeals for more equitable apportionment of electoral districts should be directed not to the Court, but "to an informed, civically militant electorate. In a democratic society like ours, relief must come through an aroused popular conscience that sears the conscience of the people's representatives."[107]

Explicit discussions of public opinion in judicial restraint opinions have also appeared in several other controversies, such as labor union and strike disputes. Many involved railway strike procedures regulated under either Title III of the 1920 Transportation Act, or, later, the 1926 Railway Labor Act.[108] In a long series of decisions, the Court reviewed the extent to which railway strikes were to be regulated by states, federal agencies, or lower courts, versus their being regulated by public opinion and the railroad or union's own actions.[109] Several other labor cases also weighed the effectiveness of the role that public opinion plays in pressuring unions and companies to end strikes.[110]

The theory that courts should defer to elected officials and public opinion clearly predated both the New Deal period and the development of scientific public opinion polling.[111] This theory was already well developed in the late 1800s, most notably in lottery and alcohol regulation decisions,[112] and in business and wage regulation cases such as *Munn v. Illinois* (1876),[113] *Holden v. Hardy* (1898),[114] *Lochner v. New York* (1905),[115] or *Mueller v. Oregon* (1908).[116]

Evolving Public Opinion

The third theory involves a more complex analysis than the second. In this third theory, the Court compares some law (or policy) against contemporary or evolving public opinion and may strike down laws or policies held to be inconsistent with public opinion. This third theory requires that the Court assess public attitudes, and existing laws or policies separately, and that it not simply assume, ipso facto, that a law reflects public opinion. This theme appeared in about one-fifth (21 percent) of modern Court opinions that directly mention public opinion.

The Court's reading of contemporary public opinion need not be based upon specific poll results. Justices more often rely on indirect measures of public opinion, such as legislative statutes, lower court rulings, referendum results, or even their own general, if undocumented understanding of public attitudes. As Table 3.4 suggests, this theory appeared in Supreme Court decisions long before the advent of scientific polling techniques.

During the late 1800s the Supreme Court applied this theory chiefly in two types of cases: first, in deciding what crimes required a grand jury indictment: and second, in deciding what punishments were cruel and unusual (and hence, unconstitutional). During the late 1800s and early 1900s, criminal indictments were often made without a grand jury, by information filed by a district attorney. For an "infamous" federal crime, however, the Supreme Court held that a grand jury indictment was required. What constituted an infamous crime "may be affected by the changes of public opinion from one age to another."[117] Imprisonment at hard labor, the Court held, was both legally and in the popular mind permissible only for an infamous crime.[118] In *Mackin v. U.S.* (1886) the Court later acknowledged that "...at the present day imprisonment in a State prison or penitentiary, with or without hard labor, is an infamous punishment...in the general opinion of the people."[119]

The second line of cases originating in the 1800s interpreted the Eighth Amendment ban on cruel and unusual punishments in terms of prevailing public opinion. In *O'Neil v. Vermont* (1892) Justices Field, Harlan, and Brewer, in dissent, argued that a fine of $6,637.96 or a sentence of 19,914 days at hard labor, imposed for 307 liquor sales, was cruel and unusual. Justice Field, complained "...it is hard to believe that any man of right feeling and heart can refrain from shuddering."[120] Nearly two decades later the Court dealt more explicitly with public attitudes in *Weems v. U.S.* (1910). In this case the Court held that the meaning of the cruel and unusual clause "is not fastened to the obsolete, but may acquire meaning as public opinion becomes enlightened by a humane justice."[121]

The theory that criminal procedures should be weighed against contemporary or evolving public attitudes also appeared in many later cases. In *Palko v. Connecticut* (1937) Justice Cardozo argued that the Bill of Rights should be applied to the states when the rights it outlines were fundamental to the concept of ordered liberty, but it need only include those rights "so rooted in the traditions and conscience of our people as to be ranked fundamental."[122] In *Louisiana ex rel. Francis v. Resweber* (1947), Justice Frankfurter upheld a second electrocution for a prisoner when the first attempt had failed. Argued Frankfurter, a second electrocution did not offend "the consensus of society's opinion."[123] In another 1947 decision Frankfurter wrote that "the standards of justice are not authoritatively formulated anywhere as though they were prescriptions in a pharmacopoeia" but rather they "move within the limits of accepted notions of justice."[124] In *Trop v. Dulles* (1957), Chief Justice Warren argued that expatriation for desertion was "a fate universally decried by civilized people," and that it was incompatible with "the evolving standards of decency that mark the progress of a maturing society."[125] And, in *Robinson v. California* (1962), Justice Stewart struck down a law that had made narcotics addiction illegal: "...in light of contemporary human knowledge, a law which made a criminal offence of such a disease would doubtlessly be universally thought to be an infliction of cruel and unusual punishment."[126]

The best-known debates over evolving public opinion have occurred in death penalty rulings during the 1960s and 1970s. In 1963, three justices argued that the Court should review whether the death penalty for rape violated "the 'evolving standards of decency that mark the progress of (our) maturing society' or 'evolving standards of decency more or less universally accepted.'"[127] Five years later, in *Witherspoon v. Illinois* (1968), the Court ruled that persons opposing capital punishment could not be excluded from a capital punishment jury. Wrote Justice Stewart: "...in a nation less than half of whose people believe in the death penalty, a jury composed exclusively of such people cannot speak for the community...(S)uch a jury can speak only for a distinct and dwindling minority."[128]

Furman v. Georgia (1972) represents the Court's most complete debate over contemporary American public opinion, although none of the several opinions in *Furman* hinged entirely on public opinion polls. Justice Marshall flatly asserted that the death penalty "violates the Eighth Amendment because it is morally unacceptable to the people of the United States at this time in their history,"[129] but he limited his meaning of public opinion to "people who were fully informed."[130] Justices Douglas, Stewart, White, and Brennan also held that the death penalty was, by contemporary standards, cruel and unusual, but also based their decisions partly on jury actions,[131] discriminatory effects[132], or the "freakish" inconsistency of application of the penalty.[133]

Other justices, however, have argued that contemporary public opinion — measured directly by polls, or indirectly by legislation, referendum results, or jury decisions — did not oppose the death penalty.[134] In *Gregg v. Georgia* (1976), three justices cited legislation, referenda, revised and polls results since *Furman* to argue that public opinion supported revised death penalty statutes.[135] Similar arguments, in dissent, were advanced in *Roberts v. Louisiana* (1976, 1977), against striking down a mandatory death penalty for the killing of a policeman or a prison guard.[136] In *Coker v. Georgia* (1977), Justices Burger and Rehnquist, in dissent, noted that three states had recently reenacted the death penalty for rape, and asked: "(i)f the Court is to rely on some 'public opinion' process, does this not suggest the beginning of a 'trend'?"[137]

Many other opinions also relied, at least in part, upon the theory of evolving or contemporary public opinion.[138] In 1947 the Supreme Court held that Congress, administrative agencies, court decisions, and "informed public opinion" supported the Hatch Act's ban on political activities.[139] In *Poe v. Ullman* (1961), Justice Harlan argued that Connecticut's anti-contraception law represented the bygone public opinion of the 1800s.[140] Several obscenity rulings also required that allegedly obscene materials be evaluated against "contemporary community standards"[141] — whether state[142] or national.[143] Standards such as the "common conscience of the community,"[144] the "average person,"[145] or the "contemporary notions of rudimentary decency"[146] pervade the widely varying, often elusive tests for judging obscenity.

Threats to Constitutional Rights

About one-fifth (19 percent) of the modern Court's direct mentions of public opinion reflected a fourth theory — that public opinion threatens criminal, free speech, or economic rights. Supreme Court rulings that argue that community public opinion threatens fair trial procedures may be found as early as *Patterson v. Colorado* (1907). In that case Justice Holmes held that the Fourteenth Amendment did not preclude a contempt citation for a newspaper publisher who had criticized a state court in an ongoing case.[147] Argued Holmes, "the conclusions to be reached in a case (should)...not (be induced) by any outside influence, whether of private talk or public print."[148] Juries and judges alike may be influenced by press criticism during a trial, argued Holmes, and judges may punish such "interference" by a contempt charge.

Justice Holmes's reference to "private talk or public print" did not provide direct evidence that public opinion had actually influenced the court's decision. After *Patterson*, however, a string of opinions holding that public opinion might threaten a fair trial cited more obvious threats — chiefly, outraged community opinion toward black defendants in the South. In *Frank v. Magnum* (1915) Justice Pitney, for the Court, held that "if a trial is in fact dominated by a mob, so that the jury is intimidated and the trial judge yields, and so that there is an actual interference with the course of justice, there is, in that court, a departure from due process of law..."[149] In *Frank*, the Court denied that the trial actually had involved such circumstances, despite Justice Holmes's dissent that the trial had been characterized by "mob law" and "a terrorized jury."[150] Eight years later, Justice Holmes, writing for the majority in *Moore v. Dempsey* (1923), reversed a denial of habeas corpus in the murder conviction of five Arkansas negroes. Holmes found that the trial had been characterized by mob violence, brutally forced confessions, a jury from which blacks were excluded, and "an irrestible wave of public passion."[151] In *Powell v. Alabama* (1932), the Court reversed and remanded other death penalty convictions upon evidence of effective lack of counsel and a "tense, hostile, and excited public sentiment."[152]

In later years mob actions, outraged community opinion, or prejudicial publicity led to reversed convictions in several prominent cases, such as *Shepherd v. Florida* (1951), *Estes v. Texas* (1965), and *Sheppard v. Maxwell* (1966).[153] In a later dispute the Court even held that community prejudice and massive media coverage might require a venue change in a misdemeanor case.[154] In *Gannett Co. v. DePasquale* (1979) Justice Stewart, for the majority, allowed the closing of a pre-trial hearing, which he found "could influence public opinion against a defendant and inform potential jurors of inculpatory information wholly inadmissible at the actual trial."[155] And, in 1980, an "outcry of unjustified criticism" against judges who had reduced death penalty sentences to life imprisonment without parole, helped persuade the Court to strike down an Alabama law limiting jury discretion in death penalty sentencing.[156]

In protecting defendants' trial rights the Court has often argued that the trial judge is the chief bulwark against hostile public opinion and prejudicial publicity.[157] In several instances the Court overturned convictions when a judge failed to prevent media disruption in the courtroom, or failed to prevent hostile public opinion from prejudicing the jury.[158] To counter a widespread public belief that silence implies guilt, in 1981 the Court held that a judge could be required to instruct a jury not to infer guilt from a defendant's refusal to testify.[159]

This negative view of public opinion appeared not only in criminal cases, but also in the treatment of political dissidents. During the 1950s and 1960s several Court decisions protected accused Communists from the adverse effects of public opinion. In 1955 the Court held that a federal employee, twice cleared for security, could not be disqualified from service should he be unable to confront and cross-examine his accusers at a later inquiry; the majority held that an employee should be "assured that his fate would not be decided by political appointees...more vulnerable to the pressures of heated public opinion."[160] In *Stack v. Boyle* (1951) Justice Jackson argued that public opinion pressures had brought about excessively high bail, which had caused accused Communists to be kept in jail before trial.[161] And in *Weiman v. Updegraff* (1952) the Court held that only a narrowly drawn statute could justify excluding persons from college teaching on disloyalty grounds. In part, the Court based its ruling on the severe public sanctions that might result: "In the view of the community, the stain is a deep one; indeed it has become a badge of infamy."[162]

In their efforts to protect unpopular dissidents from hostile public opinion, Justices Douglas and Black were often the Court's most outspoken members. In 1951, the two justices, in dissent, took note of the "present climate of public opinion" and the adverse effects that resulted from designating an organization as subversive.[163] In 1956, again in dissent, Black and Douglas elaborated on the penalty of infamy and adverse public opinion: "When public opinion casts a person into the outer darkness, as happens today when a person is exposed as a Communist, the government brings infamy on (a) witness when it compels disclosure."[164] Still later, in *W.E.B. DuBois Clubs v. Clark* (1967), Black, in dissent, raised the "classic" meaning of public opinion — a coerced unanimity of opinion — in protesting the club's required registration as a Communist front organization.[165]

The argument that public opinion may threaten rights appeared in other cases, as well. In *Beuharnais v. Illinois* (1952) Justice Frankfurter, for the Court, upheld the Illinois "group libel" law, as a legitimate means to prevent "the systematic manipulation of a (mobile public opinion) by the use of calculated falsehood and vilification."[166] In *Norton v. Disciplinary Committee* (1970), three justices argued in dissent, that public opinion had improperly caused several college students to be suspended for circulating leaflets critical of a university administration.[167] In 1970 Justice Douglas held that segregated lunch counters, based upon community customs and state enforcement, could be banned.[168]

The Court more vigorously protected associational privacy rights when the group did not include accused Communists. In *NAACP v. Alabama* (1958), the Court struck down Alabama's attempt to force disclosure of the NAACP membership list, on the grounds that the privacy of the list protected members from hostile public opinion and "private community pressure." [169]

In 1960 the Court again protected NAACP membership lists, citing a "fear of community hostility and economic reprisals."[170] In *Shelton v. Tucker* (1960), a closely divided Court struck down an Arkansas law that required public school and college teachers to file annual reports of organizations to which they belonged or contributed. The Arkansas law, held Justice Stewart, involved "the possibility of public pressure upon school boards to discharge teachers who belong to unpopular or minority organizations."[171]

Other Court opinions extended the argument that public opinion can be a threat to rights in economic cases. Justice Sutherland's dissents during the 1930s offer the best examples. In a mortgage moratorium dispute, Justice Sutherland, in dissent, wrote that "(I)t is with special reference to the varying moods of public opinion, and with a view to putting the fundamentals of government beyond their control, that (a written constitution was) framed."[172] Three years later, in a state minimum wage dispute, Justice Sutherland, again in dissent, wrote that "much of the benefit expected from written constitutions would be lost if their provisions were to be bent to circumstances or modified by public opinion."[173] While these views lost favor during the 1930s, they reflected a long line of earlier Supreme Court decisions.[174]

Conclusion

The modern Supreme Court has applied the concept of public opinion in a wide variety of rulings. Almost all direct mentions of public opinion reflect one of four judicial theories, although the balance among these four theories has clearly varied over the last two centuries.[175]

Most Supreme Court discussions of public opinion are not based upon any very precise reading of nationwide attitudes. Since the mid-1930s two-thirds of the Court's direct mentions have occurred in normative or theoretical discussions. The modern Court rarely cites specific polls, and, even when it does, it often gives poll results little weight.

That the modern Court usually relies upon one of the four major theories discussed in this chapter does not necessarily mean that the Court is predisposed to hand down a majoritarian ruling. In many instances, applying the first or fourth theory may lead the Court to a countermajoritarian decision — protecting an unpopular individual or group. In applying the second theory, the Court may defer to local, not nationwide majorities. In applying the third theory, the Court may simply misread contemporary attitudes. In short, the modern Court's theories of public opinion do not explain how often it reaches a majoritarian, versus a countermajoritarian decision. This question is discussed in the next chapter.

References

1 *Home Building & Loan Association v. Blaisdell* (1934), 450.
2 *Chambers v. Florida* (1940), 229.
3 Louisiana ex rel. Francis v. Resweber, Sheriff (1947), 469, 471.
4 *Irvin v. Dowd, Warden* (1961), 719, 728.
5 *Communist Party v. Subversive Activities Control Board* (1961), 102.
6 *Rideau v. Louisiana* (1963), 729.
7 *Adickes v. Kress Co.* (1970), 179.
8 References to public opinion during the 1800s were often even less direct. Examples include "the people in their sovereign capacity," *Stone v. Mississippi* (1880), 821; "the public will,"

Hurtado v. California (1884), 532; "the judgment of mankind" or "every civilized and Christian community" or "any man of right feeling and heart," *O'Neil v. Vermont* (1892), 340; and "a popular demand" or "wishes of the citizens" or "the people of each state," *Holden v. Hardy* (1898), 384–385, 387, 389. For direct mentions of public opinion during the early 1800s, see Tables 3.1 to 3.4.

9 For the modern period, percentages are based on the 142 majority, concurring, dissenting, or per curiam opinions, 1934–1986, which directly mention "public opinion." Percentages may exceed 100 percent due to multiple usages which appear in some decisions. For the period 1792–1859, the Court made 21 direct mentions of public opinion, and from 1860–1933, another 34 direct mentions. For the period 1792–1859, full printed decisions begin with *Georgia v. Brailsford* (1792).

10 Percentages here do not include indirect references to mass attitudes. If close synonyms for public opinion were also counted, the percentage of references to a specific poll result would decline.

11 These decisions are reported below, at notes 127–137.

12 See *In the Matter of James Caplinger* (1981); *Ingraham v. Wright* (1977), 660–661; *Hannegan v. Esquire* (1946), 157; *Carter v. Kentucky* (1891), 303; *Public Utilities Commission v. Pollack* (1952), 459–460. For other examples, see *Textile Workers Union v. Lincoln Mills* (1957), 517–518; *Roth v. U.S.* (1957), 509; *Branzburg v. Hayes* (1971), 694, n. 33; *Bates v. Arizona State Bar* (1977), 370–371, n. 22, 23; and *Linmark Associates, Inc. v. Willingboro* (1977), 90, n. 5.

13 *Furman v. Georgia* (1972), 360–363. Justice Marshall further cited an earlier opinion by Judge Frank, that "(T)he community's attitude — is usually an unknowable. It represents a slithery shadow, since one can seldom learn, at all accurately, what the community, or a majority actually feels. Even a carefully-taken 'public opinion poll' would be inconclusive in a case like this." Cited at 361, n. 143. See also Neil Vidmar and Phoebe Ellsworth, "Public Opinion and the Death Penalty," *Stanford Law Review* 26 (June 1974): 1245–1270; and Austin Sarat and Neil Vidmar, "Public Opinion, the Death Penalty, and the Eighth Amendment: Testing the Marshall Hypothesis," *Wisconsin Law Review* (1976): 171–197.

14 *Furman v. Georgia* (1972), 360–363.

15 *Furman v. Georgia* (1972), 441–442.

16 *Furman v. Georgia* (1972), 385: "In looking for reliable indicia of contemporary attitude, none more trustworthy has been advanced (than state and federal statutes)."

17 See, for example, *Gregg v. Georgia* (1976), 181, n. 25.

18 *Estes v. Texas* (1965), 548–549, 599; *Craig v. Harney* (1947), 370–371.

19 *Witherspoon v. Illinois* (1968), 521, n. 19.

20 *Shepherd v. Florida* (1951), 50–55.

21 *Ingraham v. Wright* (1977), 660–661, n. 17; *United Public Workers of America v. Mitchell* (1947), 102–103.

22 *Coker v. Georgia* (1977), 613–614; *Lassiter v. Department of Social Services* (1981), 34; *Rudolph v. Alabama* (1963), 889–890.
23 *National City Bank of New York v. Republic of China* (1955), 359.
24 *Norton v. Disciplinary Committee* (1970), 909.
25 *U.S. v. United Mine Workers* (1947), 349–350; *Stack v. Boyle* (1951), 10; *Dennis v. U.S.* (1951), 581; *Sweezy v. New Hampshire* (1957), 240–241, n. 6; *Frank v. Maryland* (1959), 372.
26 These overall results contrast sharply to the subset of direct mentions of public opinion that cite specific polls. Three-quarters (77 percent) of the Court's citings of specific polls have occurred after 1960.
27 For an even earlier discussion, see Jeremy Bentham, *Rationale of Judicial Evidence*, ed. by John Stuart Mill (London: Hunt and Clarke, 1827); John Stuart Mill, *On Liberty* (New York: Liberal Arts Press, 1956). For other discussions, see Alexander Meiklejohn, *Free Speech and Its Relation to Self Government* (New York: Harper & Row, 1948); and Woodrow Wilson, *Congressional Government* (1885, reprinted, Cleveland: World Publishing Co., 1967), 303–304. For a review of earlier Court rulings, see Justice Frankfurter, concurring, in *Kovacs v. Cooper* (1949), 90–95. More generally, see Thomas Emerson, *Toward A General Theory of the First Amendment* (New York: Vintage, 1966); and Martin Shapiro, *Freedom of Speech: The Supreme Court and Judicial Review* (Englewood Cliffs, N.J.: Prentice-Hall, 1966).
28 *Shenck v. U.S.* (1919), 53.
29 *Whitney v. California* (1927), 373.
30 *Whitney v. California* (1927), 376–377.
31 *Whitney v. California* (1927), 374.
32 *Whitney v. California* (1927), 375.
33 *Abrams v. U.S.* (1919), 630.
34 *De Jonge v. Oregon* (1937), 365.
35 *Cohen v. California* (1971), 24.
36 *Edwards v. South Carolina* (1963), 237.
37 *Dennis v. U.S.* (1951), 584.
38 *Cantwell v. Connecticut* (1940), 310.
39 *Tinker v. Des Moines Independent Community School District* (1969), 508–509.
40 *West Virginia v. Barnett* (1943), 637.
41 *In re: Oliver* (1948), 270, n. 24.
42 *Nebraska Press Association v. Stuart* (1976), 587. See also *Branzburg v. Hayes* (1972), 720–726.
43 *Mills v. Alabama* (1966), 218–220. For a discussion of election-day exit polls, see Clyde Spillenger, "Early Election Projections, Restrictions on Exit Polling, and the First Amendment," *Yale Law and Policy Review* 3 (Summer 1984): 210–230.
44 *Thornhill v. Alabama* (1940), 104.
45 *Virginia State Board of Pharmacy v. Virginia Citizens Consumer Council* (1976), 765; *Bates v. Arizona State Bar* (1977), 364.
46 *Grosjean v. American Press Company* (1936), 250.

47 By the standards of the early 1900s, the clear, present, and imminent danger tests were remarkably permissive. In *Abrams v. U.S.* (1919), and *Gitlow v. New York* (1925), for example, the Court majority held that advocacy of a particular belief (in that instance, criminal anarchy) was, per se, punishable. In *Abrams* the majority's opinion affirmed a conviction for anti-war leafletting based on the illicit purpose or intended effect of the speech.

   Various tests used in dissent cases were reviewed in Paul Murphy, *The Constitution in Crisis Times* (New York: Harper & Row, 1972), 21–32; and Jonathan D. Casper, *The Politics of Civil Liberties* (New York: Harper & Row, 1972), 17–86. Justice Black's absolutist position was described in his article, "The Bill of Rights," *New York University Law Review* 35, (April 1960): 865–881; see also his dissenting opinion in *Barenblatt v. U.S.* (1959), 140–154; and his concurring opinion in *Brandenburg v. Ohio* (1969), 449–450, as well as Justice Douglas's concurring opinion, 450–457.

48 See the discussion, below, at notes 63 and 64.

49 Champlinsky v. New Hampshire (1942).

50 Obscenity cases are discussed below, at notes 141–146.

51 *Valentine v. Chrestensen* (1942); *Pittsburgh Press Co. v. Pittsburgh Commission on Human Relations* (1973).

52 *Dennis v. U.S.* (1951).

53 See note 96, below, for examples from labor picketing disputes. These decisions were reviewed in Justice Frankfurter's concurring opinion, in *Dennis v. U.S.* (1951).

54 For discussions of restrictions on place, manner, and time and their bearing on efforts to influence public opinion, see *Lovell v. Griffin* (1938), 452; *Schneider v. State* (1939), 161; *Cantwell v. Connecticut* (1940), 310; *Martin v. City of Struthers* (1943), 143, 146–147; *Saia v. New York* (1948); *Terminiello v. Chicago* (1949); *Kunz v. New York* (1951); *Feiner v. New York* (1951); *Edwards v. South Carolina* (1963); *Cox v. Louisiana* (1965); and *Organization for a Better Austin v. O'Keefe* (1971), 419.

55 Court rulings for the broadcast media differ from rulings for the print media. Nonetheless, Supreme Court rulings that uphold the Federal Communications Commission requirements for rebuttal time, public affairs coverage, the equal time rule, and reply time for non-endorsed candidates also rely upon this theory. See *Red Lion Broadcasting Co. v. FCC* (1969), 390, arguing that the First Amendment's purpose is "to preserve an uninhibited marketplace of ideas in which the truth will ultimately prevail."

56 *Near v. Minnesota* (1931), 713, 716–717. See also *New York Times Co. v. U.S.* (1971), 728. In the *Pentagon Papers* dispute, Justice Stewart's opinion reflected the same argument: "(T)he only effective restraint upon executive policy and power in the areas of national defense and international affairs may lie in an enlightened citizenry — in an informed and critical public opinion

which alone can here protect the values of democratic government...(W)ithout an informed and free press there cannot be an enlightened people." See also Justice Douglas's concurring opinion, at 722–723, quoting from *Near*.

57 *Grosjean v. American Press Co.* (1936), 250: "(S)ince informed public opinion is the most potent of all restraints upon misgovernment, the suppression or abridgement of the publicity afforded by a free press cannot be regarded otherwise than with grave concern."

58 *Joseph Burstyn, Inc. v. Wilson* (1952), 501: "The importance of motion pictures as an organ of public opinion is not lessened by the fact that they are designed to entertain as well as to inform." In *Burstyn*, the Court overruled *Mutual Film Corporation v. Industrial Commission of Ohio* (1915), 244: "(T)he exhibition of moving pictures is a business pure and simple,...not to be regarded...as part of the press of the country or as organs of public opinion."

59 *U.S. v. Rumely* (1953), 46.

60 *Miami Herald Publishing Co. v. Tornillo* (1974), 250, 257.

61 *Pittsburgh Press Co. v. Pittsburgh Commission on Human Relations* (1973). In *Associated Press v. U.S.* (1945), 19–20, the Court held that news-gathering organizations were subject to antitrust action, denied that this infringed First Amendment protection, and held instead that news-gathering monopolies themselves limited freedom of the press. Justice Murphy, at 51–52, discussed the media's importance in informing public opinion, but dissented from using the Sherman Act against news-gathering organizations. For another antitrust case decided favorably to the media, see *Times-Picayune Publishing Co. v. U.S.* (1953), 602–604.

62 *Pell v. Procunier, Corrections Director* (1974), 828; *Houchins, Sheriff v. KQED* (1978), 9–10. See, however, the dissenting opinion, in *Houchins* at 32–33, that the restraint unreasonably limited the public's right to be informed on important public issues. For an opinion that censorship of prisoner mail must be judged as affecting right-to-receive claims, and as informing the public about prison conditions, see *Procunier v. Martinez* (1974), 408–419.

63 *New York Times v. Sullivan* (1964), 265–266.

64 In the *New York Times v. Sullivan* decision, the Court found for the newspaper. However, in *Curtis Publishing Co. v. Butts* (1964), 146–151, the Court upheld a lower court decision awarding libel damages to a public figure.

65 *Branzburg v. Hayes* (1972), 695. See also *Herbert v. Lando* (1979), 156–157, 169–175, for another discussion of balancing of the public's right-to-know, versus a public figure's libel claim. There, the Court held that a reporter may be forced to testify as to his thoughts and intentions in a libel suit. This complex area of law was extensively reviewed in the *Lando* ruling.

66 *Gannett Co., Inc. v. DePasquale* (1979). For another restrictive decision, see *Wiseman v. Massachusetts* (1970), 960–965.

67 *In re: Oliver* (1948), 269–270. Justice Black also argued that open trials would stimulate public knowledge of and confidence in the judicial system, encourage eyewitnesses to step forward, and protect unpopular defendants or groups.

68 *Gannett Co., Inc. v. DePasquale* (1979), also reviewed below. For an argument against closing a suppression hearing, see *Waller v. Georgia* (1984), 46.

69 *Richmond Newspapers, Inc. v. Virginia* (1980), 569–573, 575–580, 592–593; *Landmark Communications, Inc. v. Virginia* (1978), 842. In *Richmond Newspapers*, Chief Justice Burger further listed the benefits of discouraging perjury, or misconduct, or partiality, at 569; encouraging public confidence in the judiciary, at 570; and providing a "catharsis" for the community after a shocking crime, at 571. For other decisions providing for media coverage of trials, and relying on the same argument (that trial coverage informs the public, and merits protection), see *Cox Broadcasting Corp. v. Cohn* (1975), 491–495; *Nebraska Press Assn. v. Stuart* (1976), 559–560, 567–568; and *Sheppard v. Maxwell* (1966), 363.

70 *Patterson v. Colorado* (1907), 462–463; *Toledo Newspaper Co. v. U.S.* (1918), 412–415, and Justices Holmes and Brandeis dissenting, at 422–425; *Craig v. Hecht* (1923), 268–270, 277, and Justice Taft concurring, at 278. For other early cases, see *Gompers v. Buck Stove & Range Co.* (1911), or *Hitchman Coal & Coke v. Mitchell* (1917).

71 *Nye v. U.S.* (1941), 52.

72 *Times-Mirror Co. v. Superior Court* (1941). There, the Court held that "an enforced silence, however limited, solely in the name of preserving the dignity of the bench, would probably engender resentment, suspicion, and contempt more than it would enhance respect," at 170–271.

73 *Pennekamp v. Florida* (1946), 349.

74 *Craig v. Harney, Sheriff* (1947), 376.

75 *In re: Little* (1972), 555.

76 *Wood v. Georgia* (1962).

77 For a review of dissent cases from this period, see Henry Abraham, *Freedom and the Court*, 4th ed. (New York: Oxford, 1982), 176–188; Paul Murphy, *The Constitution in Crisis Times* (New York: Harper & Row, 1972), 279–309; and Jonathan D. Casper, *The Politics of Civil Liberties* (New York: Harper & Row, 1972), 17–86.

An informed public opinion is only one of many grounds upon which dissenter cases have been decided. For examples of other grounds, see *Pennsylvania v. Nelson* (1956), conflict of a state statute with a dominant federal statute; *Watkins v. U.S.* (1957), vagueness of a Congressional resolution authorizing a committee inquiry; *Deutch v. U.S.* (1961), specific inquiry not relevant to committee investigation; *Albertson v. Subversive Activities Control Board* (1965), self-incrimination; or *Weiman v. Updegraff* (1952), lack of scienter.

78 *Dennis v. U.S.* (1951), 510, citing Judge Learned Hand, 183 F. 2d at 212.

79 *Scales v. U.S.* (1961), 228–230. On the same day, however, the Court reversed a conviction for another Communist party member, holding that advocacy of an abstract doctrine, absent advocacy of present or future violence to overthrow the government, could not be punished; see *Noto v. U.S.* (1961), 297.

80 *Wilkinson v. U.S.* (1961), 414.

81 *Weiman v. Updegraff* (1952). For a description of later state court action, reading scienter into the statute, see "Evasion of Supreme Court Mandates in Cases Remanded to State Courts Since 1941," *Harvard Law Review* 67 (1954): 1251–1259, at 1255–1256.

82 *Weiman v. Updegraff* (1952), 191. Justice Black's concurring opinion cited the special importance of "habits of open-mindedness and critical inquiry...acquired in the formative years" and the role of teachers in introducing controversial views, fostering "open-mindedness" and "an enlightened and effective public opinion," at 196. For a similar argument, see *Keyishian v. Board of Regents* (1967), 601–603.

83 *Yates v. U.S.* (1957), 321, 326–327.

84 *Lamont v. Postmaster-General* (1965). Justices Brennan and Goldberg's concurring opinion raised the "right to receive" claim for political publications, as an integral part of free speech rights: "It would be a barren marketplace of ideas that had only sellers and no buyers," at 308.

85 *Terminiello v. Chicago* (1949), 5. But see *Feiner v. New York* (1951), 321, in which the conviction of a streetcorner speaker was upheld, on grounds that the speaker had passed "the bounds of argument or persuasion" and undertaken "incitement to riot." Justices Black, Douglas, and Minton dissented, on grounds that a speech's content, however excited, extravagant, or emotional, was a protected means of influencing public opinion, at 321, 329–331.

86 *Edwards v. South Carolina* (1963), 237, originally from *Terminiello v. Chicago* (1949), 4–5.

87 *Tinker v. Des Moines Independent Community School District* (1969), 508–509. Justice Fortas also held, at 510–511, that the school board had permitted symbols and expression of other political ideas.

88 *Cohen v. California* (1971), 24–25. See also *Papish v. Board of Curators of the University of Missouri* (1973).

89 *Hartzel v. U.S.* (1944), 688. See also *Keegan v. U.S.* (1945), 482.

90 *Thornhill v. Alabama* (1940), 105.

91 *Thornhill v. Alabama* (1940), 104–105: "Abridgement of the liberty of such discussion can only be justified where the clear danger of substantive evils arises under circumstances affording no opportunity to test the merits of ideas by competition for acceptance in the market of public opinion." The potential economic damage to a labor-picketed business was held insufficient to permit a

state-enforced ban on peaceful picketing. See also *A. F. of L. v. Swing* (1941), 326.

92 Various grounds include mass or excessive picketing, in *American Foundries v. Tri-City Council* (1921), and *Bakery Drivers v. Wohl* (1942), 775; actual or potential violence, in *Milk Wagon Drivers Union v. Meadowmoor Dairies* (1941); or picketing away from the site of the dispute, in *Carpenters & Joiners Union v. Ritter's Cafe* (1942).

93 *Valentine v. Chreistensen* (1942). For other examples, see the discussion in *Bigelow v. Virginia* (1975).

94 *Bigelow v. Virginia* (1975), 818; *Virginia State Board of Pharmacy v. Virginia Citizens Consumer Council* (1976); *Bates v. Arizona State Bar* (1977): "(T)he free flow of commercial information...is indispensable to the proper allocation of resources in a free enterprise system (and) to the formation of intelligent opinions as to how that system ought to be regulated or altered. Therefore, if the First Amendment were thought to be primarily an instrument to enlighten public decisionmaking in a democracy, we could not say that the free flow of information does not serve that goal," in *Virginia Board of Pharmacy*, 765; permissible restraints on commercial speech are discussed at 770–771.

95 *Buckley v. Valeo* (1976), 24–25,28–29, and 35–36.

96 *Buckley v. Valeo* (1976), 23–38, 60–68. For a discussion of reporting requirements as a threat to dissent, see 68–84.

97 *First National Bank of Boston v. Bellotti* (1978), 776–777, n. 12, and 791–792. Several justices would have extended campaign speech rights yet further, on grounds that restrictions limit the public's right to be fully informed. See Justice Douglas, dissenting in *Broadrick v. Oklahoma* (1973), 620–621, on political activity by public employees; Justices Brennan and Marshall, dissenting in *Greer v. Spock* (1976), 868, on political campaigning at a military base; and Justices Black, Reed, Douglas, and Murphy, all dissenting in *McDonald v. Commissioner of Internal Revenue* (1944), on allowing an income tax deduction for political party assessments of candidates.

98 For a review of the grounds of judicial review and judicial activism, see Henry Abraham, *The Judicial Process*, 4th ed., (New York: Oxford University Press, 1980), 295–400; *Ashwander v. Tennessee Valley Authority* (1936), 346–348; Philip Kurland, *Mr. Justice Frankfurter and the Constitution* (Chicago: University of Chicago Press, 1971); Alexander Bickel, "The Passive Virtues," *Harvard Law Review* 75 (November 1961): 40-79; or the several essays in Stephen Halpern and Charles Lamb, eds., *Supreme Court Activism and Restraint* (Lexington, Mass.: Lexington Books, 1982).

99 *Tyson and Brother v. Banton* (1927), 446. Justices Holmes and Brandeis argued that the "affected with a public interest" doctrine should be abandoned. Justice Holmes's view that judges should defer to the decisions of elected officials is further described in *The Common Law* (Boston: Little, Brown, 1881).

100 *U.S. v. Butler* (1936), 78–79. For a very different view by Justice
Stone in Bill of Rights disputes, see *U.S. v. Carolene Products Co.*
(1938), 152–153, n. 4.

101 *Minersville School District v. Gobitis* (1940), 600, later overruled
in *West Virginia Board of Education v. Barnette* (1943). For a view
that Justice Frankfurter's judicial restraint philosophy has been
misunderstood, see Harold Spaeth, "The Judicial Restraint of Mr.
Justice Frankfurter — Myth or Reality," *Midwest Journal of Political
Science*, 8 (February 1964): 22–38.

102 *Kovacs v. Cooper* (1949), 97.

103 *U.S. ex rel. Toth v. Quarles* (1955), 43.

104 *Wolf v. Colorado* (1949), 31, later overruled in *Mapp v. Ohio*
(1961). In explaining the difference between state and federal
standards, Justice Frankfurter argued that "(t)he public opinion
of a community can far more effectively be exerted against
oppressive conduct on the part of police directly responsible
to the community itself than can local opinion, sporadically
aroused, be brought to bear upon remote authority pervasively
exerted throughout the country," *Wolf v. Colorado*, at 32–33. For
a later discussion, see *Linkletter v. Walker, Warden* (1965), 630–631.

105 *Frank v. Maryland* (1959), 372, later overruled in *Camera v. Municipal Court* (1967).

106 Quoted in *West Virginia Board of Education v. Barnette* (1943), 669.

107 *Baker v. Carr* (1962), 270.

108 Briefly, the 1920 Act provided for arbitration and hearings in
labor disputes, but no enforceable sanctions "except through the
effect of adverse public opinion," *Pennsylvania Railroad System v.
Pennsylvania Railroad Company* (1925), 216. The 1926 Act provided
for a 30-day "cooling off" period and enforcement of awards
from voluntary arbitration. See *Virginia Railway Company v. System
Federation No. 40, A.F. of L.* (1937), 542–545.

109 See *Texas and New Orleans Railroad Co. v. Brotherhood of Railway &
Steamship Clerks* (1930); *General Committee v. Missouri-Kansas-Texas
Railroad Co.* (1943); *Switchmen's Union of North America v. National
Mediation Board* (1943); *Elgin, Joliet & Eastern Railway Co. v. Burley*
(1945); *National Labor Relations Board v. Insurance Agents' Interna-
tional Union* (1960); *Brotherhood of Railroad Trainmen v. Jacksonville
Terminal Co.* (1969); *Detroit & Toledo Shore Line Railroad Co. v. United
Transportation Union* (1969); and *Chicago & North Western Railway
Co. v. United Transportation Union* (1971).

110 See *U.S. v. United Mine Workers of America* (1947), Justice Rutledge
dissenting; and *Bus Employees v. Wisconsin Board* (1951), Justice
Frankfurter dissenting. For a similar discussion in a state right-
to-work dispute, see Justice Frankfurter's dissent in *A. F. of L. v.
American Sash & Door Co.* (1949), 549–550. See also *U.S. v. Hutcheson*
(1941), 230–231; and *Youngstown Sheet & Tube Co. v. Sawyer* (1952),
Justice Frankfurter, concurring, at 599, n. 2.

111 Explicit mentions of public opinion were less common during
the 1800s for several reasons. First, the term "public opinion" was

more often used in its "classic" meaning; see Chapter One, at note 5. Second, the Court often assumed that a legislative statute also reflected majority public opinion. Third, Court opinions were generally shorter and dissents less frequent; see Walter Murphy, *Elements of Judicial Strategy* (Chicago: University of Chicago Press, 1964), 60–65; and David O'Brien, *Storm Center* (New York: Norton, 1986), 262–273.

112 References to public opinion, or to closely related synonyms, may be found in lottery decisions in *Stone v. Mississippi* (1880), 819, 821; and *Douglas v. Kentucky* (1897), 502. For discussions in alcohol cases, see *Crowley v. Christensen* (1890), 91. For an even earlier discussion of judge-created crimes, as inconsistent with public opinion, see *U.S. v. Hudson and Goodwin* (1812), 32.

113 *Munn v. Illinois* (1876), 134: "For protection against abuses by Legislatures, the people must resort to the polls, not to the Courts."

114 *Holden v. Hardy* (1898), 387, 389, 390, 393.

115 *Lochner v. New York* (1905); see Justice Holmes, in dissent, arguing for "the right of a majority to embody their opinion in law," at 75.

116 *Mueller v. Oregon* (1908), 420–421: "Constitutional questions, it is true, are not settled by even a consensus of present public opinion...At the same time, a widespread and long continued belief concerning (a question of fact) is worthy of consideration."

117 *Ex Parte Wilson* (1885), 427. For a discussion of the importance of changing public opinion upon law, see Benjamin Cardozo, *The Growth of the Law* (New Haven, Conn.: Yale University Press, 1924), and *The Nature of the Judicial Process* (New Haven, Conn.: Yale University Press, 1928).

118 *Ex Parte Wilson* (1885), 428.

119 *Mackin v. U.S.* (1886), 352.

120 *O'Neil v. Vermont* (1892), 340.

121 *Weems v. U.S.* (1910), 378.

122 *Palko v. Connecticut* (1937), 325, quoting from *Snyder v. Massachusetts* (1934), 105.

123 *State of Louisiana ex rel. Francis v. Resweber, Sheriff* (1947), 471.

124 *Adamson v. California* (1947), 68.

125 *Trop v. Dulles* (1957), 101–102. See also *Sellars v. Beto* (1972). Justice Douglas dissented from denial of certiorari in a dispute concerning solitary confinement conditions in a Texas prison, describing the conditions as "considered inhumane at the time of Charles Dickens," at 969.

126 *Robinson v. California* (1962), 666. Justice Douglas concurred: "(t)his age of enlightenment cannot tolerate such barbarous action," at 678.

127 Justices Goldberg, Douglas, and Brennan, dissenting from denial of certiorari, in *Ruldoph v. Alabama* (1963), 889–890, and quoting from *Trop v. Dulles* (1957) and *Louisiana ex rel. Francis v. Resweber, Sheriff* (1947).

128 *Witherspoon v. Illinois* (1968), 519–520: "(O)ne of the most important functions any jury can perform...is to maintain a link

between contemporary community values and the penal system — a link without which the determination of punishment could hardly reflect 'the evolving standards of decency that mark the progress of a maturing society,'" at 519, n. 15. For a similar argument on juries' roles in accurately reflecting public opinion, see *Colegrove v. Battin* (1973), dissent at 167–168, n. 1.

129 *Furman v. Georgia* (1972), 360.

130 *Furman v. Georgia* (1972), 360–363.

131 *Furman v. Georgia* (1972), Justice Brennan, concurring, at 291–302.

132 *Furman v. Georgia* (1972), Justice Douglas, concurring, at 249–257.

133 *Furman v. Georgia* (1972), Justice Stewart, concurring, at 309–310; Justice White, concurring, at 311.

134 *Furman v. Georgia* (1972), dissenting opinions at 385–386, 409–414, 441–443, 445.

135 *Gregg v. Georgia* (1976), 180–181.

136 *Roberts v. Louisiana* (1976), 351–353, and (1977), 644-645. See also *Woodson v. North Carolina* (1976), 298–299.

137 *Coker v. Georgia* (1977), 613.

138 The Supreme Court has also applied the standard of "evolving public opinion" to business and sovereign immunity claims. See *Davis v. Pringle* (1925), holding that "(p)ublic opinion as to the peculiar rights and preferences due to the sovereign has changed," at 318; Justice Cardozo's dissent in *Ashton v. Cameron County Water Improvement District* (1936), arguing that "(a)ll these objections, so hotly and frequently asserted from period to period, were overcome either by public opinion or the Court," at 536, n. 6; *National City Bank of New York v. Republic of China* (1955), noting a "steady shift in attitude toward the American sovereign's immunity," at 359; or *Tigner v. Texas* (1940), upholding restraint-of-trade exemptions for stockmen and farmers, and arguing that "the effect of shifting tides of public opinion" could be considered by legislatures and the Court, at 149. See also the reference to "modern authority" in *Brown v. the Board of Education of Topeka, Kansas* (1954), 494–495

139 *United Public Workers of America, C. I. O., v. Mitchell* (1947), 102–103.

140 Justice Harlan, dissenting from dismissal of appeal, in *Poe v. Ullman* (1961), and arguing, on grounds of privacy, that the Connecticut law was unconstitutional as applied to married persons, at 546–549.

141 *Roth v. U.S.* (1957), 489; *Miller v. California* (1973), 33.

142 *Miller v. California* (1973), 31, 34.

143 *Jacobellis v. Ohio* (1964), 192–195; *Manual Enterprises v. Day* (1962), 488.

144 *Roth v. U.S.* (1957), 490.

145 *Pinkus v. U.S.* (1977), 297–300.

146 *Manual Enterprises v. Day* (1962), 489. Other obscenity texts rely on substantive standards, such as the "intent" test in *Ginzburg v. U.S.* (1966). For a review of these cases, see Henry Abraham,

Freedom and the Court, 4th ed., (New York: Oxford University Press, 1982), 188–204.

147 *Patterson v. Colorado* (1907). In this instance the case was pending only in that the time for motions for rehearing had not expired.

148 *Patterson v. Colorado* (1907), 462–463.

149 *Frank v. Magnum* (1915), 335.

150 *Frank v. Magnum* (1915), 347, Justices Holmes and Hughes, dissenting.

151 *Moore v. Dempsey* (1923), 86.

152 *Powell v. Alabama* (1932), 51–58. Justice Sutherland's opinion also noted the "hostile sentiment" and "especial horror (of the crime) in the community." See also *Chambers v. Florida* (1940), 229–231, 237–241.

153 *Shepherd v. Florida* (1951); *Estes v. Texas* (1965); *Sheppard v. Maxwell* (1966). For arguments that prejudicial publicity may require curbs on the press, see Justice Frankfurter, dissenting in *Craig v. Harney* (1947), 386–393; or writing respecting the denial of certiorari, in *Maryland v. Baltimore Radio Show* (1950); and concurring in *Kingsley International Pictures Corp. v. Regents of the University of the State of New York* (1959), 696–697.

154 *Groppi v. Wisconsin* (1971).

155 *Gannett Co., Inc. v. DePasquale* (1979), 378.

156 *Beck v. Alabama* (1980).

157 *Craig v. Harney, Sheriff* (1947).

158 For cases involving prejudicial publicity, see *Irvin v. Dowd, Warden* (1961), 719, 727, in which the Court held that a venue change to an adjoining county, likewise affected by "great excitement and indignation" failed to protect a defendant's right to a fair trial. See also *Rideau v. Louisiana* (1963). For cases in which the Court did not find prejudicial publicity to have affected community opinion, see *Stroble v. California* (1952) and *Murphy v. Florida* (1965).

For discussions of public opinion polling in venue changes, see Michael Nietzel and Ronald Dillehay, "Psychologists as Consultants for Change of Venue: The Use of Public Opinion Surveys," *Law and Human Behavior*, 7 (December 1983): 309–335; Brian Vargus and Bessanne Kiefer, "Public Opinion as Evidence in Court: A Case Study of a Change in Venue Motion," *Research in Legal Deviance and Social Control* 4 (1982): 241–267; and Neil Vidmar and John W. T. Judson, "The Use of Social Science Data in a Change of Venue Application: A Case Study," *Canadian Bar Review* 59 (March 1981): 76–102.

159 *Carter v. Kentucky* (1981).

160 *Peters v. Hobby* (1955), 345.

161 *Stack v. Boyle* (1951), 10.

162 *Weiman v. Updegraff* (1952), 191. See also *Sweezy v. New Hampshire* (1957), 248. Other decisions from this era recognized the adverse effects of designating a person as a member of a Communist front organization, but held the harm to be overbalanced by

other goals. Justice Frankfurter, for the Court, in *Communist Party of the U.S. v. Subversive Activities Control Board* (1961), 102–103, admitted "an angry public opinion, and the evils which it may spawn" and "the existence of an ugly public temper." Nonetheless, Frankfurter held that dangers to an individual from public opinion were overridden by "rational interests high in the scale of national concern."

163 *Joint Anti-Fascist Refugee Committee v. McGrath* (1951), 142, 175.

164 *Ullman v. U.S.* (1956), 454.

165 *W.E.B. DuBois Clubs v. Clark* (1967), 314, n. 1.

166 *Beuharnais v. Illinois* (1952), 261, n. 16.

167 *Norton v. Disciplinary Committee* (1970).

168 *Adickes v. S.H. Kress & Co.* (1970).

169 *NAACP v. Alabama* (1958), 462–463. See, however, *New York ex rel. Bryant v. Zimmerman* (1928), 465–466, in which the Court refused protection to the Ku Klux Klan's membership list.

170 *Bates v. Little Rock* (1960), 524. See also *Dombrowski v. Pfister* (1965), 488–489, enjoining a prosecution for advocacy of civil rights, under a Louisiana anti-subversion law. There the Court cited the "threatened exposure of the identity of adherents to a locally unpopular cause."

171 *Shelton v. Tucker* (1960), 486–487.

172 *Home Building & Loan Assoc. v. Blaisdell* (1934), 452.

173 *West Coast Hotel v. Parrish* (1937), 404, quoting from Judge Thomas Cooley, *Constitutional Limitations*, 8th ed., (Boston: Little, Brown, 1927), 123–124.

174 Most of these decisions involve the impairment of contract. For earlier examples, see Daniel Webster's argument in the *Dartmouth College* case (1819), 598–599; *Union Bank v. Hyde* (1821), 573–574; Slaughterhouse cases (1873), 81–82; *Loan Association v. Topeka* (1874), 662–663; *Edwards v. Kearzey* (1877), 604–607; *Walla Walla v. Walla Walla Water Company* (1898); or *Adkins v. Children's Hospital* (1923), 560: "The elucidation of (a constitutional question) cannot be aided by counting heads."

175 A few Court opinions acknowledge that government policies themselves can influence public opinion. See *Meyer v. Nebraska* (1923), 401–403; *Minersville School District v. Gobitis* (1940), 598–600; *West Virginia State Board of Education v. Barnette* (1943), 641; *Youngstown Sheet & Tube Co. v. Sawyer* (1952), 653–654; *Stein v. New York* (1953), 202; *Gravel v. U.S.* (1972), 640–641; *Paul v. Davis* (1976), 703; *Ambach v. Norwick* (1979), 78–79; and *Federal Energy Regulation Commission v. Mississippi* (1982), 779–780.

CHAPTER FOUR

Public Opinion and the Modern Court

Representation and the Judiciary

Three decades ago Robert Dahl published a now-classic article reexamining the Supreme Court's role in American democracy.[1] Dahl concluded that the Supreme Court had seldom succeeded in defending minority rights for very long against a contemporary "lawmaking majority" in Congress and the executive branch. Retirements, new appointments, and pressure from Congress and the president have usually forced the Supreme Court to give in and accept (or "legitimate") the policy choices of a lawmaking majority.

Because scientific, nationwide polls were not available for most of the Supreme Court's history, Dahl made the working assumption that laws passed by Congress and signed by the president (a "lawmaking majority") also represented nationwide public opinion (a "national majority").[2]

Dahl then examined 86 instances in which the Supreme Court had exercised judicial review to strike down a federal-level law. Except for minor cases, Court decisions striking down federal laws were usually reversed, either by congressional action, by constitutional amendment, or by the Court's own backtracking on its earlier decisions.

Further, Dahl noted, among the 86 instances of judicial activism, few instances could be found in which the Court had defended minority rights against a contemporary political majority. In short, the Supreme Court had not typically been a staunch defender of minority rights. Nor had the Court usually been able to long defy an active, national lawmaking or a national majority.[3]

Dahl's analysis clearly placed judicial review and the Supreme Court within majoritarian democratic theory, since, historically, the Court had seldom struck down laws on behalf of beleaguered minorities. Concluded Dahl:

Except for short-lived transitional periods when the old alliance is disintegrating and the new one is struggling to take control of political institutions, the Supreme Court is inevitably a part of the dominant national alliance.
(Robert Dahl, "Decision-Making in a Democracy," 293)

Dahl's article has spawned considerable research reevaluating his findings. Two decades later, Jonathan Casper challenged Dahl's methodology and conclusions, and argued that the modern Supreme Court was less a part of the dominant national alliance than Dahl's work suggested.[4] Casper argued that Dahl paid too little attention to the Court's role in striking down long-standing federal laws, in interpreting federal statutes, in eliminating state or local restrictions on minorities, in delaying new policies for lengthy time periods, and in placing new issues on the nation's political agenda. Further, he argued that the Warren and Burger Courts more aggressively defended minority rights than had earlier Courts, and those pro-minority rulings were seldom reversed.[5]

Several other authors also reevaluated Dahl's historical argument concerning the Supreme Court's behavior. David Adamany described frequent instances of conflict between holdover Courts and emerging national coalitions during four realignment periods. He noted that realignment era Courts frequently disagreed with newly elected presidents and congressional majorities over key policy measures.[6] Richard Funston reexamined Dahl's thesis by defining five critical realignment periods, and reported that the overturning of recently enacted federal laws was three times more frequent during critical realignment periods.[7] Bradley Canon and S. Sidney Ulmer, however, defined critical realignment periods differently than Funston, and argued that the Court was, on the whole, no more countermajoritarian during transitional periods.[8]

A few case studies of public opinion and specific Court rulings are available. Charles Sheldon indicated that most Court rulings on anti-communism laws during the 1950s agreed with prevailing public opinion.[9] Jonathan Casper reported that the Supreme Court's civil rights and national security decisions reflected public opinion more closely than had its criminal rights decisions; even so, in all three areas Court decisions sometimes deviated from majority sentiment.[10] Robert Weissberg reported that the Court agreed more frequently with public opinion in school integration cases and death penalty cases (until 1965) than in school prayer cases or in the later (1965–1973) death penalty decisions.[11] David Barnum identified poll trends in eleven policy areas and reported that Court decisions have usually, if not unfailingly, reflected poll majorities — or at least have followed discernible poll trends.[12] Judith Blake, Eric Uslaner, and Ronald Weber, however, indicated that the Court's abortion rulings exaggerated the level of mass support for liberal abortion policies.[13]

Several studies have tested the impact of national, regional, or statewide public opinion on federal judges' decision making. Beverly Blair Cook and Dianne Graebner reported that the sentencing behavior of federal district judges toward draft resisters during the Vietnam War era was strongly related both to national and regional poll trends and patterns.[14] Herbert Kritzer agreed that shifts in federal judges' sentencing behavior were moderately related to trends in nationwide polls, although he argued that variations in regional or local public opinion were not especially significant determinants of sentencing behavior.[15]

Less research is available on state and local courts; however, three studies suggest that state judges are at least moderately attentive to local public opinion. James Kuklinski and John Stanga compared the sentencing behavior of California county courts toward marijuana possession offenses with the results of a 1972 (county-level) statewide referendum aimed at removing criminal penalties for the personal use of marijuana.[16] Kuklinski and Stanga reported that sentencing behavior was more strongly related to local referendum results after, rather than before, the 1972 referendum. Deviant (over- or under-sentencing) courts most frequently shifted toward local referendum results.

Another state-level study indicated that criminal sentencing patterns in Iowa circuit courts were moderately related to local public opinion.[17] The linkage was markedly stronger among judges who had strong local ties, who adopted a "delegate" role orientation, or who had experienced an election loss. A third study reported that ten percent of state judges explicitly cited public opinion as an important factor in their decision making; another 14 percent cited a closely related concept, such as community values, needs, or demands.[18]

Most research on public opinion and judicial policy making, then, suggests that judges' decisions tend to reflect public opinion — especially when public opinion itself is clearly expressed, one-sided, and intense. Even so, some glaring exceptions appear,[19] and judicial decisions frequently exaggerate or lag behind poll trends.[20] The available studies are also limited because they chiefly report single case studies, focus upon rulings from the 1960s or 1970s, or concentrate upon civil rights and liberties (or noneconomic) decisions.

This book examines a much larger and more diverse sample of Supreme Court decisions for which timely, scientific, nationwide poll results are available. Because actual poll results are available, it is not necessary simply to assume, ipso facto, that the challenged laws or policies themselves reflect public opinion majorities.

This chapter first explains the study's methodology, and then reports the frequency with which modern Supreme Court decisions reflect majority public opinion. Four linkages are then tested — the state-of-public-opinion model, the federal and state/local policy process models, and the interest group model — and several additional hypotheses as well.

Chapter Five, in turn, focuses upon the 36 individual justices who have served on the Supreme Court since the mid-1930s, and asks how consistently these 36 justices have reflected majority public opinion. Five of the 12 linkages are then tested — the political socialization model, the appointment process model, the judicial roles model, the length-of-tenure model, and the realignment model. The remaining three linkages are tested in Chapters Six and Seven.

Comparing Court Decisions and the Polls

The following analysis was based upon comparisons between scientific, nationwide polls and Supreme Court decisions from

1935 through the 1985–1986 Court term. Data sources and coding rules are briefly described below.

Data Sources

No single index of scientific, nationwide polls that matches Supreme Court decisions is available. To compile as complete a listing of relevant poll questions as possible, major, nationwide polls were reviewed from published volumes of the Gallup Poll, the National Opinion Research Center (or NORC) Poll, and the Harris Poll; from *Public Opinion* magazine and "The Polls" section of *Public Opinion Quarterly;* and from other published sources. A search of the Roper Archives at the University of Connecticut provided several unpublished network and newspaper poll items.

Not only was no single listing of polls related to Court decisions available; there is also no index of Court decisions related to public opinion polls. Court decisions were identified from a wide variety of sources, including casebooks, law journals, monographs, and the annual summaries of Supreme Court decisions in the *American Political Science Review* (through 1961), *Congressional Quarterly Weekly Review* and *Almanac* (from 1972), *Harvard Law Review* (throughout this period), *Western Political Quarterly* (from 1962 through 1976), and in the *University of Chicago Law Review* (from 1947–1948 through 1953–1954). Additionally, a Lexis computer search as well as case summaries in *U.S. Reports* provided information on several cases. All together, these procedures identified 146 matches, or comparisons, between poll items and Supreme Court decisions. Of these 146 comparisons, 125 represent full, written opinions; per curiam decisions; or summary affirmations, denials, or dismissals. Another 21 matches represent denials of certiorari.

The most commonly used polls for all 146 matches, or comparisons, included the Gallup Poll (108 matches), the Harris Poll (46 matches), and NORC (10 matches). Other poll sources included the CBS-*New York Times* Poll (3 matches), Roper (4), ABC-*Washington Post* (5), *Life* magazine (2), NBC-Associated Press Poll (10), SRS (2), and SRC (1).

For several reasons, it is unlikely that the 146 matches represent a completely random sample of Supreme Court rulings. Major polling organizations are usually tied to newspapers or

Table 4.1

Number of matches, by issue area, including or excluding denials of certiorari, 1935–1986

Type of issue	(Including cert denials) Number of decisions	%	(Excluding cert denials) Number of decisions	%
Labor, unions, strikes	30	21%	25	20%
Criminal rights, courts, police	23	16%	20	16%
Education, schools	21	14%	18	14%
National security, foreign policy, communism	20	14%	14	11%
Privacy, morality, abortion	19	13%	15	12%
Race, integration, segregation	19	13%	19	15%
Business regulation, taxes	17	12%	17	14%
Elections, campaign finance	14	10%	13	10%
Intergovernmental relations	11	8%	10	8%
Free speech, dissent, media, obscenity	11	7%	11	9%
Social welfare, poverty	8	5%	7	6%
Transportation, commerce	6	4%	4	3%
Religion	4	3%	4	3%
Other	3	2%	1	1%

Note: Numbers and percentages sum down, by column, in excess of 146 and 100%, or 125 and 100%, because some decisions are counted into multiple categories.

Table 4.2
Frequency of matches, by Court period, 1935–1986

Chief Justice serving when decision was handed down	Number of cases	% of cases	Average number of cases per term
Hughes (1934/35–1940/41)	17	12	2.4
Stone (1941/42–1945/46)	13	9	2.6
Vinson (1946/47–1952/53)	19	13	2.7
Warren (1953/54–1968/69)	21	14	1.3
Burger (1969/70–1985/86)	76	52	4.5
	146	100	2.8*

* (average)

television stations, and the polls focus heavily on timely controversies. As a result, topics of greater public interest — such as civil liberties, civil rights, national security, labor, privacy, or religion cases — are overrepresented. By contrast, less colorful and more technical areas (such as bankruptcy, taxation, securities, or intergovernmental relations) inspire poll questions less frequently. Supreme Court rulings from the 1970s and 1980s are overrepresented (in the unweighted sample) because more polls were conducted during that period. For these reasons, the inferential statistics reported later should be interpreted cautiously. Nonetheless, as further described below, the nonrandom sampling does not appear to bias the overall results.

Table 4.1 lists the issue categories into which the 146 decisions fall, either including or excluding denials of certiorari. The Court decisions ranged across a wide variety of issues. Labor decisions comprised the most common single category, represented by 30 rulings. Nine other categories were represented by at least ten cases apiece.

The 146 decisions were spread over the last half century, although by no means evenly. The largest number of cases (76 of 146) were from the Burger Court period (1969–1986). The Hughes, Stone, Vinson, and Warren Court periods were represented by 13 to 21 cases apiece.[21] On the average, 2.8 cases per term were sampled, ranging from 1.3 cases per term (during the Warren Court period) to 4.5 cases per term (during the much more heavily polled Burger Court period). See Table 4.2.

Coding Rules

Coding so large and diverse a number of rulings required several coding rules, described below:

(1) When the wording of one (or more) poll items closely matched an issue raised in a Supreme Court decision, a match (or comparison) was made. The special problem of denials of certiorari is discussed in the next section. Denials of certiorari were included in the analysis in this chapter (although their exclusion would not affect the conclusions drawn in this chapter)[22]; denials of certiorari are excluded from the analysis of individual justices' voting patterns in Chapter Five.

   A Court decision that could be matched with a poll item was classified as either consistent, inconsistent, or unclear, depending on whether or not it reflected public opinion polls.

(2) A Supreme Court decision that agreed with a poll majority or plurality was classified as "consistent" (or majoritarian). One example is *Coker v. Georgia* (1977), in which a divided Court struck down the death penalty for rape. The *Coker* decision agreed with majorities in a 1978 and a 1981 Gallup Poll.[23]

(3) Decisions that disagreed, in substance, with a public opinion poll majority (or plurality) were classified as "inconsistent" (or countermajoritarian). The *Engle v. Vitale* (1962) and *Abington v. Schempp* (1963) school prayer rulings offer striking examples of rulings that disagreed with large poll majorities. In 1963, for example, a Gallup Poll reported that a 70-to-24 percent majority disapproved of the Court's rulings.[24]

(4) In a few instances public opinion was closely divided, or available polls reported conflicting results. Here, the Court's decision was classified as "unclear," since no readily apparent poll majority or plurality existed.

   To define a "clear" poll margin, the .05 statistical significance level was used — usually a margin of 3 to 5 percent for polls included here. When the poll margin was closer than this, or when available polls produced conflicting results, public opinion was classified as "unclear."

   In *Cooper v. Aaron* (1958), for example, public opinion was nearly evenly divided — 46-to-44 percent — over a federal district judge's two-year delay of Little Rock, Arkansas, school desegregation.[25] In another instance, *Harris v. McRae* (1980), different polls offered differing and inconsistent reports of attitudes toward federal abortion funding for poor women.

(5) If an earlier decision was counted, then later decisions that simply followed the precedent were not counted. For example, *Bowers v. Hardwick* (1986) was not counted separately (although timely polls were available), since it followed the earlier *Doe v. Commonwealth's Attorney for the City of Richmond* (1976).

(6)   A later Court decision that overturned an earlier-counted decision, however, might be counted. For example, on the question of federal taxation of salaries of state and local employees, both *Brush v. Commissioner of Internal Revenue* (1937) and *Helvering v. Gerhardt* (1938) were counted separately.

(7)   If a later decision followed an earlier precedent, but a poll was available only for the later decision, then the later ruling was counted, even if the precedent is better known and more often cited. For example, on the issue of forced blood tests for alleged drunk drivers, *Schmerber v. California* (1966) was counted rather than the earlier, more well-known *Breithaupt v. Abram* (1957).

(8)   If the Court ordered a lower court to apply or consider a law, then the Court was assumed to uphold the law's constitutionality — even if the Court did not expressly so hold. In *U.S. v. Malphurs* (1942), for instance, the Court ordered a federal district court to consider a recently enacted federal law making it illegal for a relief supervisor to attempt to influence the vote of a WPA reliefer.

(9)   If the Court upheld a specific application of a more general law or policy it was considered to uphold the law or policy itself. In *Cummings v. Deutsch Bank* (1937), for example, the Court upheld the federal government's efforts to collect war debts owed to the U.S. In this particular dispute the Court upheld the U.S. government's refusal to release seized property of German nationals until Germany resumed war debt payments.

(10)   A single Court decision involving two (or more) issues was treated as two (or more) separate decisions if it could thereby be better compared with available poll questions. For example, *Oregon v. Mitchell* (1970) was divided and analyzed as two separate decisions — the first decision was federal-level voting rights, and the second was state-level voting rights for 18-to-20-year-olds.

(11)   A few closely related decisions were combined and treated as a single decision. For example, *New York v. Quarles* (1984), *Nix v. Williams* (1984), and *U.S. v. Leon* (1984) — all exceptions to the exclusionary rule — were treated as a single decision.[26]

(12)   Companion decisions (typically handed down on the same day) were classified as a single case. For example, the 1954 *Brown v. Board of Education of Topeka, Kansas*, decision actually includes four companion cases.

(13)   A Court decision was classified as upholding a practice by permitting it under frequently arising, although not under all possible circumstances. *Schwartz v. State of Texas* (1952), for example, permitted wiretap evidence to be used in state trials, even though the same practice was not then permissible in federal-level prosecutions.

(14)   When public opinion polls showed a majority (or plurality) favored a policy through a more general means (such as a constitutional amendment), then public opinion was also assumed to

favor that policy through a less general means (such as a federal, state, or local law).

(15) Decisions were counted only if a poll item was available within five years of the decision's date. For most cases, (70 percent) a matching poll was identified within two years of the decision. As described below, no significant differences in the level of consistency were found between more and less timely poll matches, nor when the available poll was taken before (versus after) the decision was announced.[27]

A Note on Denials of Certiorari

Whether or not to include the 21 denials of certiorari identified here may fairly be disputed.[28] Denials of certiorari present both theoretical and practical problems.

Justice Frankfurter probably expressed the most widely shared legal view about denials of certiorari.[29] To Frankfurter, cert denials implied nothing about the Court's substantive views of a controversy:

> (A)ll that a denial of a petition for a writ of certiorari means is that fewer than four members of the Court thought it should be granted...(S)uch a denial carries with it no implication whatever regarding the Court's views on the merits of a case which it has declined to review.
> (*Maryland v. Baltimore Radio Show* (1950), at 919)

Or, as Justice Holmes contended, "The denial of a writ of certiorari imports no expression of opinion upon the merits of a case, as the bar has been told many times."[30]

A writ of certiorari might be denied for several reasons, among them, the appeal's ripeness or mootness, narrow technical issues, lack of final review by lower courts, an inadequate record, or even the petition's inadequacy.[31]

Aside from the long-standing debate among legal scholars and justices themselves about the meaning of denials of certiorari, practical problems also exist. Denials of certiorari are less often discussed in law reviews or newspapers, and less often elicit poll questions. As a result, cert denials are more difficult to identify and are likely to be undersampled. Routine denials of certiorari in certain types of cases may, in effect, let contradictory decisions stand.[32] Further, denials of certiorari provide no information about an individual justice's views — unless a justice writes separately to dissent from the denial[33] or to offer reasons for denying certiorari.[34]

These problems notwithstanding, a denial of certiorari clearly has a practical effect in a case; it lets a lower court ruling stand. The issue here is neither whether cert denials have precedent value, nor whether cert denials clearly reflect the Court's substantive views on an issue. Rather, the key issue is simply what result the cert denial will have in a specific case. Although it may have no importance as a precedent, a cert denial clearly has the effect of letting a lower court decision stand.

The 21 denials of certiorari identified here were classified by their effect. That is, they were treated as if the Supreme Court had upheld a lower court decision. In this chapter (where the Court's ruling itself is the unit of analysis), denials of certiorari were included in the analysis. In fact, however, either including or excluding them little affects the conclusions reached.[35] Later, in Chapter Five (where the individual justices' votes are examined), denials of certiorari are excluded, except in those rare instances when an individual justice wrote to explain a position.

Court Decisions and Public Opinion

Overall Results

A clear majority of the 146 Supreme Court decisions were consistent with public opinion. Depending on whether denials of certiorari are included or excluded, some 62 or 63 percent of the Court's decisions were consistent with the polls when a clear poll majority (or plurality) existed.

In the total sample of 146 decisions, some 56 percent (or 82 of 146 decisions) were consistent with public opinion, another 33 percent (48 of 146) were inconsistent, and 11 percent (16 of 146) were "unclear." If these last 16 decisions are set aside, then 63 percent (or 82 of 130) of the Court's decisions agreed with the polls, while 37 percent (48 of 130) did not.

The full 146-decision sample might also be subdivided to examine cert denials and non-cert denial decisions separately. Of the 21 cert denials, two-thirds (67 percent, or 14 of 21) had the effect of letting a consistent lower court decision stand, while 29 percent (6 of 21) had the effect of letting stand a lower court decision that was inconsistent with public opinion. In one denial of certiorari, available polls were "unclear."

In the remaining 125 decision that did not involve a cert denial, the Court's decision was consistent with public opinion 54 percent of the time, inconsistent with the polls 34 percent of the time, and unclear 12 percent of the time. If the "unclear" cases are again set aside, then 62 percent of the remaining Court decisions were consistent with public opinion, and 38 percent were not.

Sampling biases over time and in the types of issues polled do not affect these results. Because more polls were available during the 1970s and 1980s, Burger Court decisions were over-represented. If the sample is reweighted to correct for an over-time sampling bias (and if "unclear" decisions are again set aside), then 62 percent of the Court's (reweighted) decisions were consistent and the other 38 percent were inconsistent — percentages identical to the unweighted sample.

In the 146 decisions analyzed here, some types of decisions (such as business, commerce, and taxation cases) are under-sampled. If the 146-decision sample is reweighted, by type of issue, to reflect a more accurate estimate of the Court's actual decision load,[36] and if the "unclear" decisions are again set aside, the reweighted results were 66 percent consistent and 34 percent inconsistent.

The Court Versus Other Policy Makers

If these estimates are correct, how does the modern Supreme Court compare with other American policy makers? Available studies differ in their methodology, making precise comparisons difficult. However, some evidence suggests that the U.S. Supreme Court is roughly as consistent with public opinion as other U.S. decision makers.

One study by Alan Monroe compared 222 nationwide poll items from 1960 through 1974 with existing policies.[37] A consistent public policy could be identified for 64 percent of the poll items.[38] For the remaining 36 percent of poll items, public policy was inconsistent. Monroe's study did not separate judicial from non-judicial policies, although he noted that civil rights and liberties policies (which were most frequently decided by the federal judiciary) were consistent 67 percent of the time.

A later study by Benjamin Page and Robert Shapiro identified 609 instances between 1935 and 1979 in which an identically worded poll item had been repeated at least twice.[39]When policies were compared with the polls, 49 percent of the policy–poll matches were consistent at the time of the first poll measurement, and 54 percent were consistent at the time of the later poll. Sixty-one percent of the policy–poll matches were consistent within one year after the later poll, 65 percent within four years after the later poll, and 68 percent were consistent at some time during a four-year span. Page and Shapiro also reported that Congress, the executive branch, and the federal judiciary were all equally likely to reflect public opinion.

State-level policies are more difficult to compare with state-level public opinion because of the enormous costs of producing adequate state-by-state sample sizes. Very few studies are available at this level. In one study Robert Erikson reported that 73 percent of state-level policies during the 1930s were consistent with state-level public opinion on three issues: the death penalty, a child labor amendment, and female jurors.[40] In another study Robert Sutton simulated state-by-state public opinion and reported that 60 percent of 116 different state policy issues were consistent with (estimated) statewide majorities.[41]

The Scotch verdict ("not proven") may be the best way to answer the question: Is the Supreme Court more or less likely to reflect public opinion than other policy makers? In the most comparable studies, from 64 percent to 68 percent of nationwide polls were matched by similar policies — given a four-year time lag. Here, by either the unweighted or reweighted figures, from 62 percent to 66 percent of Supreme Court decisions were consistent with available polls. Against these comparisons, the modern Court appears neither markedly more nor less consistent with the polls than are other policy makers.

Explaining the Results

To this point the discussion suggests two findings. First, three-fifths to two-thirds of the modern Court's rulings have reflected prevailing public opinion. Second, the modern Supreme Court has reflected the polls as often as have other policy makers. The remainder of this chapter further evaluates the state-of-public-opinion linkage, the federal policy linkage, the state/local policy linkage, the interest groups linkage, as well as several other explanations for the Court's pattern of representing public opinion.

The State of Public Opinion

The results, just described, offer support for the first of three assumptions of the state-of-public-opinion linkage — the Court reflects public opinion significantly more often (at the .02 level) than a random-choice model would predict. The several estimates, just reported, all indicate that more than half of the modern Court's decisions have reflected public opinion, when the polls themselves were clear.

The state-of-public-opinion linkage also has two further assumptions — that the Court will be especially majoritarian when the polls are unusually one-sided, and that the Court will be especially majoritarian when public attention is closely focused upon an issue, such as during crisis times. These two assumptions are further tested below.

POLL MARGINS

Several studies suggest that public policy is more consistent with public opinion when large, one-sided poll majorities exist.[42] Supreme Court decision making, however, was not strongly influenced by the size of poll majorities. Overall, the Court has been no more majoritarian in cases in which public opinion was very one-sided than in cases in which the polls were more closely divided.

In Table 4.6 decisions for which a "landslide" margin was involved (over 30 percent) are compared with decisions in which the poll margin was significant, but less than 30 percent. In *South Carolina v. Katzenbach* (1966), for example, a Gallup Poll question indicated that a 76-to-16 percent majority favored federal registrars.[43] Accordingly, this decision was counted as an instance in which the poll margin (of 60 percent) was strongly one-sided. By contrast, in three 1984 exclusionary rule decisions, public opinion was more closely divided. One 1982 NBC-Associated Press survey reported that a 53-to-41 percent majority favored modifying the exclusionary rule to admit more evidence. These decisions were combined and counted as an instance in which the poll margin (of 12 percent) was still clear, but more closely divided.[44]

As Table 4.6 indicates, the Court was only slightly more likely to agree with public opinion when the poll margin was very one-sided. For the original (uncollapsed) poll margins, the point-biserial correlation would be an insignificant .09.

CRISIS TIMES

Whether the Court defers to public opinion during "crisis times" has also concerned both judicial scholars and Supreme Court justices. Theodore Becker, for example, argued that the Court was not sympathetic to unpopular minorities when public opinion against them was aroused and intense. Suggested Becker: "(T)he high court is not likely to protect individual liberty — when it really counts — against the politically irresponsible mass that becomes aroused so often."[45]

In an often-cited dissent,[46] Justices Black and Douglas also hinted that aroused public opinion might sway the Court's decisions:

> Public opinion being what it is now, few will protest the conviction of these Communist petitioners. There is hope, however, that in calmer times, when present pressures, passions, and fears subside, this or some later Court will restore the First Amendment liberties to the high preferred place where they belong in a free society.
> (*Dennis v. U.S.* (1951), at 580)

The indicator of crisis-times disputes was the Gallup Poll's repeatedly asked question "What do you think is the most important problem facing this country today?" Cases closely related to the leading national concerns were counted as crisis-times cases.[47] Admittedly, the small number of crisis-times disputes limits the certainty with which these results can be accepted. Nonetheless, the crisis-times thesis appears to have some validity. Court decisions are significantly more majoritarian when public attention is closely focused upon an issue.

The results in Table 4.6 suggest that two of the three assumptions of the state-of-public-opinion linkage found empirical support. The modern Court reflected the polls more often than a random-choice model would predict, and the Court was especially likely to reflect public opinion during crisis-times decisions.

The Federal Policy Process

Whether Supreme Court rulings will reflect public opinion may also depend upon the dispute's level and context. A case's "level" refers to whether the dispute originated from the federal or state/local level. A dispute's "context" refers to whether the challenged law or policy itself reflects nationwide public opinion.

The federal policy process model assumes that federal-level policies themselves usually reflect public opinion, and that the Court usually exercises judicial restraint toward federal laws and policies. As a result, through the deference norm, the Court reflects mass public opinion.

Because actual polls are used here, it is not necessary simply to assume, ipso facto, that federal laws and policies themselves reflect majority public opinion. Rather, it is possible to examine how consistent federal or state/local acts themselves are with public opinion; how consistent, by comparison, were the Court's decisions in these same cases; and whether a dispute's level and context influence how often Court decisions reflect the polls.

Seventy-four of the disputes studied involved a federal law or policy.[48] In these federal-level disputes the challenged law or policy was itself consistent with the polls in 65 percent (or 48 of 74) of instances, "unclear" in 9 percent (7 instances), and inconsistent in 26 percent (or 19 instances). Excluding instances of evenly divided or contradictory polls, the federal law itself was consistent with public opinion in 72 percent of the remaining cases, and inconsistent in 28 percent.

The Supreme Court was very likely to defer to federal policy makers, regardless of whether the federal law was itself consistent with the polls. When a challenged federal law was consistent

Table 4.3
Supreme Court treatment of federal laws and policies,
1935–1986

	[Federal law or policy was:] Majoritarian	Unclear	Counter majoritarian
Supreme Court action:			
Upheld law/policy	81%	71%	63%
Overturned law/policy	19%	29%	37%
	100%	100%	100%
Number of cases:	(48)	(7)	(19)

with the polls, the Court upheld it in four-fifths (81 percent) of all decisions. The Court, however, also upheld a large majority (63 percent) of federal laws and policies that were inconsistent with the polls. See Table 4.3.

When cases involving evenly divided or contradictory polls are excluded, 69 percent of the Court's decisions were majoritarian, and the remaining 31 percent were countermajoritarian. This level of majoritarian decision making is strikingly similar to the 72 percent figure for disputed federal laws and policies themselves.[49]

These results strongly support the federal policy process linkage. As this linkage assumes, federal laws and policies usually reflect public opinion; the Court usually exercises deference toward disputed federal laws and policies; and as a result, Court decisions usually reflect mass public opinion. Perhaps the single most critical test occurs when a federal law or policy contradicts mass public opinion. In these few cases, the Court typically supports the disputed federal action, not mass public opinion. This suggests that no direct, unmediated linkage exists between mass public opinion and Supreme Court decisions in federal-level disputes.

The State/Local Policy Process

The state/local policy process linkage assumes that a very different relationship between public opinion and Court decisions occurs in disputes originating at the state or local level. It assumes that disputed state or local policies do not reflect nationwide polls accurately; that the Court does not necessarily defer to state/local policies; and that Court decisions more often reflect nationwide polls than state/local policies whenever national polls and state or local policies differ.

Considerable support appeared for this model. First, challenged state/local laws and policies were less often consistent with nationwide polls. Of 78 disputed state/local laws, only half (50 percent, or 39 of 78) were consistent with national polls. Fourteen percent were "unclear" due to inconsistent or evenly divided polls. The remaining 36 percent (or 28 of 78 laws or policies) were inconsistent with nationwide polls. If the instances of "unclear" polls are set aside, only 58 percent (or 39 of 67) of the remaining state/local laws and policies themselves agreed with nationwide polls.

The Supreme Court was also far less deferential toward state/ local laws and policies — upholding only 49 percent (or 38 of 78) of them. The Court upheld just over half (56 percent) of the 39 state/local laws and policies that were consistent with nationwide polls, and even fewer (only 43 percent) of state/local actions that were inconsistent with national polls.

Restated differently, the Court was consistent with the polls 56 percent of the time when state/local policies agreed with the polls — versus the Court's 57 percent consistency when state/local policies disagreed with the polls. These results suggest that state and local policies do not mediate the linkage between nationwide public opinion and Supreme Court policy making as effectively as do federal policies.

Once again, the agreement between the Supreme Court and national polls can be compared to that between national polls and disputed state or local policies. Excluding unclear instances, some 57 percent of the Supreme Court's decisions in cases from the state or local level agreed with nationwide polls. By comparison, 58 percent of disputed state/local laws and policies themselves reflected nationwide public opinion.

Other Explanations

Several other variables including the Court era, the type of issue involved in a case, and measurement artifacts, could also be tested, although no theoretically based models could be con-

Table 4.4
Supreme Court agreement with public opinion, by court period,
1935–1986

	Hughes	Stone	Vinson	Warren	Burger
% majoritarian	65%	54%	68%	52%	53%
% unclear	12%	—	—	14%	15%
% counter-majoritarian	24%	46%	32%	33%	33%
	101%	100%	100%	99%	101%
(Number of cases:	(17)	(13)	(19)	(21)	(76)

Total number of cases = 146: results insignificant at .05.

structed for these variables. Each of these potential explanations
is described and evaluated below.

OVER-TIME PATTERNS

To test whether the Court's agreement with public opinion
has varied over time, the full 146-decision sample was divided
into five periods, defined by the presiding Chief Justice. All
146 decisions are examined, and are separated by time period
in Table 4.4.

Once again, the instances of evenly divided or inconsistent
polls may be set aside. If this is done, the percent of majoritarian
decisions ranged from 73 percent for the Hughes Court to 54
percent for the Stone Court. Although the Warren Court is
sometimes thought to have been less consistent with public
opinion than other modern Courts, it appears to rank near the
midpoint.[50] See Table 4.5.

Since there were so many decisions during the Burger Court
era, that period was further subdivided — before, versus after,
the Nixon-Ford appointees (Justices Burger, Blackmun, Powell,
Rehnquist, and Stevens) formed a Court majority. The differences between the early and late Burger Court were very slight
and insignificant. Before the Nixon-Ford appointees formed a
Court majority, the early (1969–1975) Burger Court was majoritarian in 65 percent, and countermajoritarian in 35 percent of
its decisions. The late (1975–1986) Burger Court was majoritarian
in 63 percent, but countermajoritarian in 37 percent of its

Table 4.5

Supreme Court agreement with public opinion, by court period,
1935–1986 (excluding instances of "unclear" polls)

	Hughes	Stone	Vinson	Warren	Burger
% majoritarian	73%	54%	68%	61%	62%
% counter-majoritarian	27%	46%	32%	39%	38%
	100%	100%	100%	100%	100%
Number of cases:	(15)	(13)	(19)	(18)	(65)

Total number of cases = 130; results insignificant at .05.

decisions.[51]

The percentage of majoritarian rulings, by time period, along with the percentages for several other variables, is reported in Table 4.6. Table 4.6 excludes "unclear" cases of evenly divided or inconsistent polls.

TYPE OF ISSUE

Does the modern Court agree with nationwide public opinion more often when certain types of issues are involved? Several studies suggest that the Court's religious liberties rulings and its criminal rights rulings less often reflect popular opinion.[52] For most types of issues, however, no clear, directional hypothesis can be offered. Table 4.7 reports the Court's percentage of agreement with public opinion for several different types of issues.

The conclusions to be drawn from Table 4.7 are admittedly limited by the small number of cases within several categories, but, overall, the differences in Table 4.7 are not statistically significant. Further, except for two areas (criminal rights and intergovernmental relations), half or more of the Court's rulings reflected public opinion.[53]

For a further analysis, the decisions were also collapsed into two much broader categories — "fundamental freedoms" cases and economic cases.

"Fundamental Freedom" Decisions Whether the Court reflects popular opinion in its Bill of Rights (or "fundamental freedoms")

Table 4.6

Percentage of majoritarian decisions, by explanatory variables, for the modern Supreme Court

% Category	% Majoritarian	Number of cases
Overall results	63%	(130)
By state of public opinion:		
Crisis times cases	76%	(29)
Non-crisis times cases	59% *	(101)
By size of poll margin:		
"Landslide" (over 30%)	65%	(82)
6–29% Poll margin	60%	(45)
By level and context:		
Consistent federal law	81%	(48)
Inconsistent federal law	37%	(19)
Consistent state/local law	56%	(39)
Inconsistent state/local law	57% ***	(28)
By chief justice period:		
Hughes Court	73%	(15)
Stone Court	54%	(13)
Vinson Court	68%	(19)
Warren Court	61%	(18)
Burger Court	62%	(65)
By type of issue:		
Fundamental freedoms cases	66%	(96)
Non-fundamental freedom cases	56%	(34)
Economic case	71%	(34)
Non-economic case	60%	(96)
By timing of poll:		
Pre-decision poll	67%	(84)
Post-decision poll	57%	(46)

Note: Percentage differences are not statistically significant unless otherwise noted. Total number of cases = 130. To compute the percentage of countermajoritarian decisions, subtract the percentage of majoritarian decisions from 100%.

  * significant at .05
 ** significant at .01
*** significant at .001

Table 4.7
Percentage of majoritarian decisions, by type of case

Type of issue	[%] Majoritarian	Number of cases
Labor, unions, strikes	69%	(25)
Criminal rights, courts, police	48%	(21)
Education, schools	65%	(20)
National security, foreign policy, communism	70%	(20)
Privacy, morality, abortion	50%	(14)
Race, segregation, integration	75%	(16)
Business regulation, taxes	77%	(13)
Elections, campaign finance	69%	(13)
Intergovernmental relations	46%	(11)
Free speech, dissent, media, obscenity	60%	(10)
Social welfare, poverty	50%	(8)
Transportation, commerce	80%	(5)
Religion	50%	(4)

Note: Table 4.7 omits instances of closely divided or inconsistent poll results. A chi-square would not be significant at the .05 level.

decisions has frequently concerned Court-watchers. Because the Court has had a well-developed rationale for countermajoritarian decisions in these cases since the 1930s, fundamental freedoms rulings were predicted to be less frequently majoritarian.[54]

Cases based upon Bill of Rights or Fourteenth Amendment claims were compared to the remaining non-fundamental freedoms cases. Contrary to the hypothesis, the Court was no less majoritarian in fundamental freedoms disputes. Sixty-six percent of the Court's fundamental freedoms decisions, versus 56 percent of the non-fundamental freedoms decisions, reflected the polls.

Economic Cases While economics cases are not as dominant a part of the Court's docket today as they were before the mid-1930s, they still comprise a large share of the Court's workload. This study separated employment, labor unions, business regulation, taxation, interstate commerce, or other economic rights cases from noneconomic cases, and examined the Court's agreement with the polls in each instance. Because the Court has tended toward judicial restraint in economic cases since the mid-1930s, the Court's economic rulings were predicted to be more often majoritarian.[55]

Table 4.6 provides little support for this hypothesis. The Court's economic decisions slightly, but not significantly more often reflected public opinion than its non-economic decisions.

MEASUREMENT ARTIFACTS

Whether the Court's decision would reflect public opinion or not is unrelated to whether the poll was taken before, versus after the decision. Court decisions and polls could be matched if a suitable poll, taken within five years of a Court decision, was available (although 74 percent of the polls used were taken within two years of the decision). To test whether post-decision poll shifts might bias the results, the 146 matches were separated into those with pre-decision versus post-decision, polls, and then compared.

Perhaps surprisingly, Court decisions were slightly more majoritarian when matched with pre-decision polls rather than with post-decision polls, although the differences were not statistically significant. As Chapter Six also suggests, there is little evidence that most Supreme Court decisions markedly affect public opinion.

Combining the Predictors

Several of the predictors just described help to explain the conditions under which the modern Supreme Court's decisions will reflect public opinion, but other predictors do not. In this section, the predictors are reexamined using a probit analysis.

Probit (or "probability unit") analysis is a technique for analyzing dichotomous (1,0) dependent variables, such as whether the Supreme Court agrees or disagrees with public opinion.[56] While ordinary least-squares regression is inappropriate for (1,0) dependent variables, probit analysis can be employed in these instances. Probit analysis estimates the effect that one or more predictors have upon achieving some specific outcome — here, that the Court will agree with mass public opinion. Probit estimates are maximum likelihood estimates (MLEs), and represent the change in the cumulative normal probability function resulting from a one-unit change in predictor. These MLEs can be divided by their standard errors to test whether the predicted change is greater than chance.

Probit analysis has several advantages over the simple, bivariate results reported in Table 4.6. Probit results can be interpreted more meaningfully, and the joint impact of several predictors can be assessed. Probit analysis also offers several summary statistics to help determine how strong the complete prediction model is.

A Full Model Test

In the full probit model reported in Table 4.8 twelve predictors are examined.[57] The predictors (and underlying models) included:

THE STATE OF PUBLIC OPINION

(1) Crisis Times? A decision involving a top national concern was coded (1); other decisions (0).
(2) Poll Margin? The actual (uncollapsed) public opinion poll margin was coded, yielding a range of (absolute) numbers from 6 to 82 percent. Instances of evenly divided or contradictory polls were excluded, leaving a sample size of 130 decisions.

FEDERAL POLICY PROCESS

(3) Federal Law Consistent? Disputed laws (or policies) at the federal level that agreed with the polls were coded (1); other decisions (0).
(4) Federal Law Inconsistent? Disputed laws (or policies) at the federal level that disagreed with the polls were coded (1); other decisions (0).

STATE/LOCAL POLICY PROCESS

(5) State Law Consistent? Disputed state or local laws or policies that agreed with the nationwide polls were coded (1); other decisions (0).
(6) State Law Inconsistent? Disputed state/local laws or policies that

Table 4.8
Full-model probit results explaining Supreme Court
agreement with public opinion

Predictor	MLE	S.E.	MLE/S.E.
Crisis Times?	.85	.41	2.07 *
Poll Margin?	.00	.01	.38
Federal Law Consistent?	.22	.40	.55
Federal Law Inconsistent?	−1.63	.52	−3.15 ***
State Law Consistent?	−.88	.44	−1.98 *
State Law Inconsistent?	−.80	.45	−1.77 *
Hughes Court?	.10	.47	.21
Stone Court?	−.06	.50	−.11
Vinson Court?	−.54	.47	−1.15
Warren Court?	.04	.37	.10
Fundamental Freedoms?	.69	.44	1.57
Economic Rights?	.31	.37	.82

Constant = .18
% of Cases Correctly Predicted = 75%
Mean of dependent variable = .63
Improvement over Base Rate = 32%
Estimated R^2 = .52
−2LLR = (significant at .05)
Number of Cases = 130

*** significant at .001
** significant at .01
* significant at .05

disagreed with nationwide polls were coded (1); other decisions
(0).

OTHER VARIABLES

(7), (8), (9), and (10). Four (1,0) dummy variables represented the
Hughes, Stone, Vinson, and Warren Court eras.
(11) Fundamental Freedoms? If the dispute raised a fundamental freedoms issue, the decision was coded (1); other decisions (0).
(12) Economic Rights? If the dispute involved an economic issue,
the decision was coded (1); other decisions (0).

The full probit model in Table 4.8 was moderately successful
in predicting when the Court would agree with nationwide
public opinion. Seventy-five percent of the Court's decisions
were correctly predicted — a 32 percent improvement over
the base rate. Nearly half the total variance was explained by
the full model, and by the -2LLR estimate, the full model was
statistically significant.[58]

Table 4.9
Reduced-model probit results explaining Supreme Court
agreement with public opinion

Predictor	MLE	S.E.	MLE/S.E.
Crisis Times?	.65	.35	1.84 *
Federal Law Consistent?	.07	.38	.19
Federal Law Inconsistent?	−1.71	.49	−3.49 ***
State Law Consistent?	−.81	.41	−1.98 *
State Law Inconsistent?	−.72	.41	−1.76 *

Constant = .86
% of Cases Correctly Predicted = 72%
Mean of dependent variable = .63
Improvement over Base Rate = 24%
Estimated R^2 = .50
−2LLR = (significant at .05)
Number of Cases = 130

Probit results may best be explained by using a specific example. Assume a (hypothetical) Warren Court case involved a consistent federal law that enjoyed a moderately large, positive (20 percent) poll margin, and that restricted a fundamental freedoms claim during crisis times. In this instance, there would be a 98 percent (predicted) probability that the Warren Court's decision would agree with public opinion by upholding the federal law.

For an otherwise identical state law reviewed during non-crisis times, the results are quite different. In this instance, there was only a 54 percent probability that the Warren Court would agree with public opinion by upholding the (hypothetical) state law.

Reducing the Model

The large number of predictors, many of them nonsignificant, suggest that the full probit model can be reduced. In Table 4.9 a more parsimonious probit model includes only the crisis-times predictor, plus the four level/context predictors. This model included only the reduced state-of-public-opinion linkage, the federal policy process linkage, and the state policy process linkage.

This reduced probit model predicted when the Court would agree with public opinion almost as successfully as the full model, but used fewer predictors. For a hypothetical decision involving a consistent federal law during crisis times, the Court would have a (predicted) 94 percent probability of agreeing with the polls by upholding the federal law. If the dispute involved a consistent state law during non-crisis times, however, the Court would have only a 52 percent probability of agreeing with nationwide polls.

The remaining variables — poll margin, Court era, and type of issue — could not successfully predict whether the Court's decisions would reflect the polls. Individually, none of these predictors was statistically significant, either in the full probit model, in a separate probit equation, or in the bivariate results.

Interest Groups and Public Opinion

The interest groups linkage is the fourth and final model tested in this chapter. This model assumes that interest group positions are unrelated to mass public opinion; that public opinion and interest groups each have an independent (positive) impact on Supreme Court decision making; and that interest groups and public opinion, together, better explain Court decisions than either does separately.

Interest groups may participate in a lawsuit in several different ways. At a minimum, a group may file an amicus curiae brief to offer its position. An interest group may, on the other hand, actively support a lawsuit by soliciting plaintiffs, providing counsel, financing the lawsuit, and organizing the appeals.[59]

A group that participated by filing an amicus brief or by providing counsel was classified as being involved in the case. Since few groups participated in more than a handful of the 146 decisions sampled here, those groups that shared similar policy goals were combined into broader categories. Nine broad categories of interest groups were involved in a sufficient number of cases to merit analysis here. They included pro-civil liberties, free speech, and media groups; pro-civil rights groups; education groups; corporations, businesses, and trade associations; labor unions; feminist, gender-oriented, or right-to-privacy groups; liberal religious groups; Catholic organizations; and pro-conservative or law enforcement groups.[60]

For each category, a simple coding scheme was applied. A category was scored (1) if any group within the category was actively involved in the case and also agreed with public opinion; (0) if no group within the category participated; and (-1) if any group within the category participated, but disagreed with mass public opinion.[61]

The results provide, at beest, mixed evidence for the interest groups model. First, interest group positions and mass public opinion are essentially unrelated. Taken together, interest group positions reflected mass public opinion only 50 percent of the time, and only a few categories of groups agreed with the polls substantially more than half the time, as Table 4.10 suggests. Further, as this chapter earlier indicated, there is some evidence that mass public opinion has a direct, unmediated effect on Court decisions, at least in state- or local-level disputes.

There is little evidence that interest groups are very successful when their positions disagree with mass public opinion. The nine categories of interest groups were successful 67 percent of the time when they agreed with the polls, but only 47 percent of the time when they disagreed with the polls. Very few groups were particularly successful when they disagreed with public opinion, and in those instances, the analysis was complicated with small numbers.

No support exists for the most critical assumption — that interest group positions have an independent effect upon Court decisions. When the nine group categories were examined jointly in a probit equation, they failed to improve upon the base-rate prediction level.[62] Nor did the nine group categories improve upon either the full or reduced probit equations that were described earlier in this chapter.[63]

Reconsidering Judicial Activism

These results also permit a reexamination of the modern Court's use of judicial activism. As Chapter One indicated, judicial activism has sometimes simply been assumed to be counter-majoritarian.[64] If "countermajoritarian" is defined as the striking down of a federal, state, or local law or policy, judicial activism is, of course, inevitably countermajoritarian.

If judicial activism is reexamined against nationwide polls, however, a different picture emerges. In this sample of deci-

Table 4.10
Interest Group Involvement and Success

Type of group	Positions taken	Agreement with public opinion		Percent success when	
		Percent majoritarian	Percent counter-majoritarian	Agreed with public opinion	Disagreed with public opinion
Civil Liberties, free speech, media	(35)	48%	52%	71%	47%
Civil Rights	(15)	60%	40%	78%	67%
Education	(8)	75%	25%	67%	50%
Corporations, business, trade associations	(19)	47%	53%	57%	30%
Labor Unions	(18)	29%	71%	50%	29%
Feminist, gender, privacy	(6)	50%	50%	100%	67%
Liberal religious	(12)	50%	50%	83%	83%
Catholic	(6)	50%	50%	33%	67%
Conservative, law enforcement	(15)	67%	33%	60%	40%

sions, the Court exercised judicial activism 49 times at the federal, state, or local level. In almost half (47 percent) of these 49 instances, the Court's judicial activism supported nationwide polls rather than a law (or policy) that was inconsistent with public opinion. In short, when judicial activism is evaluated directly against public opinion, nearly half the modern Court's judicial activism decisions were also majoritarian.

Conclusion

Chapter Four presented a relatively large and diverse sample of Supreme Court decisions from 1935 through 1986, which could be directly compared with scientific, nationwide polls. Most modern Court decisions reflect public opinion. When a clear poll majority or plurality exists, over three-fifths of the Court's decisions reflect the polls. By the available evidence, the modern Supreme Court appears to reflect public opinion as accurately as other policy makers.

Three of the four linkage models tested in this chapter won some support. The state-of-public-opinion linkage was supported in that most Court decisions reflected the polls, and the Court more strongly reflected the polls during crisis times. One-sided poll margins, however, had little effect on the Court's policy making.

The federal policy process model was also strongly supported. Most federal laws or policies reflect public opinion; the Court typically defers to federal laws; and through the deference norm, the Court typically reflects public opinion as well. At the federal level, mass public opinion is clearly mediated, or "filtered" by the intervening policy process.

The state/local "non-model" also found some support. Nationwide public opinion was not strongly related to state/local policy making; the Court was not particularly deferential toward state or local laws; and when state/local laws and policies conflicted with nationwide polls, the Court more often preferred public opinion. These results indicate that state or local policies did not have an independent effect on Court policy making, as did federal laws and policies.

Only the interest group linkage failed to garner support. Interest group positions were largely unrelated to public opinion, as predicted. Yet, on the whole, there was little evidence that interest group positions had a strong, independent effect on Court decision making.

References

1   Robert Dahl, "Decision-making in a Democracy: The Supreme Court as a National Policy-Maker," *Journal of Public Law* 6 (Fall 1957): 279–295.
2   Dahl, "Decision-making in a Democracy," 284. Dahl admits that this assumption is a problematic one, as have other authors who proceeded without actual polling data.
3   Dahl, "Decision-making in a Democracy," 293.
4   Jonathan Casper, "The Supreme Court and National Policy Making," *American Political Science Review* 70 (March 1976): 50–63.
5   Casper, "The Supreme Court and National Policy Making," 52–54.
6   David Adamany, "Legitimacy, Realigning Elections, and the Supreme Court," *Wisconsin Law Review* 1973 (1973): 790–846.
7   Richard Funston, "The Supreme Court and Critical Elections," *American Political Science Review* 69 (September 1975): 795–811. Funston's views are further explained in *A Vital National Seminar: The Supreme Court in American Political Life* (Palo Alto, CA: Mayfield, 1978), esp. 33–53.
8   Bradley Canon and S. Sidney Ulmer, "The Supreme Court and Critical Elections: A Dissent," *American Political Science Review* 70 (December 1976): 1215–1218. See also Paul Allen Beck, "Critical Elections and the Supreme Court: Putting the Cart after the Horse," *American Political Science Review* 70 (September 1976): 930–932, and replies by Professor Funston. See also Gregory Caldeira and Donald McCrone, "Of Time and Judicial Activism," in Stephen Halpern and Charles Lamb, eds., *Supreme Court Activism and Restraint* (Lexington, Mass.: Lexington Books 1982), 103–128.
9   Charles H. Sheldon, "Public Opinion and High Courts: Communist Party Cases in Four Constitutional Systems," *Western Political Quarterly* 15 (June 1967): 341–360.
10 Jonathan Casper, *The Politics of Civil Liberties* (New York: Harper & Row, 1972).
11 Robert Weissberg, *Public Opinion and Popular Government* (Englewood Cliffs, N.J.: Prentice-Hall, 1976).
12 David Barnum, "The Supreme Court and Public Opinion: Judicial Decision Making in the Post-New Deal Period," *Journal of Politics* 47 (May 1985): 652–666.
13 Judith Blake, "The Abortion Decisions: Judicial Review and Public Opinion," in Edward Manier, William Liu, and David Solomon, eds., *Abortion — New Directions for Policy Studies* (Notre Dame, Ind.: Notre Dame Press, 1977), 51–82. For similar views, see John

Jackson and Maris Vinovskis, "Public Opinion, Elections, and the 'Single Issue'," in Gilbert Steiner, ed., *The Abortion Dispute and the American System* (Washington, D.C.: Brookings Institute, 1984), 64–81: and Eric Uslaner and Ronald Weber, "Public Support for Pro-Choice Abortion Policies in the Nation and States: Changes and Stability after the Roe and Doe Decisions," in Carl Schneider and Maris Vinovskis, eds., *The Law and Politics of Abortion* (Lexington, Mass.: Lexington Books, 1980), 206–223.

14   Beverly Blair Cook, "Public Opinion and Federal Judicial Policy," *American Journal of Political Science* 21 (August 1977): 567–600, and "Sentencing Behavior of Federal Judges: Draft Cases — 1972," *University of Cincinnati Law Review* 42 (Fall 1973): 597–633: Dianne Graebner, "Judicial Activity and Public Attitude: A Quantitative Study of Selective Service Sentencing in the Vietnam War Period," *Buffalo Law Review* 23 (Winter 1973): 465–498.

15   Herbert Kritzer, "Political Correlates of the Behavior of Federal District Judges: A 'Best Case' Analysis," *Journal of Politics* 40 (February 1978): 25–58. For an exchange, see Herbert Kritzer, "Federal Judges and Their Political Environments: The Influence of Public Opinion," *American Journal of Political Science* 23 (February 1979): 194–207; and Beverley Blair Cook, "Judicial Policy: Change Over Time," *American Journal of Political Science* 23 (February 1979): 203–214.

16   James Kuklinski and John Stanga, "Political Participation and Government Responsiveness: The Behavior of California Superior Courts," *American Political Science Review* 73 (December 1979): 1090–1099.

17   James Gibson, "Environmental Constraints on the Behavior of Judges: A Representational Model of Judicial Decision Making," *Law & Society Review* 14 (Winter 1980): 343–370. Gibson's measure of local public opinion was an estimate, not based on actual poll data.

18   Charles Sheldon, *The American Judicial Process* (New York: Dodd, Mead & Co., 1974), 192–193.

19   The most notable instance of a prolonged, countermajoritarian Court decision is the school prayer decision: see Robert Weissberg, *Public Opinion and Popular Government*, 121–126.

20   See especially Casper, *The Politics of Civil Liberties*; Barnum, "The Supreme Court and Public Opinion"; and Blake, "The Supreme Court's Abortion Decisions and Public Opinion in the United States," *Population and Development Review* 3 (March/June 1977): 45–62

21   Although Chief Justice Hughes's (second) tenure on the Court began in 1930, the first decision counted here dated from the 1934–1935 term — *A.L.A. Schencter Poultry Corporation v. United States* (1935) The chief justice's tenures were adjusted when necessary to include all the terms. Chief Justice Stone was counted until the end of the 1945–1946 term; Vinson was counted from the beginning of the 1946–1947 term until the end of the 1952–1953

term; Warren was included from the start of the 1953–1954 term until the end of the 1968–1969 term; and Burger was counted from the start of the 1969–1970 term until the end of the 1985–1986 term.

22   For results with denials of certiorari excluded, see Thomas Marshall, "Public Opinion, Representation, and the Modern Supreme Court," *American Politics Quarterly* (1988, forthcoming).

23   The Gallup Poll question was "Are you in favor of the death penalty for persons convicted of rape?" In a March 3–6, 1978 survey, some 56 percent said no and 32 percent said yes. In another Gallup survey,1/30/81–2/2/81, 53 percent said no and 37 percent said yes.

24   The Gallup Poll, June 21–26, 1963; for a longer discussion, see Robert Weissberg, *Public Opinion ad Popular Government*, 121–126.

25   The Gallup Poll, 7/10/58–7/15/58.

26   Nine such combinations of multiple decisions into a single comparison (or match) occurred here.

27   This issue is described and examined at greater length in Chapter Six.

28   To the twenty denials of certiorari was added one per curiam decision, *Shapiro v. Doe* (1970), in which an appeal was dismissed on highly technical grounds (timeliness of appeal) over the dissents of Justices Black and Douglas.

29   *Maryland v. Baltimore Radio Show* (1950), at 919. See also *Agoston v. Pennsylvania* (1950).

30   *United States v. Carver* (1923), at 490.

31   See *Maryland v. Baltimore Radio Show* (1950), at 917–918; *Tiger v. Lozier* (1927); and *Zap v. U.S.* (1945). More generally, see Stephen Wasby, *The Supreme Court in the Federal Judicial System* (New York: Holt, Rinehart, and Winston, 1984), 158–167 and Fowler Harper and Arnold Leibowitz, "What the Supreme Court Did Not Do During the 1951 Term," *University of Pennsylvania Law Review* 102 (February 1954): 427–463, and earlier articles in this series.

32   No such decisions were identified here, however. If contradictory rulings between circuits resulted, the Court might address those discrepancies under its certiorari rules. However, see Robert Stern, "Denial of Certiorari Despite a Conflict," *Harvard Law Review* 66 (January 1953): 468–472; S. Sidney Ulmer, "The Supreme Court's Certiorari Decisions: Conflict as a Predictive Variable," *American Political Science Review* 78 (December 1984): 901–911.

33   In recent years, for instance, Justices Brennan and Marshall have repeatedly dissented from denials of certiorari in death penalty cases.

34   See, for example, Justice Blackmun's opinion in *Kerr-McGee Chemical Corp. v. Illinois* (1982), at 1049–50.

35   Marshall, "Public Opinion, Representation, and the Modern Court."

36   David O'Brien, *Storm Center* (New York: W.W Norton, 1986), 205.

37   Alan Monroe, "Consistency Between Public Preferences and National Policy Decisions," *American Politics Quarterly* 7 (January

1979): 3–19. In the same (1960–1974) period, some 58 percent of available polls were matched by a consistent Supreme Court decision, and 42 percent were matched by an inconsistent decision. Instances of inconsistent or evenly divided polls were excluded.

38   This figure excludes 26 instances in which spending decisions were compared with opinion preferences. In these 26 cases, only 11 of 26 cases were judged as consistent. See Monroe, "Consistency Between Public Preferences and National Policy Decisions," Table 4.

39   Benjamin Page and Robert Shapiro, "Effects of Public Opinion on Policy," *American Political Science Review* 77 (March 1983): 175–190.

40   These figures were re-computed from Robert Erikson, "The Relationship Between Public Opinion and State Policy," *American Journal of Political Science* 20 (February 1976): 25–36.

41   Richard Sutton, "The States and the People: Measuring and Accounting for 'State Representativeness,'" *Polity* 5 (Summer 1973): 451–76. Sutton allowed a two-year time lag from the poll to the policy measurement.

42   Alan Monroe, "Consistency Between Public Preferences and National Policy Decisions"; Christopher Hewitt, "Policy Making in Postwar Britain", *British Journal of Political Science* 4 (April 1974): 187–216; and Robert Erikson, "The Relationship Between Public Opinion and State Policy" all showed a consistent, if only marginal tendency for greater policy–opinion agreement to exist when the poll margin was extremely one-sided.

43   The Gallup Poll, March 18–23, 1965.

44   *New York v. Quarles* (1984), *Nix v. Williams* (1984), and *U.S. v. Leon* (1984): see also the NBC/Associated Press Poll, 1/18/82–1/19/82.

45   Theodore Becker, *Comparative Judicial Politics* (Chicago: Rand McNally, 1970), 229.

46   *Dennis v. United States* (1951), dissent at 580. For another example, see the dissent by Justice Murphy in *Korematsu v. United States* (1944) at 239–240.

47   For a recent summary, see *The Gallup Report*, Report no. 243 (Princeton, N.J.: Gallup, December 1985), 14.

48   A few cases that involved conflicts between different branches of the federal government were excluded. Cases involving a conflict between the federal government and a state/local law or policy were counted in both categories.

49   A subset of these cases closely parallelled Robert Dahl's sample. Of the federal-level cases, 51 involved a challenge to a federal law clearly passed by Congress and signed by the president. These 51 cases most nearly matched Dahl's definition of a "national majority." Some 71 percent of the 51 Dahl-like federal laws were consistent with the polls, 16 percent were inconsistent, and the remaining 14 percent were unclear, due to closely divided or contradictory polls.

In the 51 Dahl-like rulings, the Supreme Court upheld 86 percent of the 36 consistent federal laws, 75 percent of the 8 inconsistent ones, and 71 percent of the 7 cases where polls were unclear. Excluding the latter 7 cases, the Court decision was a majoritarian one in 75 percent (or 33 of 44) of the remaining cases. By contrast, if unclear cases are also set aside, some 82 percent (or 36 of 44) of remaining federal laws were consistent with the polls — once again, a figure quite similar to the Supreme Court's record.

50 As David Barnum has noted, public opinion changed dramatically on many key issues during the Warren Court period; see Barnum, "The Supreme Court and Public Opinion."

51 Percentages were based on Burger Court decisions, excluding cases in which polls were closely divided or inconsistent.

52 For a discussion of countermajoritarian Court decisions, see Casper, *The Politics of Civil Liberties*; Weissberg, *Public Opinion and Popular Government*; and Barnum, "The Supreme Court and Public Opinion."

53 If the denials of certiorari were excluded from Table 4.3, the numbers of cases and percentage majoritarian were civil liberties (6, 67 percent); civil rights (16, 75 percent) labor (21, 62 percent); national security (14, 71 percent); intergovernmental relations (10, 50 percent); business regulation (13, 77 percent); social welfare (7, 57 percent); privacy (10, 50 percent); education (17, 59 percent); criminal rights (18, 44 percent); elections (12, 75 percent); religion (4, 50 percent); media (4, 50 percent); transportation (13, 100 percent); and other (1, 100 percent).

54 *U.S. v. Carolene Products* (1938), at 152.

55 For examples of the Supreme Court's changing doctrine, see *Nebbia v. New York* (1934), *West Coast Hotel v. Parrish* (1937), *U.S. v. Carolene Products* (1938), and *Federal Power Commission v. Hope Natural Gas Co.* (1944). This hypothesis also rests upon the assumption that federal and state regulations will themselves reflect nationwide public opinion.

56 Probit estimation procedures were further discussed in Richard McKelvey and William Zavoina, "A Statistical Model for the Analysis of Ordinal Level Dependent Variables," *Journal of Mathematical Sociology* 4 (1975): 103–120; John Aldrich and Charles Cnudde, "Probing the Bounds of Conventional Wisdom: A Comparison of Regression, Probit and Discriminant Analysis," *American Journal of Political Science* 19 (August 1975): 571–608; and John Aldrich and Forrest Nelson, *Linear Probability, Logit, and Probit Models* (Sage: Beverly Hills, Calif., 1984). A logit (logistical regression) analysis provides very similar results to the probit results here.

57 The final indicator, pre- versus post-decision polls, was tested as a measurement artifact. Because it was not significantly related to the Court's agreement with public opinion, it is not included in the following probit analysis.

58 See McKelvey and Zavoina, "A Statistical Model"; and Aldrich and Nelson, *Linear Probability*, for a discussion of the pseudo-R^2 technique.

59 For an overview of the role of interest groups in Supreme Court policy making, see Stephen Wasby, *The Supreme Court in the Federal Judicial System*, 109–120; Karen O'Connor and Lee Epstein, "Amicus Curiae Participation in U.S. Supreme Court Litigation," *Law & Society Review* 16 (1981–1982): 311–320; Lee Epstein, *Conservatives in Court* (Knoxville, Tenn.: University of Tennessee Press, 1985); Samuel Krislov, "The Amicus Brief: From Friendship to Advocacy," *Yale Law Journal* 72 (March 1963): 694–721; and Nathan Hakman, "Lobbying the Supreme Court – An Appraisal of the Political Science 'Folklore,'" *Fordham Law Review* 35 (1966): 15–50.

60 Examples of specific interest groups within the nine categories included: pro-civil liberties, free speech, and media (ACLU, Amnesty International, American Newspaper Guild, American Newspaper Publishers Association, National Lawyers Guild); pro-civil rights (NAACP, MALDEF, National Urban Coalition, Japanese American Citizens League); education (NEA, AFT, National School Board Association, Classroom Teachers Association); corporations, businesses, and trade associations (National Right to Work Legal Defense Fund, Chamber of Commerce, and specific businesses or trade associations); labor unions (AFL-CIO, UAW, American Federation of Musicians, United Mine Workers); feminist, gender and privacy (Planned Parenthood, Human Rights for Women, NOW, ZPG, WEAL); liberal religious (National Council of Churches of Christ, Anti-defamation League of B'Nai B'Rith, American Jewish Congress, Unitarian Fellowship); and conservative or law enforcement (National District Attorneys Association; FOP; Southeastern or Pacific or Mountain States Legal Foundation; National Right to Life.)

61 In rare instances different groups within the same category took conflicting positions. Where this occurred, the category position was scored (0).

62 When the nine interest group categories were jointly entered in a probit equation, -2LLR was not significant, the percentage of correctly predicted cases was only 64 percent (versus a 63 percent base rate), and only the feminist-gender-privacy category was statistically significant at .05.

63 When the nine interest group categories were added to the seven-variable (party, context, and case type) probit equation, the R^2, percent of cases correctly predicted, and the -2LLR figure did not improve.

64 See Chapter One, at notes 36–38.

CHAPTER FIVE

Public Opinion and Supreme Court Justices

Why do Supreme Court justices vote as they do? As any Supreme Court term demonstrates, individual justices often vote quite differently. Court observers may try to explain these voting patterns in a variety of ways, among them, by examining the justices' political party ties, their ideology or judicial philosophy, their role on the Court, or their personal, career, or political backgrounds.

Chapter Four tried to explain why the Court makes majoritarian rulings in some instances, but not in others. Chapter Five focuses not on the Court's collective rulings, but rather on the 36 individual justices who served on the Supreme Court during the period 1935–1986.

This chapter asks two questions. First, do some justices agree with public opinion more often than do other justices? Second, if so, why? Five different models are tested, each focusing on the individual justice. The five models include a justice's political socialization, the appointment process, on-the-Court roles, length of tenure, and political realignments.

The Individual Justice and Public Opinion

Just as the Supreme Court, as a collective body, can hand down a majoritarian or countermajoritarian ruling, so, too, can an individual justice's votes agree or disagree with the polls. In the landmark (but countermajoritarian) *Engle* and *Abington* school prayer decisions, for example, Justices Clark, Black,

Warren, Harlan, White, Brennan, Douglas, and Goldberg wrote or joined opinions that disagreed with nationwide polls. By contrast, Justice Stewart, alone in dissent, reflected nationwide public opinion.

In this chapter each of the votes of the modern Court's 36 justices was coded as either consistent (majoritarian) or inconsistent (countermajoritarian) with nationwide polls. Only full, written opinions were counted.[1] Denials of certiorari and summary affirmations, reversals, or dismissals were not counted, except in those rare instances in which an individual justice wrote to explain a dissenting or concurring vote; nor were votes counted if the available polls were evenly divided or inconsistent, or if a justice did not participate in a decision.

How consistently have the modern Court's justices reflected public opinion? For all 36 justices, some 59 percent (or 529 of 901) of individual votes were majoritarian. The remaining 327 individual votes (or 41 percent of the total) disagreed with available polls.[2]

Twenty-five justices authored or joined at least ten opinions for which available polls showed a clear public opinion majority or plurality. Table 5.1 ranks these 25 justices in order of their agreement with nationwide public opinion. The remaining justices (for whom fewer than ten votes could be coded) are listed at the bottom of Table 5.1. For the twenty-five justices ranked in Table 5.1, the average (percent) agreement with public opinion was 59 percent, with a standard deviation of 12 percent.

The modern Court's justices have varied considerably in the frequency with which they have agreed with nationwide public opinion. At one extreme, Chief Justices Hughes and Vinson agreed with the polls in more than three-quarters of their votes. At the other extreme, Justices Black, Murphy, Harlan, McReynolds, Stevens, and Rutledge agreed with poll majorities or pluralities in fewer than one-half of their votes.

While these results should be interpreted cautiously, they suggest that some modern Supreme Court justices may have been considerably more majoritarian than others. Yet what accounts for these differences? Are some types of justices particularly prone toward majoritarian opinions, while others are not?

The remainder of this chapter addresses the second question — whether some types of justices are more majoritarian than

Table 5.1
Justices ranked by their level of agreement with public opinion

Rank	Justice	% Majoritarian	Number of votes
1	Hughes	86%	14
2	Vinson	77%	13
3	Frankfurter	72%	29
4	Burton	71%	17
5 (tie)	Roberts	68%	22
	Stone	68%	25
	Jackson	68%	19
	White	68%	62
9	Powell	67%	45
10	Blackmun	65%	51
11	Reed	61%	31
12 (tie)	Clark	60%	15
	Stewart	60%	58
	Rehnquist	60%	43
15	Douglas	56%	61
16	Brennan	55%	65
17 (tie)	Warren	53%	15
	Marshall	53%	58
19	Burger	52%	54
20	Black	49%	53
21	Murphy	47%	17
22 (tie)	Harlan	45%	20
	McReynolds	45%	11
24	Stevens	44%	25
25	Rutledge	30%	10

Note: Table 5.1 excludes denials of certiorari, decisions where public opinion polls were contradictory or evenly divided, decisions where an individual justice's vote could not be determined, and decisions in which a justice did not participate.

The remaining justices each participated in nine or fewer votes for which a clear poll margin existed. The number of votes for each justice, and the percent of majoritarian votes is: Brandeis (9 votes — 78% consistent), Cardozo (7—71%), Minton (9—67%), Goldberg (3—67%), VanDevanter (7—57%), Sutherland (8—50%), O'Connor (8—38%), Butler (9—33%), Byrnes (3—33%), and Fortas (5—20%). Justice Whittaker participated in no decisions which could be scored here.

others. In turn, five linkage models are explored: political socialization, the appointment process, on-the-Court roles, length of tenure, and realignments.

Political Socialization

A justice's pre-Court socialization experiences might influence Court voting behavior. Here, a variety of pre-Court socialization experiences and values were tested, including a justice's political party ties, ideology, and personal, career, or political background. Experiences and values that exposed a justice to a majority-oriented culture, or that attuned a justice to mass public opinion, were predicted to be linked to majoritarian voting behavior on the Supreme Court.

Taken together, the modern Court's justices are an excellent group upon which to test hypotheses about majoritarian voting. At least by the Supreme Court's own exclusive standards, the modern Court's justices are a relatively diverse group.[3] Since the mid-1930s, the Court's first black (Marshall) and first female (O'Connor) justices joined the previously all-white, all-male brethren. The Court's five Jewish justices (Brandeis, Cardozo, Frankfurter, Goldberg, and Fortas) all sat during this period, as did three (Butler, Murphy, and Brennan) of the Court's six Catholic members to 1986. While most justices hailed from top-ranked law schools, Justice Byrnes was the last in a long line of self-taught justices. Republican and Democratic justices, and even one self-described (if arguably) Independent justice, (Frankfurter) were included. Some justices (such as Murphy, Marshall, or Douglas) were renowned liberals, while others (such as McReynolds or Rehnquist) have been equally staunch conservatives. A few justices (such as Cardozo) boasted long and distinguished judicial careers before joining the Court; others (Warren and Burton, for example) had no previous judicial experience at all.

POLITICAL PARTY

As Stuart Nagel, Sheldon Goldman, and others have demonstrated, political party affiliation is a critical variable in examining judicial behavior. Political party ties affect a Supreme Court justice's career in several ways.[4] With rare exceptions presidents choose Supreme Court justices from the ranks of their own party. Further, Democratic justices more often support liberal economic decisions, pro-civil rights and civil liberties rulings, and pro-criminal defendant rulings than do their Republican brethren. Here, three different indicators were examined to test whether political party is linked to majoritarian voting patterns: a justice's own political party, the appointing president's political party, and the (combined) era and party of the appointing president.

Hypotheses about the linkage between political party and majoritarian voting patterns can be offered only tentatively. Yet since the 1930s the Democratic party can reasonably be counted as the nation's dominant party. Democratic party identifiers have consistently numbered at least a plurality, and at times an outright majority of all Americans. Democrats have also usually organized both houses of Congress, as well as most state legislatures.[5]

Accordingly, Democratic justices and justices appointed by Democratic presidents were predicted to be more consistent with nationwide public opinion than were their Republican (or Republican-appointed) counterparts. Because pre-New Deal Republican and laissez-faire values were so thoroughly abandoned during and after the Great Depression, the appointees of pre-New Deal Republican presidents were predicted to be the least majoritarian justices.

Justices' Own Party Preferences The justices were first examined by their own self-designated party preference.[6] Contrary to the earlier hypothesis, Democratic justices were not more majoritarian than their Republican brethren. As Table 5.2 indicates, the sixteen GOP justices reflected poll majorities (or pluralities) in 60 percent of their 376 votes, and the 19 self-described Democratic justices did so in 57 percent of their 496 votes — a statistically insignificant difference.

In two instances, a justice's self-designated party ties can reasonably be disputed. Upon appointment, Justice Brandeis was a registered Republican, and Justice Frankfurter, a self-described Independent. If both Brandeis and Frankfurter are instead counted as Democrats, then the 21 Democratic justices were majoritarian in 59 percent of their votes, while the 15 GOP justices were consistent with the polls in an identical 59 percent of their votes.

Party of the Appointing President When the justices were compared by their appointing president's political party, no significant differences appeared. The 18 justices appointed by GOP presidents were majoritarian in 59 percent of their votes — a figure identical to that for the 18 justices appointed by Democratic presidents.

Era and Party of the Appointing President Because the justices' appointments span so long a time period (from 1910 to 1981), the combined era and party of the appointing president was also examined. Presidents Taft, Harding, Coolidge, and Hoover's seven appointees were combined into a category of pre-New Deal GOP presidential designees. Woodrow Wilson's two appointees were counted as pre-New Deal Democratic presidential appointees. Presidents Roosevelt and Truman's 12 appointees formed the New Deal Democratic category. Presidents Eisenhower, Nixon, Ford, and Reagan together appointed 11 justices (the post-New Deal Republican category). Presidents Kennedy and Johnson's four choices rounded out the post-New Deal Democratic presidential appointee category.

Contrary to the hypothesis, the seven justices appointed by the pre-New Deal GOP presidents were slightly more likely to reflect popular opinion than were other justices. The differences, however, are not statistically significant.

A justice's political party ties, then, cannot explain why some justices are more majoritarian than others. Party affiliation may help explain a justice's initial appointment or a justice's economic, civil liberties, or criminal rights voting patterns. Yet party ties are unrelated to a justice's tendency to reflect nationwide public opinion while serving on the Supreme Court.

IDEOLOGY

Judicial scholars have examined judges' ideologies in several ways — through specially constructed scales and clustering techniques, bloc analysis, content analysis, or, occasionally, interviews or mailed questionnaires.[7] In this study a justice's ideology was evaluated by classifying each vote as either liberal or conservative. A liberal vote was one upholding an individual's civil rights, civil liberties, or criminal rights claim;

upholding government regulation of business; or upholding a labor claim against either business or government. A conservative vote was the reverse.[8] Only a handful of votes could not be so classified, and were excluded from the analysis.

Each justice was grouped into a conservative, moderate, or liberal category, numbering 11, 13 or 12 justices, respectively.[9] The percentage of majoritarian votes from each group was then examined. As hypothesized, moderate justices were marginally more majoritarian than conservative or liberal justices. Politically moderate justices were consistent in 63 percent of their votes, versus 58 percent for more conservative justices, or 54 percent for more liberal justices.

JUDICIAL BACKGROUND

Whether a justice's personal, career, or political background is tied to on-the-bench voting behavior has long concerned practicing politicians and judicial scholars alike.[10] Here, a wide variety of personal, career, and political socialization experiences were examined.

The available literature does not clearly identify which of a justice's pre-Court experiences may be most strongly related to on-the-bench majoritarian voting. Generally, background traits that place a justice in a more majority-oriented culture, a more contemporary age group, or a more actively politicized role were predicted to sensitize that justice to majority-oriented values — and, in turn, lead to majoritarian voting while on the Supreme Court.

Accordingly, nonSouthern, nonminority, and younger justices were predicted to be more majoritarian than Southern, minority, or older justices. Justices from more prestigious law schools, those who had held appointed or elected public office, and justices who held high-level presidential appointments or served as presidential confidants were also predicted to be more majoritarian.

Personal Background
Region The justices were first compared by their regional background, according to where they spent most of their pre-Court careers. Contrary to the hypothesis, a justice's home region was not significantly related to majoritarian voting on the

Court. Southern justices were neither more nor less majoritarian than Eastern, Midwestern, or Western justices.[11]

Minority Status   Supreme Court justices have historically comprised the nation's most exclusive fraternity — entirely white and male, and overwhelmingly Protestant and Anglo-Saxon. Yet during the 1935–1986 period a record number of ten "minority" justices served on the high court, including three Catholic justices, five Jewish justices, and the Court's first black justice and its first female justice.[12]

Contrary to the hypothesis, the Court's Catholic Jewish, black, and female "minority" justices were only slightly, but not significantly less majoritarian than their white, male, Protestant counterparts. Together, the ten minority appointees reflected nationwide polls in 56 percent of their votes, compared with 60 percent for the nonminority justices.

Generation and Age   An individual's age and political cohort have often been tied to political attitudes and electoral choices.[13] Supreme Court justices may reflect their own generation's political experiences, values, norms, and milieu upon reaching the bench.[14] Two indicators of a justice's age were examined — the justice's age group (or cohort) and the justice's age at appointment.

The modern Court's justices span a remarkable number of years. Justices Brandeis and VanDevanter were born before the Civil War — in 1856 and 1859, respectively. The youngest justice (O'Connor) was born almost three-quarters of a century later — shortly after the October 1929 stock market crash.

The justices were divided into three cohorts. The oldest cohort includes the 20 justices born before 1895. These justices were already well into middle age (or older) when the Great Depression, the New Deal political realignment, and scientific, nationwide polling all appeared almost simultaneously. The middle cohort — born between 1895 and 1910 — numbers 10 justices who were less advanced into their careers by the mid-1930s. The youngest cohort — six justices born after 1910 — were still younger when the Great Depression transformed American political life.

Contrary to the hypothesis that the oldest cohort would be the least majoritarian, no significant differences appeared when

111

the justices were divided by political generation. Nor could on-the-bench majoritarianism be explained by the justices' ages upon appointment.

Career Background A justice's career patterns may also affect a justice's later tendency to reflect majority opinion. Here, four career patterns were examined: the prestige of a justice's law school, occupation upon appointment, career experiences, and law school teaching experience.

Law School Prestige Law schools may shape a lawyer's later outlook by exposing the student to a broader or narrower perspective on the law.[15] Top-ranking law schools may expose students to national, rather than state law, and may also expose them to more modern legal theories. Here, justices from more prestigious law schools were compared with those from less prominent schools, or those with no law school training at all. Justices from more prestigious law schools were significantly more majoritarian than were justices who graduated from less prestigious law schools, or justices who had no law school training.

Occupation Upon Appointment The modern Court's 36 justices pursued markedly different careers before joining the Court. Upon appointment, seven justices were in private practice, 12 held a lower state or federal court post, four served in an elected (nonjudicial) office, 12 held an appointed position, and one was a law school professor. Contrary to the hypothesis that elected or appointed officeholders would be more majoritarian, no significant differences appeared.

Overall Career Patterns In many instances a justice's position at the time of appointment did not accurately reflect the justice's entire career. Justice Rutledge, for example, long served as a law school professor and dean, but four years before his Supreme Court appointment he was named to the Court of Appeals for the District of Columbia. As an alternate measure of a justice's career pattern, the number of years each justice spent in private practice, appointed office, elective office, a judicial position, or in a (full-time) law school post was measured, then correlated with the percentage of majoritarian votes for each justice. Once again, none of these measures was significantly related to a justice's majoritarian tendencies.

Law School Teaching   Ten justices had some law school teaching experience, although often only briefly, intermittently, or early in the justice's career. Law school teaching, however, was not related to a justice's later majoritarian behavior.

Political Background   Five types of pre-Court political experiences were examined: prior candidacy, prior election loss, holding an appointed or elected public office, holding a high-level presidential appointment, or serving as a close presidential confidant. Justices with politicized careers were predicted to be more majoritarian than their less politicized brethren.

Election Experience   Twenty of the thirty-six justices had campaigned for elective office before coming to the Court. While office seeking was predicted to heighten a justice's sensitivity to public opinion, no such relationship appeared. Previous candidates were neither more nor less majoritarian than justices who had never campaigned for an elective office.

Electoral Defeat   Of the twenty justices who had earlier sought political office, not all were successful. Six justices had been defeated at least once, ranging from Justice McReynolds (who ran in 1896 as a Gold Democrat for Congress) to Justice Warren (who made his vice-presidential bid in 1948). Previously defeated justices, however, did not differ significantly from the remaining justices in their agreement with public opinion.

Public Office Holding   Twenty-nine of the thirty-six justices had held some elected or appointed public post. Contrary to the hypothesis, previous officeholders were slightly, but not significantly less majoritarian than justices who had not held an elected or appointed office.

High Ranking Presidential Appointment ˍTwelve justices held a high-level, non-judicial appointment at the time they joined the Court. Typically, this included the post of attorney general (McReynolds, Stone, Murphy, Jackson, and Clark), solicitor general (Reed and Marshall), deputy or assistant attorney general (White and Rehnquist), or in other instances, Treasury Secretary (Vinson), Securities and Exchange Commission chair (Douglas), or Labor Secretary (Goldberg). Top-ranking presidential appointees were predicted to be more "politicized" (and hence, more majoritarian), but no significant differences appeared.

Presidential Confidant Nearly half the justices could fairly be termed close presidential confidants or advisors. Justice Fortas, a Lyndon Johnson confidant, perhaps best exemplifies the close relationship which presidents and their appointees sometimes enjoy.[16] By contrast, other appointees, such as Justices O'Connor and Stevens, were barely known to their appointing presidents. As hypothesized, presidential confidants were more majoritarian than other justices.

The Appointment Process

The appointment process may also serve as a rough indicator of which justices will reflect public opinion. Potential nominees who are perceived as out-of-line with public opinion may not be nominated at all, or if nominated, may be rejected by the Senate. Justices who show a broad appeal during the confirmation process may later prove to be more attuned to public opinion while on the Supreme Court. Here, two types of justices were predicted to be the most majoritarian — first, justices chosen by a president of the opposite party; and second, justices who received unanimous or near-unanimous Senate confirmation.

CROSSOVER APPOINTMENTS

On rare occasions a president strays from his own party to tap a personal friend (Burton), an unusually well-respected contender (Cardozo), a politically attractive regional or religious nominee (Butler, Brennan and Powell), or a justice who is only nominally from the opposition party (Brandeis and again, Butler). Crossover appointees were predicted to be more majoritarian than same-party nominees. The six crossover appointees, however, were not significantly more majoritarian than justices from the appointing president's own party.[17]

SENATE CONFIRMATION MARGIN

Most Supreme Court justices are confirmed with little, or no Senate opposition. Yet a handful of justices faced divisive confirmation battles — perhaps none more rancorous than Justice Brandeis's eventual 47-to-22 Senate confirmation (with 27 Senators not voting), or Justice Hughes's 52-to-26 confirmation (with 18 abstentions).[18]

Justices who faced divisive confirmation battles were predicted to be less majoritarian during their tenure on the Court. Unexpectedly, however, justices with less one-sided confirmation margins were slightly, albeit not significantly more majoritarian.

To be sure, the nomination and confirmation process may still serve to screen out potentially countermajoritarian justices. Presidents may decline to nominate, and Senators may decline to confirm such candidates if they are nominated.For justices who are actually confirmed and who serve on the Supreme Court, however, the appointment process provides no clue as to the justices' tendency to reflect public opinion.

Judicial Roles

How frequently a Supreme Court justice reflects popular opinion may be related to a justice's role on the Court. As David Danelski, Walter Murphy, and others have argued, Supreme Court justices pursue a variety of roles and strategies.[19] Some justices are task leaders, others social leaders, and still others policy leaders. Some justices exercise no apparent influence at all, and at least one justice is best known for antagonizing his colleagues.[20] A few justices pursue off-the-Court ambitions. Some achieve a lasting fame; others drift into historical obscurity.

Because they may be more sensitive to the Court's image and more frequently speak for the Court, chief justices were predicted to be more majoritarian than associate justices. Politically ambitious justices and highly regarded justices were also predicted to reflect public opinion more often.

CHIEF JUSTICES

The chief justice travels more widely, speaks more often, and assumes a spokesman role for the Court, both in Congress and elsewhere.[21] This role as spokesman for the Court might attune the Chief Justice more finely to public opinion. In fact, the modern Court's five Chief Justices (Hughes, Stone, Vinson, Warren, and Burger) were slightly more likely to agree with public opinion than were the 31 remaining associate justices. Alone, the differences were slight, but when combined with other predictors (later in this chapter), the differences between Chief Justices and associate justices proved to be more significant.

AMBITION

For most justices the Court is plainly the culmination of a career. A handful of justices, however, were nominated from associate to chief justice (Stone, Rehnquist, and Fortas), left the Court for another prominent post (Byrnes and Goldberg), or flirted with an off-the-Court political bid (Douglas). Contrary to the hypothesis that "ambitious" justices would be more responsive to public opinion, the six "ambitious" justices were no more majoritarian than were the remaining 30 justices.[22]

REPUTATION

A third on-the-Court variable taps the justice's reputation among Court observers and scholars. A 1972 *American Bar Association Journal* article surveyed 65 prominent law school deans and professors who ranked each of the first 96 justices as "great," "near-great," "average," "below average," or as "a failure." Thirty of the 36 justices in this study were so ranked.[23]

No significant differences appeared on this measure. Great or near-great justices agreed no more often with public opinion than did their less well-regarded brethren.

Length of Tenure

Robert Dahl's now-classic article suggested that deaths, resignations, and new appointments typically bring the Supreme Court back into line with prevailing public opinion. Long-tenured justices who resist newly emerging national values eventually are replaced by justices who reflect more contemporary social and economic norms. As a result, the Supreme Court will seldom long defy Congress, the president, and nationwide public opinion.[24]

The length-of-tenure model suggests that justices grow less responsive to public opinion during their career on the Supreme Court. In this model, long-tenured justices should be less majoritarian than recently appointed justices. Here, the justices' earlier and later votes were compared in four different ways.

EARLY AND LATE COURT TENURE

The first test compared the justices' votes during their first four years on the Court with their votes in later years.[25] During their first four years the 36 justices collectively wrote or joined 227 opinions that could be counted here. Later in their Court careers the 36 justices collectively produced another 674 votes. This test did not support the Dahl thesis. Justices were as consistent with the polls during their later years on the Court as they were during their first four years of service.

FIRST AND SECOND HALF-TENURE

As a second test, each justice's Court tenure was divided into two equal halves. The justices' record during their first half-tenure was then compared with their second half-tenure. Again, there were no significant differences. The justices wrote or joined majoritarian opinions equally often during their first or second half-tenure.

SENIOR JUSTICES

As a third test, the length-of-tenure model was reexamined even more narrowly. Eight of the 36 justices sat on the Court longer than twenty years. After their twentieth year on the Court, these eight justices collectively cast 119 votes, of which 56 percent were consistent with the polls. Once again, no evidence suggested that justices grow less majoritarian during their Court tenure, even during their last years on the Court.

AGING AND CONSERVATISM

Finally, some studies hint that longer-tenured justices may become more conservative and hence, less representative of an increasingly less conservative American public. This version of the length-of-tenure model can be tested only in a limited way, given the differing judicial issues that arise over time. Even so, little support appeared for this thesis. Eighteen of the 36 justices served for at last ten years within the period 1935–1986. For these 18 justices, 57 percent of their 417 first half-tenure votes, versus 67 percent of their 341 second half-tenure votes, were politically liberal. Individually, three of the justices became significantly more liberal, two became significantly more conservative, and 13 showed no significant change over time. In short, there was no evidence that the modern Court's justices grew either less majoritarian or more conservative over their tenure on the Court.

Realignment

In the realignment model, periodic economic or social upheavals cause rapid changes in mass public opinion. Sitting justices, however, are less likely to change their well-settled views; as a result, during realignment periods, sitting justices rapidly grow less representative of mass public opinion.

Unfortunately, scientific public opinion polls did not exist before the mid-1930s, and it is impossible to measure how well individual justices or the Court as a whole represented public opinion before the mid-1930s. Even so, two limited tests of the realignment model are possible. The first compares pre-New Deal Republican presidential appointees with later appointees. A second, more limited test examines justices' majoritarian behavior before, versus after White House party turnovers. Justices appointed by pre-New Deal GOP presidents were predicted to be less representative than post-New Deal appointees. Justices were also predicted to be more majoritarian before their appointing president's party lost control of the White House.

THE NEW DEAL REALIGNMENT

Seven justices were appointed by pre-New Deal GOP presidents and continued to serve after the 1932 election. These seven justices, however, were slightly more, not less majoritarian than justices appointed after the 1932 presidential election.[26]

PARTY TURNOVERS AT THE WHITE HOUSE

From 1935 to 1986 the White House moved from Democrat to Republican (or vice versa) five times: in 1952, 1960, 1968, 1976, and 1980. While these shifts are not usually described as realignments, they do offer an alternate, indirect test of the realignment model. To test whether justices' agreement with public opinion is linked to these electoral swings, each justice's votes were examined before, versus after the appointing president's party lost control of the presidency.

Once again, no significant differences appeared. The justices reflected public opinion no less often after the appointing president's party lost control of the presidency than before a White House turnover occurred.[27]

The results from the length-of-tenure and realignment models may be surprising. There was no evidence to indicate that Supreme Court justices grow less majoritarian or more conservative over their tenure on the Court. Nor were justices less likely to reflect public opinion after their appointing president's party lost control of the White House. Indeed, even appointees of pre-new Deal GOP presidents reflected nationwide polls as frequently as did justices appointed after the 1932 election. In short, there was no evidence to suggest that deaths, retirements, and new appointments bring the Court back into line with public opinion, or that the justices appointed before 1932 were, on the whole, unrepresentative of public opinion after the New Deal realignment period.

Combining the Predictors

As in Chapter Four, the individual predictors can be combined into more complex models. In Table 5.3 the dependent variable is the percentage of majoritarian opinions of each justice. The independent variables, or predictors, described earlier in this chapter, were entered in groups in stepwise regression models.[28]

Because only a small number of justices served on the modern Court, an attractive regression model should contain as few

Table 5.2
Percent majoritarian, by category of justice

Category	% of Majoritarian votes	Number of (justices/votes)
Political Socialization Model		
Justice's political party:		
Republican	60%	(16/376)
Democrat	57%	(19/496)
Independent	72%	(1/29)
Appointing president's political party:		
Republican	59%	(18/476)
Democrat	59%	(18/425)
Party and era of appointing president:		
Pre-New Deal Republican	65%	(7/92)
Pre-New Deal Democrat	60%	(2/20)
New Deal Democrat	58%	(12/277)
Post-New Deal Republican	57%	(11/384)
Post-New Deal Democrat	59%	(4/128)
Ideology of justice:		
Conservative	58%	(11/198)
Moderate	63%	(13/375)
Liberal	54%	((12/328)
	(significant at .05)	
Four-part region:		
East	60%	(12/334)
Midwest	56%	(11/253)
West	61%	(6/143)
South	58%	(7/171)
Two-part region:		
South	58%	(7/171)
Non-South	59%	(29/730)
Minority appointment:		
Minority appointee	56%	(10/210)
Not a minority	60%	(26/691)
Cohort:		
Oldest (pre-1895)	61%	(20/328)
Middle (1895–1909)	57%	(10/372)
Youngest (1910 or later)	59%	(6/201)
Law school prestige:		
Top-ranked	61%	(26/679)
Less prestigious	52%	(10/222)
	(significant at 0.5)	

Table 5.2
Continued

Category	% of Majoritarian votes	Number of (justices/votes)
Occupation upon appointment:		
Private practice	64%	(7/112)
Judge	55%	(12/314)
Elected office	53%	(4/88)
Appointed office	60%	(12/358)
Law school	72%	(1/29)
Law school teaching:		
Prior law school		
Teaching experience	58%	(10/256)
No experience	59%	(26/645)
Prior candidacy:		
Previously a candidate	58%	(16/280)
Never a candidate	59%	(20/621)
Prior election loss:		
Previously defeated	58%	(6/74)
No electoral defeat	59%	(30/827)
Appointed or elected public service:		
Some such service	58%	(29/734)
No such service	60%	(7/167)
High-level appointment:		
Yes	60%	(12/358)
No	58%	(24/543)
Presidential confidant:		
Confidant	64%	(15/309)
Not a confidant	56%	(21/592)
	(significant at .05)	
Appointments process model		
Crossover appointments		
Crossover appointees	61%	(6/152)
Same-party appointees	58%	(30/749)
Judicial roles model		
Chief justice:		
Yes, chief justice	62%	(5/121)
Associate justice	58%	(31/780)
Ambition:		
Yes, "ambitious"	60%	(6/154)
Not "ambitious"	58%	(30/747)

Table 5.2
Continued

Category	% of Majoritarian votes	Number of (justices/votes)
Reputation:		
Great	63%	(7/152)
Near-great	53%	(7/188)
Average	60%	(7/244)
Below average	—	(0/0)
Failure	59%	(8/69)
Length of tenure model		
First four years or later:		
First four years	59%	(—/227)
Later tenure	59%	(—/674)
First half/second half:		
First half tenure	60%	(—/447)
Second half tenure	58%	(—/454)
Senior justices:		
Prior to 20th year	56%	(8/119)
20th year or later	59%	(36/782)
Realignment model		
New Deal realignment:		
Pre-New Deal GOP justices	65%	(7/92)
Later appointees	58%	(27/789)
White House party shift:		
Prior to shift	59%	(—/439)
After shift	59%	(—/462)

Ratio-level measures Category	Pearson product-moment correlation
(Recomputed) Moderate Ideology	+.19
Age at appointment	+.20
Prior career patterns: (in years)	
Private practice	+.23
Appointed office	−.07
Judicial position	+.26
Elected office	−.17
Law school teaching	.00
Senate confirmation margin	−.23

Note: The variables listed in Table 5.2 are not significant at the .05 level, unless so indicated. The realignment and tenure variables are reported for all the justices, as are the ratio-level variables.

predictors as possible. At the same time the predictors should also be as distinct (or noncollinear) as possible, exhibit strong explanatory power, and yield a straightforward interpretation.

Table 5.3 reports several alternative regression models, each based upon only a single set of predictors, such as a justice's political party; ideology[29]; personal, career, or political background; or on-the-Court role.[30] None of these "pure" models,

Table 5.3
Alternative models of the justices' voting behavior,
1935–1986

Model description	Variables included	R^2/Adjusted R^2
2-variable Political Party:	Justice's party + Appointing president's party + "Crossover"	.03/.00
3-variable political party model:	(above) + Era and party of appointing president	.08/.00
Ideology:	3-categories (dummy variables)	.04/.00
Ideology:	Re-computed measure	.05/.01
Personal background:	2-part Region + Cohort + Age at appointment + "Minority" appointment	.12/.00
Career background:	Law school prestige + Years in appointed post + Years as judge + Years in elected post + Years in private practice + Years, law school teaching	.21/.04
Political background:	Ever ran for office + (If so) ever defeated + Held appointed or elected position + Presidential confidant + High-level appointment	.17/.00
On-the-court role:	Chief justice + Reputation + Ambition	.18/.08

Note: None of the models in Table 5.3 was significant at the .05 significance level.

however, could adequately explain how often a justice would reflect public opinion.

Several alternative regression models were also tested. The only significant regression model incorporated just three variables — whether the justice attended a prestigious law school, served as a presidential confidant, and held the chief justice post.[31] Adding further variables failed to improve upon this model.

Percent   (.44)
Majoritarian←←←←←   + (.11) if prestigious law school
                            + (.06) if presidential confidant
                            + (.14) if Chief Justice

$(R^2) = .24$: Adjusted $R^2) = .17$: F-significance $= .03)$

Figure 5.1   Regression model predicting majoritarian
votes of individual justices

In this model, a (hypothetical) chief justice who hailed from a top-ranking law school, and had been a close presidential advisor, would be predicted to agree with public opinion 75 percent of the time. At the other extreme, a (still hypothetical) associate justice from a less prestigious law school who had not been a close presidential confidant would be the least majoritarian justice — agreeing with the polls only 44 percent of the time.

Conclusion

The modern Court's 36 justices have differed considerably in how often their votes reflected public opinion. Perhaps surprisingly, however, few of the variables or models examined here were closely linked to an individual justice's tendency to reflect mass public opinion.

No support at all was found for the appointment model, the length-of-tenure model, or the realignment model. For the socialization model and the roles model, limited support appeared. Politically moderate justices, chief justices, justices from prestigious law schools, and justices who had served as close presidential advisors were all somewhat more majoritarian than their remaining brethren.

References

1 An earlier Court norm held that a justice might disagree, but not file a separate dissent. However, by the mid-1930s, that norm was clearly in decline. See Walter Murphy, *Elements of Judicial Strategy* (Chicago: University of Chicago Press, 1964), 60–68; and David O'Brien, *Storm Center: The Supreme Court in American Politics* (New York: Norton, 1986), 262–273. For a discussion of problems in inferring values from justices' votes, see J. Woodford Howard, "On the Fluidity of Judicial Choice," *American Political Science Review* 62 (March 1968): 43–56; and Robert Sickels, "The Illusion of Judicial Consensus," *American Political Science Review* 59 (March 1965): 100–104.

2 Because Chapter Four was based on 146 collective decisions and Chapter Five upon 901 individual justices' votes, the 59 percent majoritarian figure in Chapter Five differs slightly from the 63 percent figure cited in Chapter Four.

3 Biographical data has been taken from a variety of sources, including John Schmidhauser, "The Justices of the Supreme Court: A Collective Portrait," *Midwest Journal of Political Science* 3 (February 1959): 1–57; and *Judges and Justices* (Boston: Little, Brown, 1979); Henry Abraham, *Justices and Presidents: A Political History of Appointments to the Supreme Court* (New York: Oxford University Press, 1985); Robert Scigliano, *The Supreme Court and the Presidency* (New York: Free Press, 1971); *Congressional Quarterly Guide to the U.S. Supreme Court* (Washington, D.C.: Congressional Quarterly Press, 1979); Stephan Elliot, ed., *A Reference Guide to the United States Supreme Court* (New York: Facts on File Publications, 1986); and Leon Friedman and Fred Israel, eds., *The Justices of the United States Supreme Court, 1789–1969*, 5 vols. (New York: Chelsea House, 1969).

4 The literature on political party and judicial behavior is extensive. For evidence that political party is significantly linked to judges' voting behavior, see Stuart Nagel, "Political Party Affiliation and Judges' Decisions," *American Political Science Review* 55 (December 1961): 843–850; "Judicial Backgrounds and Criminal Cases," *Journal of Criminal Law, Criminology, and Political Science* 53 (June 1962): 333–339; "Testing Relations Between Judicial Characteristics and Judicial Policy-Making," *Western Political Quarterly* 15 (September 1962): 425–427; and "Multiple Correlation of Judicial Backgrounds and Decisions," *Florida State University Law Review* 2 (Spring 1974): 258–288; Sheldon Goldman, "Voting Behavior on the United States Courts of Appeals, 1961–1964," *American Political Science Review* 60 (June 1966): 374–383; and "Voting Behavior on the United States

Courts of Appeals Revisited," *American Political Science Review* 69 (June 1975): 491–506; Sheldon Goldman and Thomas Jahnige, *The Federal Courts as a Political System*, 3rd ed., (New York: Harper & Row, 1985); Kenneth Vines, "Federal District Judges and Race Relations Cases in the South," *Journal of Politics* 26 (May 1964): 338–357; C. Neal Tate, "Personal Attribute Models of the Voting Behavior of U.S. Supreme Court Justices: Liberalism in Civil Liberties and Economic Decisions 1946–1978," *American Political Science Review* 75 (June 1981): 355–367; and S. Sidney Ulmer, "Social Background as an Indicator to the Votes of Supreme Court Justices in Criminal Cases: 1947–56 Terms," *American Journal of Political Science* 17 (August 1973): 622–630.

For the importance of political party in judicial appointments and Court voting since the early days of the federal judiciary, see Henry Abraham, *Justices and Presidents*; John Schmidhauser, "Judicial Behavior and the Sectional Crisis of 1837–1860," *Journal of Politics* 23 (November 1961): 615–640; Stuart Nagel, "Political Parties and Judicial Review in American History," *Journal of Public Law* 11 (2, 1962): 328–340; and Kermit Hall, "The Children of the Cabins: The Lower Federal Judiciary, Modernization, and the Political Culture, 1789–1899," *Northwestern University Law Review* 75 (October 1980): 423–471.

For state-level studies reporting that political parties are less important, see Malcolm Feeley, "Another Look at the 'Party Variable' in Judicial Decision-Making: An Analysis of the Michigan Supreme Court," *Polity* 4 (Fall 1971): 91–104; David Adamany, "The Party Variable in Judges' Voting: Conceptual Notes and a Case Study," *American Political Science Review* 63 (March 1969): 57–73; and Edward Beiser and Jonathan Silberman, "The Political Party Variable: Workmen's Compensation Cases in the New York Court of Appeals," *Polity* 3 (Summer 1971): 521–531.

5   See "Political Parties," *The Gallup Report* (January/ February 1985), no. 232/233, 21; and John Bibby, Thomas Mann, and Norman Ornstein, *Vital Statistics on Congress, 1980* (Washington, D.C.: American Enterprise Institute, 1980).

6   Abraham, *Justices and Presidents*, 386–391.

7   Most studies report two separate liberal-conservative scales — one measuring a civil liberties (C) dimension, and the other, an economic (E) dimension. The small number of 146 decisions here, however, compelled the use of a single ideology scale. The correlation between this scale and Glendon Schubert's C-Scale (ranked) values was .58 (Kendall's Tau), and with Schubert's E-Scale, .33, both significant at .05; see Glendon Schubert, *The Judicial Mind Revisited* (New York: Oxford University Press, 1974), 60, reporting data for 20 justices.

For justices who cast more than ten votes in both the economics and civil liberties areas, the Pearson product–moment correlation between the two scale values was .72, significant at .001. For a comparison, see Goldman, "Voting Behavior, 1961–1964."

8   These categories and voting positions were consistent with Gold-
    man, "Voting Behavior, Revisited," 492.

9   Justices who cast liberal votes less than 40 percent of the time were
    included in the most conservative group. Justices who cast liberal
    votes from 40 percent to 70 percent of the time were counted
    in the moderate group, and justices who cast liberal votes more
    than 70 percent of the time, were counted as liberals.

    The resulting conservative group included Justices VanDevanter,
    McReynolds, Butler, Sutherland, Jackson, Burton, Vinson, Min-
    ton, Burger, Rehnquist, and O'Connor. Moderates include Jus-
    tices Hughes, Roberts, Reed, Frankfurter, Byrnes, Clark, Harlan,
    Whittaker, Stewart, Powell, White, Blackmun, and Stevens. The
    liberal group included Justices Stone, Brandeis, Cardozo, Black,
    Douglas, Murphy, Rutledge, Warren, Brennan, Goldberg, Fortas,
    and Marshall.

10 For conflicting evidence on the impact of judicial backgrounds,
    see Joel Grossman, "Social Backgrounds and Judicial Decision-
    Making," *Harvard Law Review* 79 (June 1966): 1551–1564; Sheldon
    Goldman and Austin Sarat, eds., *American Court Systems: Readings
    in Judicial Process and Behavior* (San Francisco: W. H. Freeman,
    1978), 372–375; but also S. Sidney Ulmer, "Social Background as
    an Indicator" and C. Neal Tate, "Personal Attribute Models." For
    a general overview and discussion of judicial background studies,
    see Joel Grossman, "Social Backgrounds and Judicial Decisions:
    Notes for a Theory," *Journal of Politics* 29 (May 1967): 334–351; and
    Walter Murphy and Joseph Tanenhaus, *The Study of Public Law*
    (New York: Random House, 1972), 105–115. For an argument that
    judicial background analysis may be time-bound, see S. Sidney
    Ulmer, "Are Social Background Models Time-Bound?" *American
    Political Science Review* 80 (September 1986): 957–967.

11 Regional classification was based upon the region in which a
    justice spent most of his or her life — usually, but not always,
    the childhood region as well. Thus, Justices Douglas and Fortas
    were both counted as Easterners, not as a Westerner and a
    Southerner, respectively. A childhood-based classification did
    not produce results significantly different from those reported
    in Table 5.2

12 Justice Byrnes, an Episcopalian convert, was not counted as a
    minority (Catholic) appointee.

13 See, for example, Paul Allen Beck, "A Socialization Theory of
    Partisan Realignment," in Richard Niemi, ed., *The Politics of Future
    Citizens* (San Francisco: Jossey-Bass, 1974), 199–219; Russell Dal-
    ton, Scott Flanagan, and Paul Allen Beck, eds., *Electoral Change in
    Advanced Industrial Democracies: Realignment or Dealignment?* (Prince-
    ton: Princeton University Press, 1985); Norman Nie, Sidney Verba,
    and John Petrocik, *The Changing American Voter* (Cambridge, Mass.:
    Harvard University Press, 1979), 74–95; and Ronald Inglehart, *The
    Silent Revolution: Changing Values and Political Styles among Western
    Publics* (Princeton: Princeton University Press, 1977).

14 Judicial research that explicitly considers age includes Malcolm Feeley, "Another Look at the Party Variable"; Glendon Schubert, "Two Causal Models of Decision-Making by the High Court of Australia," in Glendon Schubert and David Danelski, eds., *Comparative Judicial Behavior* (New York: Oxford University Press, 1969), 340–341; Glendon Schubert, *The Constitutional Polity* (Boston: Boston University Press, 1970), 118–129; and *The Judicial Mind Revisited*, 142–144; S. Sidney Ulmer, "The Longitudinal Behavior of Hugo LaFayette Black: Parabolic Support for Civil Liberties, 1937–1971," *Florida State University Law Review* 1 (Winter 1973): 131–153; Charles Lamb, "Exploring the Conservatism of Federal Appeals Court Judges," *Indiana Law Journal* 51 (Winter 1976): 257–279; and Sheldon Goldman, "Voting Behavior, 1961–1964" and "Voting Behavior, Revisited."

15 The classification of law school prestige was updated from Schmidhauser, "A Collective Portrait," 25. See also Jerome Corsi, *An Introduction to Judicial Politics* (Englewood Cliffs, N.J.: Prentice-Hall, 1984), 62, for a description of the development and impact of American law Schools.

16 David O'Brien, *Storm Center*, 87–92.

17 If Justice Brandeis is excluded, the five remaining crossover appointees cast majoritarian votes 60 percent of the time — insignificantly more than the 58 percent figure for the remaining 31 justices.

18 A.L. Todd, *Justice on Trial: The Case of Louis D. Brandeis* (New York: McGraw-Hill, 1964); and Samuel Hendel, *Charles Evans Hughes and the Supreme Court* (New York: Columbia University Press, 1951), 78–90. For an analysis of partisan and institutional politics in Supreme Court confirmations, see Jeffrey Segal, "Senate Confirmation of Supreme Court Justices: Partisan and Institutional Politics," *Journal of Politics* 49 (November 1987): 998–1015.

19 Murphy, *Elements of Judicial Strategy*, 82–89; David Danelski, "The Influence of the Chief Justice in the Decisional Process," in Walter Murphy and C. Herman Pritchett, eds., *Courts, Judges, and Politics* (New York: Random House, 1961), 497–508.

A fourth judicial role variable was also tested, comparing the percent majoritarian scores with the "judicial power" (or judicial activism) scale reported for Warren Court-era justices; see Harold Spaeth, "Judicial Power as a Variable Motivating Supreme Court Behavior," *Midwest Journal of Political Science* 6 (February 1962): 59–62. The Pearson product-moment correlation between percent majoritarian opinions and judicial activism score was -.45 (significant at .1), indicating that activist justices during the Warren Court were marginally less majoritarian than restraint-oriented justices.

20 Justice McReynolds's behavior toward his fellow justices, especially Justices Clarke and Brandeis, was particularly notorious. See Murphy, *Elements of Judicial Strategy*, 52–55; and O'Brien, *Storm Center*, 112–121, 236, 253–254.

21 Murphy, *Elements of Judicial Strategy*, 100–104, 132–145; Stephen Wasby, *The Supreme Court in the Federal Judicial System*, 2nd ed., (New York: Holt, Rinehart & Winston, 1984), 52–54.

22 None of the modern Court's justices were as ambitious as the doughty Justice John McClean, who was nominated for president four times while serving on the Court between 1829 and 1861; see Abraham, *Justices and Presidents*, 96. Justice Douglas's flirtation with the presidency and vice-presidency is described in James Simon, *Independent Journey: The Life of William O. Douglas* (New York: Harper & Row, 1980), 257–275. The limited off-Court service of Justices Roberts, Reed, Jackson, and Warren was not counted as "ambitious" here. However, if Justice Jackson is also counted as "ambitious," for his well-known aspirations to be chief justice, the results in Table 5.2 would not change significantly.

23 Justices Burger, Blackmun, Powell, Rehnquist, O'Connor, and Stevens were not included in this reputational ranking. See Roy Mersky and Albert Blaustein, "Rating Supreme Court Justices," *American Bar Association Journal* 58 (November 1972): 1183–1189; and *The First One Hundred Justices* (Hamden, Conn.: Archon Books, 1978).

24 Robert Dahl, "Decision Making in a Democracy: The Supreme Court as a National Policy Maker," *Journal of Public Law* 6 (Fall 1957): 279–295; and Richard Funston, "The Supreme Court and Critical Elections," *American Political Science Review* 69 (September 1975): 793-811.

25 For justices appointed before 1931, all votes were counted in the later categories. For justices who served fewer than four years, all votes were counted in the earlier category.

26 The seven appointees of pre-New Deal Republican presidents included Justices VanDevanter, Sutherland, Butler, Stone, Hughes, Roberts, and Cardozo. If Justices Butler and Cardozo (both Democrats) are excluded, then 68 percent of the remaining five justices' votes were consistent with public opinion, compared to 58 percent consistent for the other 31 justices.

27 The presidential elections after 1932 or 1936 are not usually considered "realigning" elections, but rather "maintaining" or "deviating" elections. See Angus Campbell, "A Classification of the Presidential Elections," in Angus Campbell, Philip Converse, Warren Miller, and Donald Stokes, *Elections and the Political Order* (New York: John Wiley and Sons, 1966), 63–77.

28 Because no votes were counted for Justice Whittaker, the number of justices included in this section is actually 35, not 36. If the following regressions were computed only for those 25 justices with 10 or more votes in Table 5.1, the conclusions, below, would not change.

29 The recomputed ideology variable was recoded so that a score halfway between the most liberal and most conservative value was transformed to 1.00, and the extreme conservative or liberal

score values transformed to 0.00. Hence, higher values indicate more moderate, or centrist voting patterns.

30 Statistical results vary slightly between Tables 5.2 and 5.3. Table 5.2 is based upon a total of 901 individual votes. Table 5.3 is based upon the thirty-six justices' (average) percentage of majoritarian votes. The different methods each have slightly different biases. Table 5.2 "overweights" justices who cast more votes; Table 5.3 "overweights" justices who cast fewer votes. Overall, the two tables' results vary only slightly.

31 When other variables were added, the equation suffered from insignificant T-tests, added multicollinearity, or a loss of explained variance.

CHAPTER SIX

Legitimacy, Public Opinion, and the Supreme Court

A political system's ability to win broad, voluntary public approval and acceptance for its decisions is commonly described as legitimation. The concept of legitimacy was first popularized by Max Weber, David Easton, and Seymour Martin Lipset to explain why stable political systems survived, even during stressful times.[1]

To Weber, Easton, and Lipset, legitimacy was a widely shared belief in the political system's appropriateness. When the public believed that their government was legitimate, they willingly accepted and obeyed its policies — even specific laws which were not popular ones. In stable governments whose legitimacy was widely accepted, public policies were accepted without the need for overt force and coercion.

Not surprisingly, the concept of legitimacy has been applied to the American judiciary and to the Supreme Court. Lacking the enforcement powers of "sword or purse," the U.S. Supreme Court depends upon lower courts, other officeholders, or public acceptance to enforce its decisions. Over the last half century, the idea of legitimacy has been applied in several different ways to help explain why officeholders, political activists, and ordinary citizens accept Supreme Court decisions.

At least five different versions of the legitimacy thesis have been applied to the Supreme Court. Each version seeks to explain how Supreme Court decisions come to be accepted. The fifth version of the legitimacy thesis, described later in this chapter, focuses directly on the key question here: Do Supreme Court rulings favorably influence mass public opinion?

The evidence below suggests that most Supreme Court decisions do not greatly influence American public opinion. In recent years no more than half of all Americans have held clearly favorable opinions toward the Supreme Court. Few Court decisions are widely perceived and understood by most Americans. As a result, Supreme Court decisions ordinarily do not greatly affect mass public opinion in either the short term or the long term. The modern Court usually cannot "legitimate" its decisions in that sense.

Understanding Legitimacy

Legitimacy as Myth

Perhaps the earliest and most vivid description of the legitimacy thesis is that the Supreme Court represents a symbol of security and safety to most Americans. "(The) Constitution and Supreme Court are symbols of an ancient sureness and a comforting stability," wrote Max Lerner.[2] In Lerner's view, the Supreme Court symbolically fulfilled a deep-seated human need for assurance, stability, and security in a rapidly changing secular democracy. Jerome Frank went even further, and argued that the Court symbolically represented the unconscious adult need for a strong, infallible father figure.[3]

Max Lerner, Thurman Arnold, Jerome Frank, and Edward Corwin — the best-known proponents of this view — did not claim that the mass public blindly accepted all the Court's decisions. Nor did they argue that Supreme Court decisions inevitably endured. They did, however, suggest that during normal political times the Supreme Court occupied an important "mythic" role in American life, and that most Americans gave the Court broad respect and deference.

These authors suggested that mythic views of the Court include several widely shared stereotypes. Justices are seen as possessing special wisdom and insight into the Constitution's

132

meaning. The Supreme Court's imposing setting and its use of judicial symbols and robes encourage popular deference — even awe. Justices are viewed as fair, neutral, and even-handed. The mythic belief in "mechanical jurisprudence" holds that the justices do not simply impose their own values in reaching decisions, but merely "discover" the Constitution's intended meaning. Not surprisingly, Americans who accept these mythic beliefs may regard Court decisions as proper and legitimate.

Although judicial realists have criticized these mythic beliefs for over half a century, a substantial number of Americans still hold some mythic beliefs about the Supreme Court. In one study Gregory Casey reported that 60 percent of Missouri residents described the Supreme Court in terms of its symbolic and constitutional role.[4] Perhaps unexpectedly, better-educated respondents more often held mythic beliefs. In another study some 40 percent of the respondents explained the Supreme Court's role in constitutional terms, compared to 26 percent who viewed the Court from a policy-making or law court perspective.[5]

Legitimacy and Public Policy

Some years after Lerner, Arnold, Frank, and Corwin first argued that mythic beliefs about the Supreme Court were widely held, Charles Black sought to link those popular attitudes to the Court's impact on national policy making.[6] Black accepted the idea that most Americans viewed the Supreme Court as an impartial, tradition-minded arbitrar of the Constitution. Because the Court enjoyed such broad popular support, it could also influence both public opinion and the nation's policy agenda.

Occasionally, Black conceded, the Supreme Court struck down a law, holding it inconsistent with the Constitution — hence, illegitimate. More often, though, the Court upheld challenged federal laws, and in so doing, stamped those laws as constitutionally valid, or legitimate.

In Black's view, the Supreme Court could legitimate a law in two ways. First, the court directly influenced public opinion. Second, and equally important, the Court affected the nation's policy agenda in a strategic sense. By upholding (legitimating) laws, the Court prevented entrenched, status quo elites from vetoing political change. In so doing, the Supreme Court conferred constitutional approval upon newly emerging majority coalitions, and permitted them to implement their policies under the Constitution's auspices.

In practice, the Court's legitimating power was most critical during periodic political realignments — when a new political majority coalition was replacing an older, declining coalition. Black pointed to the New Deal period as a clear example. By upholding key New Deal measures during the mid and late 1930s, the Court deprived conservatives of their only remaining means of blocking new and more liberal policies. At the same time, the Court approved the New Deal coalition's policies as constitutionally valid, or legitimate.

In a well-known essay, Robert Dahl further elaborated on Black's view,[7] and argued that the Court had, in fact, seldom long withheld its constitutional approval from a contemporary majority coalition. Retirements, new appointments, and steady pressure from Congress and the President usually forced the Court to accept an active majority coalition's prefered policies.[8]

Legitimacy As Deference

In a third version of the legitimacy thesis, the Court's presumed popular appeal contributes to its political influence by discouraging court-curbing attacks either on its decisions or on its appellate jurisdiction. Because the Court enjoys broad support as an institution, political activists and officeholders (especially members of Congress) are reluctant to limit the Court. When court-curbing efforts do arise, the Court's legitimacy dissuades marginally committed elites from joining the attack. As a result, court-curbing efforts rarely succeed.[9]

This version of the legitimation thesis is applied most frequently in studying congressional reactions to Court decisions. To be sure, bills to overturn specific Supreme Court rulings or to limit the Court's appellate jurisdiction are often introduced in Congress, especially during occasional periods of intense antagonism toward the Court.[10] However, court-curbing constitutional amendments or limits upon the Court's appellate jurisdiction rarely succeed. Although Congress sometimes revises statutes that the Court has interpreted to congressional displeasure, even statutory revision seems more the exception than the norm.[11]

Recently, David Adamany and Joel Grossman argued that the Court's presumed legitimacy, alone, cannot explain why Congress so seldom limits or overturns the Court.[12] Instead, they argued that the Court itself does not enjoy sufficient popularity to defer court-curbing attacks. More important, they argued, the Court's policy supporters (chiefly, liberals and Northern Democrats) take advantage of the exceedingly cumbersome procedures of Congress to obstruct attacks on the Court's liberal decisions, of which they approve.

Legitimacy and Compliance

Several authors use the concept of legitimacy to explain why Court decisions win popular compliance. Michael Petrick and Richard Johnson argued that the Court's popularity, or legitimacy, helps to explain why its decisions are obeyed, even when those decisions are not particularly popular.[13]

This fourth version of the legitimacy thesis is most often applied in impact and compliance studies, which typically report a rising level of compliance with Supreme Court decisions over time. Even so, widespread misunderstanding of some decisions,[14] grudging and narrow interpretations by lower courts and local officials,[15] and long delays before actual compliance occurs have also been reported.[16] In a few instances, determined efforts at outright evasion of Court decisions have been apparent.[17]

Inferring legitimacy from the level of compliance with Court policies, alone, has several drawbacks, however. These problems are especially serious when applying the concept of legitimacy to the mass public. As Alan Hyde and others have argued, compliance alone does not explain the motivation for compliance.[18] Compliance with Supreme Court decisions may occur for a number of reasons other than from a general respect for the Court — among them, fear of penalties, habit, expediency, or agreement with the decision itself.

Inferring that compliance results from a general acceptance of the Supreme Court's legitimacy is especially problematic when studying the mass public.[19] Few Americans are ever faced with a decision of whether or not to comply with a Supreme Court decision, per se. Instead, average Americans typically confront Supreme Court decisions only as those decisions are interpreted, implemented, and enforced by lower-level courts and by other public officials or agencies. As a result, it is almost impossible to determine why most Americans comply with Supreme Court decisions — even if it can be determined that, in fact, they actually do comply.

Only a few studies have asked respondents to indicate their willingness to comply with Supreme Court decisions that, in substance, the respondents opposed. The results indicate that the Supreme Court's general popularity, or legitimacy, probably influences only a minority of Americans.

In one small Midwestern town, for example, community leaders were asked, first, whether they agreed with the Supreme Court's school prayer decisions and second, whether they felt obliged to accept that decision. Of those who disagreed with the school prayer ruling, only a third (38 percent) also reported that they had a "duty to accept the decision and act accordingly."[20]

In short, it is difficult to use the concept of legitimacy to explain popular compliance with Court rulings — especially when studying the mass public. Most Americans seldom face the decision of whether or not to comply with a Supreme Court decision, except as that decision has been interpreted by other officials. Nor is there much empirical evidence that a majority of Americans would change their actual behavior in response to a Court decision they dislike, merely because they regard the Court itself favorably.

Legitimacy and Mass Public Opinion

To this point four different versions of the legitimation thesis have been reviewed.[21] Each explored a different aspect of the Supreme Court's ability to influence mass public opinion, other elites, or the nation's policy agenda. Yet none of these four versions completely resolves the question of whether Supreme Court decisions influence mass public opinion.

The remainder of this chapter defines legitimation in the context of mass public opinion. Legitimation is conceptualized as involving three key conditions. First, the Supreme Court itself must (for whatever reason) be favorably perceived. Second, Court rulings must be recognized. Third, persons who meet the first two conditions must adjust their issue attitudes to conform more closely to the Supreme Court's announced position.[22]

Defining legitimacy in this way has considerable advantages for the study of mass public opinion. It helps to define the concept of legitimacy more narrowly, and permits a review of the empirical evidence concerning the three conditions for legitimacy. It also suggest limits on the Court's ability to legitimate its decisions.

Defined in this way, at least four limits on the Court's legitimating ability are apparent. First, Court decisions must be perceived. As noted below, however, many (and probably nearly all) Supreme Court decisions pass by virtually unnoticed by most Americans — either because the decision receives little press attention, or because many Americans pay little attention to the Court itself.

Second, some Americans who become aware of a Court decision, and even perceive that it contradicts their own opinion, may still perceive the discrepancy only fleetingly and passively. They may so little understand or so briefly consider the decision's meaning that they never adjust their personal opinions at all.[23]

Third, for Americans who view the Supreme Court with indifference or hostility, legitimation may not occur at all. As recent polls indicate, only a third to a half of all Americans hold particularly positive attitudes toward the Court, and nearly as many Americans view the Court unfavorably.

Fourth, detecting legitimation from available poll items is often very difficult. Comparable pre- and post-decision poll questions are available for very few Supreme Court decisions. Further, almost all the available poll questions are "forced choice" items — in which a respondent is either forced to agree or disagree with a statement, or allowed to choose only one of two fixed answers.

Forced-choice questions cannot detect evidence of legitimation, short of actual attitude change. Forced-choice questions, for example, fail to identify instances in which a (hypothetical) respondent already agrees with the Court's position and then further strengthens her attitude upon learning of the ruling. The only confirming evidence for legitimation in forced-choice questions occurs when a previously undecided respondent shifts to favoring the Court's position, or when a respondent who earlier disagreed with the Court shifts to being undecided or to favoring the Court's position. Forced-choice items cannot identify the more subtle, reinforcement effects of a Court ruling.[24]

Defined as a three-part process, legitimation can be described and examined empirically. Chapter Six examines the evidence for legitimation — first, by reviewing previously published studies, then by examining actual pre- to post-decision poll shifts for Court rulings since the mid-1930s.

Popular Views of the Court

The first condition for legitimation, described above, is that Americans have a favorable view toward the Court itself. Americans need not think of the Court solely in its constitutional role, or have much factual information about the Court or how it operates, nor necessarily hold any mythic beliefs about the Court. This condition simply requires that Americans hold favorable, albeit perhaps unsophisticated attitudes toward the Court.

Before the 1960s few poll questions were asked to tap the Supreme Court's popularity. As a result, describing the Hughes, Stone, or Vinson Court's public support is somewhat speculative. Nonetheless, available poll results did not suggest that the Court was any more popular during the 1930s or 1940s than it was during later decades.

During the mid-1930s "court-packing" fight, only a minority (of 31 percent or 41 percent in two separate Gallup polls) favored an outright limit on the Court's power to declare congressional acts unconstitutional.[25] However, nearly equal numbers favored or opposed President Roosevelt's plan to reorganize the Court.[26] A two-to-one majority approved forcing elderly justices to retire.[27] A clear majority (59 percent) preferred that the Supreme Court be more liberal in its treatment of New Deal policies.[28]

From the Hughes Court's 1937 "switch in time" until the 1960s, very few poll questions tapped the Court's popularity

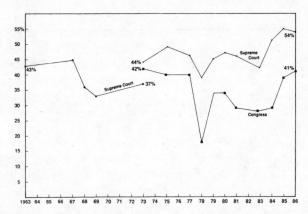

Figure 6.1 Percentage holding "excellent" or "good" views of
the Supreme Court, 1963-1973, and a "good deal" or
"quite a lot" of confidence in the Supreme Court
and Congress, 1973-1986.

and prestige. In one 1946 Gallup Poll, 43 percent agreed that the
Supreme Court "decides many questions largely on the basis of
politics," while 36 percent disagreed, and 21 percent ventured
no opinion.[29] In a 1957 poll, some 30 percent reported greater
respect for the Court; another 29 percent reported greater
respect for Congress; 23 percent reported an equal respect for
both; and 18 percent offered no opinion.[30]

Since the 1960s the Gallup Poll has repeatedly posed two
questions to measure the Court's popularity. Form 1963 to
1973 respondents were asked: "In general, what kind of ratings
would you give the Supreme Court — excellent, good, fair, or
poor?" Since 1973 Gallup has asked respondents to rate their
level of confidence, both in the Court and in the Congress, as
"a great deal, quite a lot, some, very little, or none." Overall
trends are reported in Figure 6.1.[31]

From 1972 to 1986 the National Opinion Research Center
(NORC) asked respondents another Court-related question —
whether they had "a great deal, only some, or hardly any
confidence at all in the people running the Supreme Court."
Because NORC polls also asked the same question for Congress
and the executive branch of the federal government, the three
institutions' relative popularity can be directly compared. See
Figure 6.2.[32]

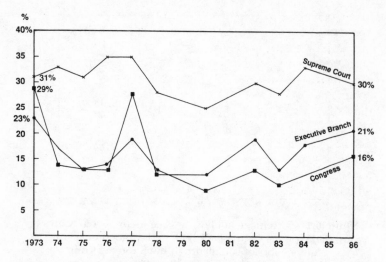

Figure 6.2 Percentage expressing "a great deal" of confidence in the Supreme Court, Congress, and the executive branch, 1973-1986

Figures 6.1 and 6.2 present a mixed picture of the Court's recent popularity. In both the NORC and Gallup Polls, the Supreme Court always receives at least marginally more support than Congress or the executive branch. In the 1973–1986 Gallup Polls, an average of 14 percent more respondents reported "a great deal" or "quite a lot" of confidence in the Court than in Congress. In the NORC surveys the Court received an average of 17 percent more support than Congress, and 14 percent more support than the executive branch.

On the other hand, seldom have more than half of all Americans given the Supreme Court clearly positive marks on the Gallup surveys. No more than 35 percent ever did so on the NORC measure. On the average, only 39 percent of respondents rated the Court as "excellent" or "good" in the 1963–1967 Gallup Polls. An average of only 47 percent said they had "a great deal" or "quite a lot" of confidence in the Court in the 1973–1986 Gallup polls. On the average, only 31 percent of respondents gave the Court clearly positive marks in the NORC polls.

By contrast, in the 1963–1973 Gallup polls, an average of 49 percent of respondents rated the Court's performance as "only fair" or "poor." In the 1973–1986 Gallup questions, an average of 46 percent reported having "only some," "very little," or "no confidence" in the Court. In the NORC polls, an average of 65 percent of respondents indicated "only some" or "hardly any" confidence in the Court. In addition, an average of 12 percent (Gallup, 1963–1973), 7 percent (Gallup, 1973–1985), or 4 percent (NORC, 1972–1986) reported "no opinion" toward the Court.

In recent years a few other poll questions about popular perceptions of the Court have also been reported. In a 1982 CBS/*New York Times* Poll, two-fifths (39 percent) of respondents felt that the Court was "carrying out its proper responsibilities," while only 17 percent felt that the Court "has taken on too much power." A plurality of respondents (42 percent), however, offered no opinion.[33]

A June 1986 CBS/*New York Times* poll again asked respondents to rate the Court.[34] Some 46 percent of respondents rated the Court as "excellent" or "good," but almost as many (48 percent) described the Court as "only fair" or "poor."

If favorable, although perhaps unsophisticated views are a precondition for legitimacy, then available polls do not indicate overwhelmingly positive views toward the Court. True, the Court has consistently won more approval than Congress or the executive branch (at least since the 1970s). Yet only a third to a half of Americans have held clearly favorable views of the Court. The remainder either have held mixed or negative opinions, or have seemed disinterested and indifferent.

Public attitudes toward the Court vary considerably between groups and over time, and Court rulings may well affect how different groups perceive it. Black/white perceptions offer a notable example. During the 1960s blacks were especially supportive of the Court, perhaps in response to a decade of favorable Court ruling in racial cases. Whites, particularly Southern whites, were much more negative. In one mid-1960s survey, blacks offered over twice as many favorable as unfavorable specific comments on Court decisions. By contrast, whites reported over twice as many unfavorable comments. Southern whites gave over seven times as many unfavorable as favorable comments on Court decisions.[35]

A decade later, these racial differences had largely disappeared. Blacks were no more likely than whites to name the

Supreme Court as the part of government that they most often trusted.[36]

Court-related attitudes also vary depending upon a respondents' social status and political views. In recent decades, ideology has been the most consistent predictor of Court perceptions. At least since the mid-1960s, self-described liberals have consistently given the Court higher evaluations than have conservatives, although at times the differences were slight. Patterns of Court support are less strongly related to education or party identification.[37]

In examining trend data from Harris and NORC polls, Greg Caldeira suggested that Court-related attitudes are not so stable as sometimes thought.[38] Further, a handful of variables explain most (79 percent) of the variation in levels of Court approval. Specific events (such as Watergate), political eras (the Johnson Administration), presidential popularity, and media coverage have been related to increases in the Supreme Court's popularity. Declines in Court support were related both to rulings supporting defendants' rights and to rulings invalidating federal laws. Changes in the crime rate, inflation, or in the unemployment rate were not related to changes in public confidence in the Court.

Public Knowledge of Court Decisions

The second requirement for legitimation offered here is that the public must be aware of Court decisions. Americans who are unaware that the Court has even ruled on an issue cannot possibly follow the Court's lead, although attitude shifts might still occur for other reasons. Knowledge of Court decisions, in short, is a necessary, but not sufficient condition for legitimation.

Public awareness of Supreme Court decisions depends heavily on the quality of coverage provided by the mass media — especially that of newspapers and television. In the mid-1970s, a Florida study found that about three-quarters of respondents reported that they relied either on newspapers (76 percent) or on television (71 percent) for news of Court decisions.[39]

Press coverage of the Court is generally spotty. Only a few newspapers (most notably, the *New York Times* and the *Washington Post*) regularly assign a Supreme Court reporter.

Most other papers rely on wire service accounts or general beat reporters. Relatively few Court cases each term receive extensive coverage or analysis. Denials of certiorari and nonunanimous, plurality opinions are especially difficult for reporters to cover.[40]

Television coverage of the Court is at least as sketchy as newspaper coverage. One study reported that only about one-fifth of all Court rulings are reported by the major networks. Only one ruling in ten was reported or analyzed by a network legal affairs correspondent, with accordingly, longer coverage — one to three minutes, versus only 10 to 30 seconds for most anchor stories. Like newspapers, the networks rarely cover cert denials or oral arguments. Economic cases, criminal cases, collective bargaining disputes, and antitrust or corporate tax cases are also seldom covered. By contrast, network newscasts spend considerably more time on death penalty cases and individual rights cases.[41]

Most accounts attribute the sketchy press coverage of Supreme Court decisions to several causes. Few reporters are well trained to cover judicial decision making. Reporting is also complicated by the Supreme Court's own procedures: the increasing number of separate opinions, the complexity and length of legal prose, the number of decisions handed down on traditional opinion days, and the heavy schedule of decisions announced near the end of the Court's regular term.[42]

Since few rulings are extensively covered, it is not surprising that many Americans little recognize or little remember the Court's rulings. On open-ended questions that probe for specific likes or dislikes about Court rulings, only about half (or fewer) of Americans can offer an opinion on even the most prominent Supreme Court decisions.

In one 1966 survey, Walter Murphy and Joseph Tanenhaus reported that 71 percent of respondents offered an opinion of the Supreme Court's overall performance.[43] However, fewer than half — 41 percent in 1964 and 45 percent in 1966 — could name a specific ruling that they liked or disliked, typically a civil rights ruling or the school prayer decision. Predictably, the number of specific likes or dislikes which a respondent offered was closely linked to a respondent's formal education and level of political knowledge. Among college graduates,

78 percent named a Court ruling they liked or disliked, but among those with less than nine years of schooling, only 27 percent did.

That a Court decision is recognized does not ensure that it will be popular. In the Murphy and Tanenhaus study, a two-to-one majority of those respondents who offered a specific opinion of a Court decision gave an unfavorable opinion.[44] Indeed, for the best-recognized decisions, public opinion was, on balance, favorable only for civil rights decisions (in a 1966 survey), and for the abortion and Watergate decisions (in a 1975 partial follow-up study).[45]

Other studies report similar findings. In a 1965 study of Seattle, Washington, area residents, John Kessel reported that barely a handful of decisions elicited specific comments by respondents.[46] Again, civil rights and school prayer rulings, together, received about two-thirds (62 percent) of all the specific mentions offered.

Several studies measure the public's understanding of Court rulings by asking respondents either to describe specific rulings or to indicate whether or not the Court had handed down a ruling at all in some areas. A 1966 study asked Wisconsin respondents whether or not the Court had handed down a ruling in eight controversies (for half of which it actually had handed down a ruling, and for half of which it had not). Only 15 percent of the respondents correctly answered a majority of the eight questions; only 2 percent correctly answered all eight questions.[47]

Admittedly, open-ended questions may underestimate the amount of knowledge that respondents have about Court rulings. A less demanding test of public awareness would first name a specific decision and then ask respondents to describe their understanding of that decision. In a 1968 Missouri study, Gregory Casey reported that about two-thirds (68 percent) of the respondents both knew that the Court had made a ruling about organized prayer in public schools, and also had a roughly correct view of that decision.[48] Some 41 percent of the Missouri respondents both understood that the Court had made a criminal rights ruling, and could also accurately describe the ruling. Casey suggested that about one-third of the Missouri public was relatively well informed, that 25 to 30 percent knew virtually nothing about even the Court's most prominent rulings, and that the remainder probably had at least sketchy impressions about landmark decisions.

A 1982 CBS/*New York Times* nationwide poll asked factual questions about the highly publicized school prayer rulings and the *Roe* and *Doe* abortion decisions.[49] Some 57 percent correctly understood that the Court had forbidden organized prayer in public schools. Few respondents (only 8 percent) incorrectly claimed that the Court allowed such prayers, but a full one-third (35 percent) of the respondents ventured no opinion on what the Court had actually ruled.

On the abortion rulings, 41 percent of the respondents correctly understood that the Supreme Court permitted first-trimester abortions. Only 10 percent of the respondents mistakenly perceived that the Court had banned first-trimester abortions. Yet nearly half (49 percent) did not offer an understanding of what the Court had ruled.

In short, the evidence concerning public knowledge of Court decisions is quite mixed. The major news media cover relatively few Court decisions. Few Americans volunteer more than a single like or dislike about particular Court rulings. Only about two-fifths of Americans can, unprompted, describe any specific Court ruling that they like or dislike, and only half to two-thirds of the mass public can accurately describe even landmark Court decisions.

Pre- and Post-Decision Poll Shifts

Earlier in this chapter legitimation was defined by three conditions. First, the Court itself must be favorably regarded. Second, specific rulings must be visible. Third, persons who meet the first two conditions must also readjust their own attitudes to conform more closely with the Court's rulings.

The available evidence just reviewed, indicated that the first two conditions are fulfilled only in limited degree. Only one-third to one-half of all Americans view the Court favorably. Barely a handful of Court rulings are widely and accurately understood.

The third condition for legitimation can be examined only indirectly — by examining pre- and post-decision polls for evidence of public opinion shifts. To be sure, the pre- and post-decision polls, analyzed below, are based on different samples, and not on panel studies. As well, respondents were not queried for their opinion of the Court itself, nor as to whether they actually understood that the Court had issued a specific ruling on that issue (before the post-decision poll). As a result, the size and direction of pre- to post-decision poll shifts can be examined. However, it cannot simply be assumed that the observed poll shift is entirely due to the Court's influence alone.

Perhaps surprisingly, relatively few identical pre- and post-decision poll questions have been asked for Supreme Court decisions. In Chapters Four and Five, some 146 instances were reported in which at least one poll could be matched with part (or all) of a Court ruling. Yet in only eighteen instances were identical (or virtually identical) polls taken both before and after the Court's ruling.

If these 18 instances of short-term poll shifts make up only a small sample of all Supreme Court decisions since the mid-1930s, they do provide a diverse sampling of the Court's decisions. In time, they span from 1937 to 1983. In substance, they include economic, privacy, criminal, and civil rights cases. They include both unanimous and closely divided cases, and both well-known and little-publicized rulings. Figure 6.3 lists the 18 instances, along with the pre- to post-decision poll shifts.

As Figure 6.3 suggests, the pattern of poll shifts offers no support for the short-term manipulation model. In nine instances the poll shift was away from the Court's announced position. In three instances no measurable poll shift occurred. In only six of the eighteen instances did the polls shift toward the Court's announced position. Overall, the average poll shift was virtually zero — a bare (+) .06, or six one-hundredths of one percent.

These results provide little evidence that Court rulings influence mass public opinion. The polls shifted away from the Court's position more often than toward it, and the average poll shift was almost zero. As with the studies discussed earlier in this chapter, these results do not suggest that Supreme Court decisions strongly influence American public opinion.[50] By another standard, these poll shifts are relatively insignificant

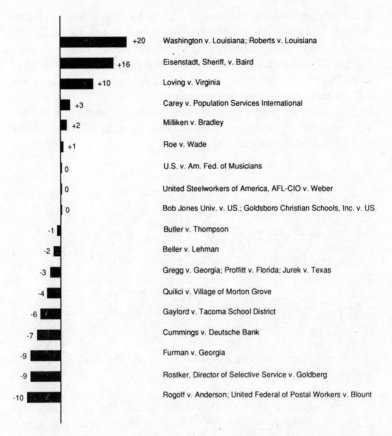

Figure 6.3 Short-term pre- to post-decision poll shifts, by size

when compared to poll shifts observed for televised presidential news appearances — which average nearly 17 percent.[51]

Explaining Legitimation

So far there has been no evidence of uniform poll shifts toward the Supreme Court's announced position. Nonetheless, it is possible that positive poll shifts occur in some instances, but negative shifts occur in other instances. The results in Figure 6.3 suggest that this is a real possibility, since the poll shifts vary greatly in size and direction. At one extreme a 20 percent swing toward the Court's announced position occurred. At the other extreme, there were several shifts of 9 or 10 percent away from the Court's position.

Exactly when legitimation might be expected to occur is not altogether clear from the existing literature, which has not yet demonstrated that legitimation is strongly related to any individual-level traits, such as a respondent's ideology, political activism, or knowledge. Nonetheless, eleven hypotheses can be offered from the judicial literature.

(1) UNANIMITY

Considerable evidence suggests that Supreme Court justices strive for unanimity when they set major precedents or when they expect serious opposition to their decisions. In the desegregation cases, for instance, both Chief Justices Vinson and Warren aimed at unanimous decisions, even if that meant making concessions to fellow justices who were less enthusiastic about ending racial segregation.[52] Other accounts suggest that Chief Justice Burger likewise sought unanimity in highly controversial decisions.[53] Unanimity may increase the clarity with which Court rulings are perceived, while plurality decisions and dissenting opinions create confusion as to the ruling's meaning and reduce the ruling's impact on mass public opinion.[54]

Here, unanimous decisions were coded (1); nonunanimous decisions were coded as (0). The hypothesis was that larger, positive poll shifts (toward the Court's position) would occur for unanimous decisions.

(2) FULL, WRITTEN OPINIONS

Some evidence suggests that full, written decisions facilitate public understanding of Court opinions. By contrast, memorandum opinions, denials of certiorari, and short (usually one paragraph) summary affirmations or denials of lower court decisions provide less evidence of the justices' intent. Further, the media typically give little attention to memorandum opinions, cert denials, and summary affirmations or denials.[55]

The hypothesis, tested below, was that greater, positive poll shifts would occur for full, written opinions (coded 1), rather than for memorandum opinions, cert denials, or summary affirmations or denials (all coded 0).

(3 AND 4) LIBERAL AND ACTIVIST DECISIONS

Among the Court's best-known and most controversial decisions have been its liberal, activist rulings on school prayer, civil rights, and criminal defendants' rights. Judicial scholars, however, have disagreed as to whether, on the one hand, activist decisions typically erode public support for the Court, or whether on the other hand, liberal activist decisions mobilize public opinion.

Alexander Bickel and Carl Swisher have advised against the Court's liberal, activist tendencies, arguing that a string of such decisions reduces the clarity of Court rulings, undermines the Court's ability to enforce its decisions, and erodes respect for the Court as an institution.[56] Challenging those views are other judicial scholars, among them C. Hermann Pritchett, who argue that Americans have come to accept the Supreme Court's role in defending unpopular groups. Pritchett and others argued that liberal, activist decisions may well mobilize public opinion toward the Court's viewpoint.[57]

The hypothesis here was that greater positive poll shifts would occur for liberal or activist decisions (both coded 1), rather than for politically conservative or judicial restraint decisions (both coded 0).

(5) PRIVACY AND GENDER CASES

Since the landmark Griswold ruling nearly two decades ago, the Supreme Court has handed down an unprecedented number of decisions in gender-related and sexual privacy cases. Some of these decisions created significant new constitutional rights, while others upheld conservative laws or policies.

Several authors have suggested that the Court has, by now, become an accepted policy maker in privacy and gender cases, or at least that opposition to the Supreme Court's noneconomic decisions has been more ineffectual and diffuse than in New Deal-era economic cases.[58] Yet other accounts of privacy and gender cases have challenged the idea that these Court rulings have greatly influenced public opinion.[59] Here, all sex, privacy, or reproductive rights cases were scored (1); others were scored (0). The hypothesis was that greater positive poll shifts would occur in gender and privacy cases.

(6) CIVIL RIGHTS CASES

The Court's civil rights and race-related rulings have been among its most prominent ones in recent years. What effect those decisions may have had on mass public opinion is less clear. While public support for the *Brown* decision grew during the 1950s, other Court decisions (such as the school busing decisions) remained steadily unpopular.[60] Here, civil rights and racial cases were coded (1); others were coded (0). No directional hypothesis was offered for civil rights cases, nor for the criminal rights, or for the death penalty cases, described below.

(7) CRIMINAL RIGHTS CASES

Rulings involving the rights of criminal defendants have also been among the Court's most controversial rulings. Some polling evidence has suggested that the Court's major rulings in this area have been generally unpopular.[61] Here, criminal rights cases were coded (1); others were coded (0).

(8) DEATH PENALTY CASES

The Court's death penalty decisions, such as *Furman*, *Coker*, and *Gregg*, have attracted considerably more attention than most decisions. Yet several authors have questioned whether polls have followed the Court's opinion, at least in its landmark *Furman* ruling.[62] Here, death penalty cases were scored (1); and others were scored (0).

(9) PUBLICITY

As noted earlier in this chapter, the media cover relatively few Court decisions, and barely a handful of the Court's decisions are frequently mentioned by survey respondents as ones that they specifically like or dislike. Several authors have suggested that media attention is a precondition for legitimation, and others have suggested that publicity is at least a correlate of compliance.[63]

The indicator for publicity was the (combined) number of front-page column inches given to each ruling by the *New York Times* and the *Washington Post* during the two days immediately following the decision's announcement. The hypothesis was that the greater the media coverage, the greater the poll shift toward the Court's position.

(10) TIME LAG

Most impact and compliance studies report that compliance with Court decisions increases over time — as specialized journals, professional workshops, training sessions, or even word-of-mouth help spread understanding of and compliance with the Court's rulings. Even so, compliance with Supreme Court decisions often remains incomplete.[64] A positive relationship was predicted between poll shifts and the number of months elapsed from a decision until the post-decision poll. The short-term time lags here averaged 27 months, with a standard deviation of 17 months.

(11) INITIAL POLL SUPPORT

A final predictor taps the initial (pre-decision) poll support for the Court's position. This variable indicated the percentage of respondents who, in a pre-decision poll, supported the Court's later ruling. No hypothesis was offered.

Data Results

Table 6.1 reports the results when the eleven predictors are compared, one-by-one, to the pre- to post-decision poll shift. For the dichotomous predictors (coded 0,1), the average poll shift is indicated, along with the F-test significance level. For the ratio-level predictors the Pearson product-moment correlation and significance levels are indicated.

As Table 6.1 indicates, only three of the eleven predictors were strongly related to public opinion poll shifts: liberal decisions, activist decisions, and the post-decision time lag. Larger poll shifts toward the Court's position occur when the Court hands down either a liberal or an activist decision, or when a longer time lag occurs between the Court's decision and the post-decision poll.

Table 6.1
Individual explanations for short-term pre- to
post-decision poll shifts

For dichotomous predictors: Variables, values, and number of cases	Average poll shift
(1) Unanimity:	
Unanimous rulings (2)	+1.5%
Non-unanimous rulings (16)	−.1%
(2) Type of opinion:	
Full, written opinion (12)	+2.0%
Cert denial, summ. affd. (6)	−3.8%
(3) Ideology:	
Liberal ruling (10)	+3.7%
Non-liberal ruling (7)	−4.1%*
(4) Activist or restraint:	
Activist ruling (7)	+6.8%
Restraint ruling (11)	−3.3%**
(5) Privacy or gender:	
Privacy, sex, or gender (7)	+1.9%
Issue not involved (11)	−1.1%
(6) Civil rights:	
Civil rights, race (4)	+3.0%
Issue not involved (14)	−.8%
(7) Criminal rights:	
Criminal rights (9)	+2.7%
Issue not involved (9)	−2.6%
(8) Death penalty:	
Death penalty (3)	+2.7%
Issue not involved (15)	−.5%

For ratio-level predictors: Variables	Pearson correlation
(9) Publicity (in combined column inches)	−.15
(10) Time lag from decision until post-decision poll	+.53**
(11) Pre-decision poll support for ruling	+.07

*** significant at .001
** significant at .01
* significant at .05

Combining the Predictors

The eleven predictors can also be combined to build a multivariate model. Given the small number of 18 cases, this model should be powerful and theoretically clear, but it should also contain as few predictors as possible.

Several models were tested, each using a different combination of variables. Overall, the strongest models used just two predictors: the post-decision time lag variable, and either the judicial activism or the liberalism variable.

The model using the time lag variable, plus the judicial activism variable, explained nearly one-half the total variance in poll shifts. See Figure 6.4

Poll Shifts←←←←←←   − 7.4%
                      + 8.2% (if an activist decision)
                      + 2.2% (per lag year)

(R^2 = .49; adjusted R-2 = .42; F-test significant at .01)

Figure 6.4 Regression model predicting pre- to post-decision poll shifts

For a (hypothetical) activist decision overturning a challenged law or policy, the predicted poll shift (three years after the decision) would be 7.4 percent toward the Court's position.[65]

An alternative model combines the variables representing the time lag and the liberal decisions. See Figure 6.5.

Poll Shifts←←←←←←   − 10.4%
                      + 7.7% (if a liberal decision)
                      + 2.8% (per lag year)

(R^2 = .48; adjusted R-2 = .41; F-test significant at .01)

Figure 6.5 Alternate regression model predicting pre- to post-decision poll shifts

Because the predictors representing liberal decisions and activist decisions are so highly intercorrelated, adding both these predictors to the time lag variable did not result in an improved, three-variable model.[66]

Other models were not so successful. Combining the variables for civil rights and privacy-gender cases did not produce a statistically significant model. Nor were the results improved when the model included both the criminal penalties and the death penalty variables. Another model representing full, written, and unanimous decisions was likewise insignificant.[67]

These results suggest that only a few Supreme Court decisions produce favorable poll shifts. When the Court hands down a liberal, activist decision, however, the polls may shift toward the Court's announced position — perhaps by several percentage points. In most other instances no regular pattern of poll shifts can be expected. These results correspond most closely to the "mobilization" argument, which holds that the Court can lead (or mobilize) public opinion by handing down liberal, activist rulings. The magnitude of the poll shifts in liberal, activist rulings may not be sweeping, but they are significant, and suggest that further inquiry may be worthwhile.

A Note on Long-Term Opinion Manipulation

To this point the evidence suggests that Supreme Court decisions strongly influence short-term public opinion changes only when the Court hands down liberal, activist rulings. The long-term manipulation model is more difficult to examine, for both conceptual and practical reasons.

At the conceptual level, a "long-term" attitude change can be defined only somewhat arbitrarily. Over long periods of time it is also difficult to control for the effect that other political actors or events may have on poll shifts. At the practical level, pollsters seldom repeat identically worded poll items over long time periods, especially when issues fade from public attention. Repeat-item poll questions are usually drawn from civil liberties, criminal rights, and civil rights issues. As a result, serious problems occur in testing the long-term manipulation model, and these problems may not be satisfactorily resolved within the foreseeable future.

In eleven instances, however, it was possible to locate an identically worded poll item that had been repeated several times over a ten-year period (or longer) following a Supreme Court ruling.[68] This post-decision period of ten years (or longer) was taken as a rough indicator of a "long term" opinion shift.

The eleven long-term poll shifts, depicted in Figure 6.6, offer no support for the long-term manipulation model. In six of eleven instances the polls shifted toward the Court's decision, but in the other five instances the polls shifted away from the Court's decision. Overall, the average long-term poll shift was almost zero — a bare 2.2 percent average shift toward the Court's position. While better poll data may become available in future years, these results offer no stronger support for the long-term model than for the short-term manipulation model.

Conclusion

The short-term and the long-term opinion manipulation models gained little support here. By themselves, Supreme Court decisions seldom greatly influence American public opinion either over the short term or the long term. Only a handful

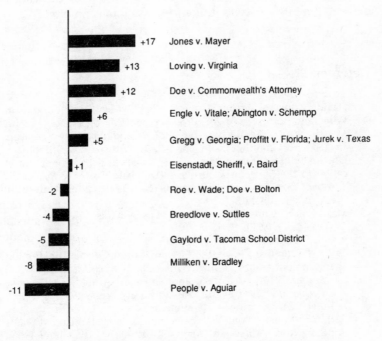

Figure 6.6 Long-Term poll shifts, by Size

of liberal, activist rulings appear to strongly influence the polls. The Court's inability to legitimate its own policies by manipulating public opinion may result both from the Court's limited visibility and popularity, and from the scant coverage that most rulings receive.

To suggest that Supreme Court decisions seldom influence public attitudes on specific issues does not deny that Court rulings influence the polls in other ways. Rulings may affect the Court's own popularity — either generally or among specific groups. A handful of Court decisions may also spur political elites and interest groups to greater activity and create greater issue clarity; eventually, these elites and interest groups may, in turn, influence mass public opinion.[69] In this way occasional Court rulings may indirectly trigger a long-term change in the nation's issue agenda in ways not captured by this analysis.[70] Yet, by the available evidence presented in this chapter, direct short- or long-term manipulation of public opinion by the modern Court has more often been the exception than the rule. The modern Court's success as a policy maker cannot be wholly explained by its ability to influence mass public opinion.[71]

References

1   David Easton, *A Systems Analysis of Political Life* (New York: John Wiley and Sons, 1965), 208, 288; Seymour Martin Lipset, *Political Man* (New York: Doubleday, 1960), 22, 64; and Max Weber, *Economy and Society*, Guenther Roth and Claus Wittich, eds., (Berkeley: University of California Press, 1968), 31–38, 212–216. For an application to the Supreme Court, see Archibald Cox, *The Role of the Supreme Court in American Government* (New York, Oxford University Press, 1976), 103–110.

2   Max Lerner, "Constitution and Court as Symbols," *Yale Law Journal* 46 (December 1937): 1291.

3   Jerome Frank, *Law and the Modern Mind* (New York: Brentano, 1930), 13–21. For similar views, see Edward Corwin, "The Constitution as Instrument and as Symbol," *American Political Science Review* 30 (December 1936): 1071–1085; and Thurman Arnold, *The Symbols of Government* (New Haven, Yale University Press, 1935), 196–197, 203–206, 224. For other statements of Supreme Court myths, see Arthur S. Miller, "Some Pervasive Myths about the United States Supreme Court," *St. Louis University Law Journal* 10 (Winter 1965): 153–189; Alpheus T. Mason, "Myth and Reality in Supreme Court

Decisions," *Virginia Law Review* 48 (December 1962): 1385–1406; Sanford Levison, "The Constitution in American Civil Religion," *Supreme Court Review* 1979 (1980): 123–151; and Larry Baas, "The Constitution as Symbol," *American Politics Quarterly* 8 (April 1980): 237–256.

4   Gregory Casey, "The Supreme Court and Myth: An Empirical Investigation," *Law & Society Review* 8 (Spring 1974): 385–419.

5   Walter F. Murphy and Joseph Tanenhaus, "Public Opinion and the Supreme Court: A Preliminary Mapping of Some Prerequisites for Court Legitimation of Regime Changes," in Joel Grossman and Joseph Tanenhaus, eds., *Frontiers of Judicial Research* (New York: John Wiley and Sons, 1969), 280–282.

6   Charles L. Black, Jr., *The People and the Court* (New York: Macmillan, 1960), 34–67.

7   Robert Dahl, "Decision-making in a Democracy: The Supreme Court as a National Policy-Maker," *Journal of Public Law* 6 (Fall 1957): 279–295.

8   Dahl's argument has been criticized by Jonathan Casper as taking an excessively narrow view of the Court's role; see "The Supreme Court and National Policy Making," *American Political Science Review* 70 (March 1976): 50–63.

    This version of the legitimation thesis has also been examined in a historical context. See Richard Funston, "The Supreme Court and Critical Elections," *American Political Science Review* 69 (September 1975): 795–811; Paul Allen Beck, "Critical Elections and the Supreme Court: Putting the Cart after the Horse," *American Political Science Review* 70 (September 1976): 930–932; and Bradley Canon and S. Sidney Ulmer, "The Supreme Court and Critical Elections: A Dissent," *American Political Science Review* 70 (December 1976): 1215–1218.

9   Walter Murphy and C. Herman Pritchett, *Courts, Judges, and Politics: An Introduction to the Judicial Process* (New York: Random House, 1961), 554–555; and C. Herman Pritchett, *Congress versus the Supreme Court, 1957–1961* (Minneapolis: University of Minnesota Press, 1961), 119–120.

10 The literature on Court-curbing efforts is extensive. See, for example, Stuart Nagel, "Court Curbing Periods in American History," in *The Legal Process from a Behavioral Perspective* (Homewood, Ill.: Dorsey, 1969), 285–293; Stuart Nagel, "Court Curbing Periods in American History," *Vanderbilt Law Review* 18 (June 1965): 925–944; and Roger Handberg and Harold Hill, "Court Curbing, Court Reversals, and Judicial Review: The Supreme Court versus Congress," *Law & Society Review* 14 (Winter 1980): 309–322.

    For an in-depth analysis of Court-curbing effects during a particularly intense period of conflict, see John Schmidhauser and Larry Berg, *The Supreme Court and Congress: Conflict and Interaction* (New York: The Free Press, 1972); and C. Herman Pritchett, *Congress versus the Supreme Court.*

11 For an analysis, see "Congressional Reversals of Supreme Court

Decisions, 1945–1957, "*Harvard Law Review* 71 (May 1958): 1324–1337; Beth Henschen, "Statutory Interpretations of the Supreme Court — Congressional Response," *American Politics Quarterly* 11 (October 1983): 441–458; and Samuel Krislov, *The Supreme Court in the Political Process* (New York: Macmillan, 1965), 143.

At the rhetorical level, the Supreme Court's legitimacy or "sacrosanctity" is apparently only rarely invoked during floor debates, although it may be invoked more often during committee testimony and hearings. For an exchange, see Harry Stumpf, "The Political Efficacy of Judicial Symbolism," *Western Political Quarterly* 19 (June 1966): 293–303; and Glendon Schubert, *Constitutional Politics: The Political Behavior of Supreme Court Justices and the Constitutional Policies They Make* (New York: Holt, Rinehart, and Winston, 1960), esp. 257–258; and "Reply with Rejoinder to H.P. Stumpf — The Political Efficacy of Judicial Symbolism," *Western Political Quarterly* 20 (September 1967): 792–794.

12 David Adamany and Joel Grossman, "Support for the Supreme Court as a National Policymaker," *Law & Policy Quarterly* 5 (October 1983): 405–437.

13 Michael Petrick, "The Supreme Court and Authority Acceptance," *Western Political Quarterly* 21 (March 1968): 5–19; and Richard M. Johnson, "Compliance and Supreme Court Decision-Making," *Wisconsin Law Review* 1967 (Winter 1967): 170–185.

14 James P. Levine, "Constitutional Law and Obscene Literature: An Investigation of Bookstore Censorship Practices," in Theodore Becker and Malcolm Feeley, eds., *The Impact of Supreme Court Decisions*, 2nd ed., (New York: Oxford University Press, 1973), 119–138; Frank Sorauf, "*Zorach v. Clauson*: The Impact of a Supreme Court Decision," *American Political Science Review* 53 (September 1959): 777–791; and Thomas Barth, "Perception and Acceptance of Supreme Court Decisions at the State and Local Level," *Journal of Public Law* 17 (1968): 308–350.

15 Gordon Patric, "The Impact of a Court Decision: Aftermath of the *McCollum* Case" *Journal of Public Law* 6 (Fall 1957): 455–464; Robert Birkby, "The Supreme Court and the Bible Belt: Tennessee Reaction to the *Schempp* Decision," *Midwest Journal of Political Science* 10 (August 1966): 304–315; Lawrence Baum, "Implementation of Judicial Decisions: An Organizational Analysis," *American Politics Quarterly* 4 (January, 1976): 86–114; Bradley Canon, "Organizational Contumacy in the Transmission of Judicial Policies: The *Mapp, Escobedo, Miranda*, and *Gault* Cases," *Villanova Law Review* 20 (November 1974): 50–79; Neil Romans "The State of State Supreme Courts in Judicial Policy-Making: *Escobedo, Miranda* and the Use of Judicial Impact Analysis," *Western Political Quarterly* 27 (March 1974): 38–59; and Walter Murphy, "Lower Court Checks on Supreme Court Power," *American Political Science Review* 53 (December 1959): 1017–1031.

16 Kenneth Dolbeare and Phillip Hammond, *The School Prayer Decisions: From Court Policy to Local Practice* (Chicago: University of

Chicago Press, 1971); Michael Wald, et. al., "Interrogations in New Haven: the Impact of *Miranda*," in Theodore Becker, ed., *The Impact of Supreme Court Decisions* (New York: Oxford University Press, 1969), 149–164; Frank Way, "Survey Research on Judicial Decisions," *Western Political Quarterly* 21 (June 1968): 189–205.

17 Albert Blaustein and Clarence Ferguson, Jr., *Desegregation and the Law* (New Brunswick, N.J.: Rutgers University Press, 1957); Harrell Rodgers and Charles Bullock, "School Desegregation: A Multivariate Test of the Role of Law in Effectuating Social Change," *American Politics Quarterly* 4 (April 1976): 153–175; Martin Shapiro, *The Court and Administrative Agencies* (New York: Macmillan, 1968), esp. 143–226; Bernard Taper, *Gomillion versus Lightfoot*: *Apartheid in Alabama* (New York: McGraw-Hill, 1962); Frederick Wirt, *The Politics of Southern Equality: Law and Social Change in a Mississippi County* (Chicago: Aldine, 1970).

18 Alan Hyde, "The Concept of Legitimation in the Sociology of Law," *Wisconsin Law Review* 1983 (1983): 379–426. For other statements of this problem, see David Easton, *A Systems Analysis*, 303; and John Griffiths, "Is Law Important?" *New York University Law Review* 54 (May 1979): 339–374, esp. 361–363. For a challenge to Hyde's views, see David Friedrichs, "The Concept of Legitimation and the Legal Order: A Response to Hyde's Critique," *Justice Quarterly* 3 (March 1986): 33–50.

19 Hyde, "The Concept of Legitimacy in the Sociology of Law," and Griffiths, "Is Law Important?"

20 Richard Johnson, "Compliance and Supreme Court Decision-Making." Percentages were recomputed from Table One, in which 30 of 84 respondents who disagreed with the Court's school prayer decision also acknowledged a duty to accept the decision. By contrast, 92 percent (or 39 of 43 respondents) who agreed with the school prayer decision accepted a duty of public compliance. Half (50 percent) of those who were neutral toward the decision also indicated a duty of public compliance.

In another study, about two-fifths of a group of Kentucky college students were willing to comply with a hypothetical Court decision on school busing or a restrictive curfew. However, almost one-third of respondents indicated a low level of willingness to obey the hypothetical decision. See Dean Jaros and Robert Roper, "The U.S. Supreme Court: Myth, Diffuse Support, Specific Support, and Legitimacy," *American Politics Quarterly* 8 (January 1980): 85–105. Data are recomputed from Table One.

21 The terms "legitimate" or "illegitimate" are also often used to indicate a personal opinion toward a Court decision, an opinion that a specific decision should (or should not) be complied with, or an opinion that a specific Court ruling was (or was not) properly arrived at. See Alan Hyde, "The Concept of Legitimation," 419–420.

22 These standards differ slightly from the more stringent tests for legitimation posed in Walter Murphy and Joseph Tanenhaus,

"Public Opinion and the Supreme Court," 275–294. In their well-known analysis, Murphy and Tanenhaus argue, first, that Court decisions be visible; second, that the Court be perceived in its constitutional role; and third, that the Court be viewed as operating in an impartial and competent manner.

23 As several authors have argued, public opinion among the mass public is not particularly well-integrated or constrained. For a classic statement, see Philip Converse "The Nature of Belief Systems in Mass Publics," in David Apter, ed., *Ideology and Discontent* (New York: Free Press, 1965), 206–261. For a more recent review of this literature, see Norman Nie and James Rabjohn, "Revisiting Mass Belief Systems Revisited; or, Doing Research is Like Watching a Tennis Match," *American Journal of Political Science* 23 (February 1979): 139–175. For a brief review of cognitive dissonance theory in judicial politics, see Charles Johnson and Bradley Canon, *Judicial Policies: Implementation and Impact* (Washington, D.C.: Congressional Quarterly Press, 1984), 196–197.

24 The few articles that go beyond forced-choice questions do not, however, provide much evidence for the legitimation thesis. See Dean Jaros and Robert Roper, "The U.S. Supreme Court"; Dan Thomas, "The Supreme Court and Legitimacy: Opinion and Behavioral Effects," American Political Science Association Annual Meeting (New Orleans, La., 1985); and Thomas Hensley, Joyce Baugh, and Steven Brown, "Testing Supreme Court Legitimacy Theory: The 1986 Abortion Case," paper presented at the American Political Science Association Annual Meeting (Washington, D.C., 1986).

25 George H. Gallup, ed., *The Gallup Poll — Public Opinion 1935–71*, and subsequent vol. (New York: Random House, 1972), September 10–15, 1935 and November 15–20, 1936. Throughout this chapter Gallup Polls were taken from the published series of Gallup Poll reports, and were referenced by the date of the specific poll. For a more general review of attitude change toward the Court during the 1930s, see Gregory Caldeira, "Public Opinion and the U.S. Supreme Court: FDR's Court-Packing Plan," *American Political Science Review* 81 (December 1987): 1139–1155.

26 The Gallup Poll, May 5–10, 1937; February 17–22, 1937; March 3–8, 1937; March 17–22, 1937; April 1–6, 1937; April 21–26, 1937; and May 5–10, 1937.

27 The Gallup Poll, April 15–20, 1938 and April 7–12, 1937.

28 The Gallup Poll, November, 15–20, 1936.

29 The Gallup Poll, June 14–19, 1946.

30 The Gallup Poll, June 27–July 2, 1957.

31 The Gallup Poll, July 18–23, 1963; June 22–27, 1967; June 26–July 1, 1968; May 22–27, 1969; July 6–9, 1973; then May 4–7, 1973; May 30–June 2, 1975; January 7–10, 1977; April 21–24, 1978; April 6–9, 1979; October 10–13, 1980; August 5–8, 1983; May 17–20, 1985; and July 11–14, 1986. More generally, see Seymour Martin Lipset and

William Schneider, *The Confidence Gap* (Baltimore: Johns Hopkins University Press, 1987), esp. 42–79, for confidence and approval trends.

32 National Opinion Research Center, *General Social Surveys, 1972-1986* (Chicago: University of Chicago Press, 1986), 175–182; and *General Social Surveys, 1972–1982, Cumulative Codebook* (Chicago: University of Chicago Press, 1982), 111–114. For the Supreme Court, surveys are available for 1973–1978, 1980, 1982–1984, and 1986.

33 CBS News/*New York Times* poll, "Part IV–The Supreme Court," New York, 1982, 4 pp. (xeroxed).

34 "Public Evenly Split over Supreme Court," *New York Times*, 13 July, 1986, 11.

35 Herbert Hirsch and Lewis Donohew, "A Note on Negro-White Differences on Attitudes Toward the Supreme Court," *Social Science Quarterly* 49 (December 1968): 557–562. See also Walter F. Murphy, Joseph Tanenhaus, and Daniel Kastner, *Public Evaluations of Constitutional Courts: Alternative Explanations* (Beverly Hills, Calif.: Sage, 1973). The Gallup Polls, cited in note 31, also indicated a pronounced pattern of black-white differences.

36 Roger Handberg and William Maddox, "Public Support for the Supreme Court in the 1970s," *American Politics Quarterly* 10 (July 1982): 333–346; and Lee Sigelman, "Black-White Differences in Attitudes Toward the Supreme Court: A Replication in the 1970s" *Social Science Quarterly* 60 (June 1979): 113–119.

   For over-time views of the Court's popularity, see Jack Dennis, "Mass Public Support for the U.S. Supreme Court," paper presented at the American Association for Public Opinion Research (Itasca, Ill., 1975); and Robert Lehnen, *American Institutions, Political Opinion, and Public Policy* (Hinsdale, Ill.: Dryden, 1976), 136–140.

   For an argument that the Supreme Court is not especially salient to American children, see Greg Caldeira, "Children's Images of the Supreme Court: A Preliminary Mapping," *Law & Society Review* 11 (Summer 1977): 851–871; and Jack Dennis and Carol Webster, "Children's Images of the President and of Government in 1962 and 1974," *American Politics Quarterly* 3 (October 1975): 396–398.

37 Kenneth Dolbeare and Phillip Hammond, "The Political Party Basis of Attitudes Toward the Supreme Court," *Public Opinion Quarterly* 32 (Spring 1968): 26; John Kessel, "Public Perceptions of the Supreme Court," *Midwest Journal of Political Science* 10 (May 1966): 167–191; Walter Murphy and Joseph Tanenhaus, "Public Opinion and the Supreme Court: The Goldwater Campaign," *Public Opinion Quarterly* 32 (Spring 1968): 41–44; and "Public Opinion and the Supreme Court," 293; Roger Handberg and William Maddox, "Public Support for the Supreme Court," 340–344; Walter Murphy, Joseph Tanenhaus, and Daniel Kastner, *Public Evaluations of Constitutional Courts*, 47–49; Gregory Casey, "Popular Perceptions of Supreme Court Rulings," *American Politics Quarterly* 4 (January 1976): 25–26; and Barbara Luck Graham, "Institutional Popularity

of the Supreme Court: A Reassessment," paper presented at the American Political Science Association Annual Meeting (New Orleans, La., 1985), 17.

38 Greg Caldeira, "Neither the Purse nor the Sword: Dynamics of Public Confidence in the Supreme Court," *American Political Science Review* 80 (December 1986): 1209–1226.

39 Larry C. Berkson, *The Supreme Court and Its Publics* (Lexington, Mass.: Lexington Books, 1978), 64.

40 Chester Newland, "Press Coverage of the United States Supreme Court," *Western Political Quarterly* 17 (March 1964): 15–36; David Grey, *The Supreme Court and the News Media* (Evanston, Ill.: Northwestern University Press, 1968); and Ethan Katsh, "The Supreme Court Beat: How Television Covers the U.S. Supreme Court," *Judicature* 67 (June–July 1983): 6–12.

41 Ethan Katsh, "The Supreme Court Beat".

42 Chester Newland "Press Coverage of the United States Supreme Court," 34–35; and David Grey, *The Supreme Court and The News Media*.

43 Walter Murphy and Joseph Tanenhaus, "Public Opinion and the United States Supreme Court," 276–280, 290–291; William Daniels, "The Supreme Court and Its Publics," *Albany Law Review* 37 (1973): 632–661; Roger Handberg, "Public Opinion and the United States Supreme Court, 1935–1981," *International Social Science Review* 59 (Winter 1984): 3–13; and Austin Sarat, "Studying American Legal Culture: An Assessment of Survey Evidence," *Law & Society Review* 11 (Winter 1977): 427–488. For a recent review of public opinion and the Supreme Court, see Stephen Wasby, *The Supreme Court in the Federal Judicial System* (New York: CBS College Publishing, 1984), 276–311.

44 Joseph Tanenhaus and Walter F. Murphy, "Patterns of Public Support for the Supreme Court: A Panel Study," *The Journal of Politics* 43 (February 1981): 24–39.

45 Joseph Tanenhaus and Walter F. Murphy, "Patterns of Public Support for the Supreme Court," 32.

46 John Kessel, "Public Perceptions of the Supreme Court."

47 Kenneth Dolbeare, "The Public Views of the Supreme Court," in Herbert Jacob, ed., *Law, Politics, and the Federal Courts* (Boston: Little, Brown, 1967), 194–212.

48 Gregory Casey, "Popular Perceptions of Supreme Court Rulings," recomputed from pages 8–14.

49 CBS News/*New York Times* poll, "Part IV — The Supreme Court."

50 Dean Jaros and Robert Roper, "The U.S. Supreme Court"; Larry Baas and Dan Thomas, "The Supreme Court and Policy Legitimation," *American Politics Quarterly* 12 (July 1984): 335–360; and "The Supreme Court and Legitimacy," paper presented at the American Political Science Association Annual Meeting (New Orleans, La., 1985).

51 Robert Weissberg, *Public Opinion and Popular Government* (Englewood Cliffs, N.J.: Prentice-Hall, 1976), 234–237. See also Benjamin

Page, Robert Shapiro, and Glenn Dempsey, "What Moves Public Opinion?" *American Political Science Review* 81 (March 1987): 23–44.

52 Dennis Hutchinson, "Unanimity and Desegregation: Decision-making in the Supreme Court, 1948–1958," *Georgetown Law Journal* 68 (October 1979): 1–96; and S. Sidney Ulmer, "Earl Warren and the Brown Decision," *Journal of Politics* 33 (August 1971): 692–696.

53 For an anecdotal description of unanimity within the Burger Court, see Bob Woodward and Scott Armstrong, *The Brethren: Inside the Supreme Court* (New York: Simon and Schuster, 1979), 53–56, 97–100, 295–296, and 345–347.

54 Unanimity has been less widely valued since the New Deal period. For a historical review, see Walter F. Murphy, *Elements of Judicial Strategy* (Chicago: University of Chicago Press, 1964); and David Danielski, "The Influence of the Chief Justice in the Decisional Process of the Supreme Court," in Sheldon Goldman and Austin Sarat, eds., *Readings in Judicial Process and Behavior* (San Francisco, Calif.: W. H. Freeman, 1978), 506–519. For an empirical analysis of unanimity in the modern Court, see David Rohde, *Supreme Court Decision Making* (San Francisco: W. H. Freeman and Company, 1976), 193–210. For an overview, see Stephen L. Wasby, *The Supreme Court in the Federal Judicial Process*, 2nd ed., (New York: Holt, Rinehart, and Winston, 1984), 180–188; and Loren Beth, *Politics, the Constitution, and the Supreme Court* (Evanston, Ill.: Row, Peterson & Co., 1962), 47–48. For a comparison with appellate courts, see Richard Richardson and Kenneth Vines, "Review, Dissent, and the Appellate Process," *Journal of Politics* 29 (August 1967): 597–616. For a view disputing the impact of unanimity on lower court compliance, see Charles A. Johnson, "Lower Court Reactions to Supreme Court Decisions: A Quantitative Examination," *American Journal of Political Science* 23 (November 1979): 792–804; and Bradley C. Canon, "Reactions of State Supreme Courts to a U.S. Civil Liberties Decision," *Law and Society Review* 8 (1973): 121–125. For a general review of the impact of dissents, see Steven Peterson, "Dissent in American Courts," *Journal of Politics* 43 (May 1981): 412–434, esp. 425–433.

55 Ethan Katsh, "The Supreme Court Beat."

56 Alexander Bickel, *The Least Dangerous Branch: The Supreme Court at the Bar of Politics* (New Haven, Conn.: Yale University Press, 1962), 29–31; and *The Supreme Court and the Idea of Progress* (New Haven, Conn.: Yale University Press, 1978); Carl Brent Swisher, "Dred Scott One Hundred Years After," *Journal of Politics* 19 (May 1957): 167–183, esp. 168–170, 183. See also Raoul Berger, *Government by Judiciary — The Transformation of the Fourteenth Amendment* (Cambridge, Mass.: Harvard University Press, 1977), 299. For a similar view, see Justice Felix Frankfurter's argument in *Baker v. Carr*, 369 U.S. 186 (1962), dissenting at 267: "Disregard of inherent limits in the exercise of the Court's 'judicial power'...may well impair the Court's position as the ultimate organ of 'the supreme law of the land.'"

57 C. Herman Pritchett, "The Supreme Court Today: Constitutional
    Interpretation and Judicial Self Restraint," *South Dakota Law Review*
    3 (Spring 1958): 51–79; and *The Political Offender and the Warren Court*
    (Boston: Boston University Press, 1958), 69–74; William K. Muir,
    Jr., *Law and Attitude Change* (Chicago: University of Chicago Press,
    1973); Stuart Scheingold, *The Politics of Rights: Lawyers, Public Policy,
    and Political Change* (New Haven, Conn.: Yale University Press,
    1974). See also Corwin, "The Constitution as Instrument and
    Symbol"; Arnold, *The Symbols of Government*, 197–224; and Eugene
    Rostow, "The Democratic Character of Judicial Review," *Harvard
    Law Review* 66 (1952): 208–214.

    For a comparison to Justice Frankfurter's quote in note 56, above,
    see Justice Tom Clark, writing for the majority in *Baker v. Carr*
    (1962), at 262: "National respect for the courts is more enhanced
    through the forthright enforcement of those rights (equitable
    representation) rather than by rendering them nugatory through
    the interposition of subterfuge."

    Although the Supreme Court sometimes hands down activist rul-
    ings that are, in substance, conservative, all the activist decisions
    here are liberal decisions. Hence, activist opinions are a subset of
    liberal decisions.
58 Michael Petrick, "The Supreme Court and Authority Accept-
    ance"; and Thomas Barth, "Perception and Acceptance of Su-
    preme Court Decisions."
59 Judith Blake, "The Supreme Court's Abortion Decisions and
    Public Opinion in the United States," *Population and Development
    Review* 3 (March/June 1977): 45–62.
60 For evidence that the Court's civil rights decisions are among its
    best-recognized decisions, see, for example, Joseph Tanenhaus
    and Walter F. Murphy, "Patterns of Public Support for the Su-
    preme Court," and John Kessel, "Public Perceptions of the Su-
    preme Court." For a review of polling evidence concerning
    school integration, see Robert Weissberg, *Public Opinion and Popu-
    lar Government*, 110–121. For a suggestion that Court rulings may
    have favorably affected public opinion on racial issues, see
    Robert McCloskey, *The Modern Supreme Court* (Cambridge, Mass.:
    Harvard University Press, 1972), 361–363.
61 See Joseph Tanenhaus and Walter F. Murphy, "Patterns of Public
    Support for the Supreme Court," and John Kessel, "Public Per-
    ceptions of the Supreme Court."
62 Robert Weissberg, *Public Opinion and Popular Government*, 132–136;
    and "The Death Penalty," *The Gallup Report*, January/February 1985,
    3–11.
63 Theodore Becker, ed., *The Impact of Supreme Court Decisions* (New
    York: Oxford University Press, 1969), 190–191; Thomas Barth, "Per-
    ceptions and Acceptance of Supreme Court Decisions," 315–318;
    Stephen Wasby, *The Impact of the United States Supreme Court*
    (Homewood, Ill: Dorsey 1970), 83–99; and Kathleen Kemp, Robert
    Carp, and David Brady, "The Supreme Court and Social Change:

The Case of Abortion," *Western Political Quarterly* 31 (March 1978): 19–31. For a suggestion that high levels of publicity reduce the Court's legitimacy and appeal, however, see Gregory Casey, "The Supreme Court and Myth."

64 See notes 13–17, above. For evidence of specialized communications networks, see Thomas Barth, "Perception and Acceptance of Supreme Court Decisions"; Neil Milner, *The Court and Local Law Enforcement: The Impact of* Miranda (Beverly Hills, Calif.: Sage, 1971). For evidence of word-of-mouth, see Gregory Casey, "Popular Perceptions of Supreme Court Rulings."

65 The average time lag, in months, between the Court's announced decision and the post-decision poll was 27 months, with a standard deviation of 17 months. Results of the regression model cannot be generalized beyond this time frame.

66 The (phi) correlation between the liberal decisions and the judicial activism variables was .62. In this sample of 18 cases, the judicial activist decisions are also all liberal decisions.

67 For a two-variable "social issues" model, combining the civil rights and privacy-gender variables, the R^2 was an insignificant .08 (adjusted R^2 = .03). In the "criminal issues" model, incorporating the criminal penalties and death penalty variables, the R^2 was .11 (adjusted R^2 = .01), also statistically insignificant. In the "consensus" model, representing full, written, and unanimous decisions, the R^2 was .12 (adjusted R^2 = .00), also insignificant. See Thomas R. Marshall, "The Supreme Court as an Opinion Leader," *American Politics Quarterly* 15 (January 1987): 147–168.

68 The eleven long-term poll items, the poll source, the initial and final poll dates, and percentages supporting the Court's position included: (1) Poll Taxes: Gallup 1941 — 25 percent, and 1953 —21 percent; (2) School Prayer; Survey Research Center, 1964 — 15 percent, and 1984 — 21 percent; (3) Miscegenation: NORC, 1972 — 59 percent, and 1985 — 72 percent; (4) Open Housing: NORC, 1973 — 34 percent, and 1986 — 51 percent; (5) Marijuana Usage: Gallup, 1969 — 84 percent, and 1985 — 73 percent; (6) Contraceptives: NORC, 1974 — 91 percent, and 1983 — 92 percent; (7) First Trimester Abortions: Gallup, 1974 — 47 percent, and 1986 — 45 percent; (8) Cross-district School Busing: NORC, 1974 — 76 percent, and 1986 — 68 percent; (9) Death Penalty for Murder: Gallup, 1976 — 65 percent, and 1986 — 70 percent; (10) Homosexual Relations: Gallup, 1977 — 43 percent, and 1987 — 55 percent; and (11) Homosexual School Teachers: Gallup, 1977 — 65 percent, and 1987 — 60 percent.

69 For arguments that the *Roe* and *Doe* abortion rulings led to polarization of public opinion and to the increased activism of anti-abortion groups, see Judith Blake, "The Abortion Decisions: Judicial Review and Public Opinion," Edward Manier, William Liu, and David Solomon, eds., *Abortion — New Directions for Policy Studies* (Notre Dame, Ind.: University of Notre Dame Press, 1977), 51–82; Eric Uslaner and Ronald Weber, "Public Support

for Pro-choice Abortion Policies in the Nation and the States: Changes and Stability After the *Roe* and *Doe* Decisions," in Carl Schneider and Maris Vinkvskis, eds., *The Law and Politics of Abortion* (Lexington, Mass.: Lexington Books, 1980), 206–223; and Charles Franklin and Liane Kosaki, "The Supreme Court and Public Opinion: The Abortion Issue," Midwest Political Science Association Annual Meeting (Chicago, Ill.: 1986).

70 See Edward Carmines and James Stimson, "On The Structure and Sequence of Issue Evolution," *American Political Science Review* 80 (September 1986): 901–920. Carmines and Stimson considered the case of racial desegregation, focusing on congressional and party elites as catalysts, not the Court. The model, however, might also be applied to occasional Court rulings; see also note 69, above.

71 For a discussion of other explanations for the Court's policy-making success, see Chapter Seven, at notes 4, 8, and 24–28.

CHAPTER SEVEN

Public Opinion and Supreme Court Policy Making

The Supreme Court as a Policy Maker

The Influential Court

At first view, the United States Supreme Court appears to enjoy an enviable position as a policy maker. Overriding a Supreme Court decision through a constitutional amendment requires cumbersome, time-consuming efforts, and very few attempts have ever succeeded. In recent decades many of the Court's best-known and most controversial rulings, such as the school integration, school prayer, or abortion decisions, have prevailed (at least to date), despite well-publicized, well-organized efforts to reverse them. Still other attempts to reverse specific Court rulings by limiting the Court's jurisdiction or by changing the size of the Court are occasionally attempted, but within this century these attempts have never succeeded.

The Court's nine justices themselves also appear well insulated from direct public pressure. The justices enjoy life tenure ("during good behavior"). Congress may not reduce the justices' salaries to express displeasure at specific rulings. Unlike the president, members of Congress, or most state or local judges, Supreme Court justices cannot be turned out by an irate electorate. Nor can specific Supreme Court rulings be overturned by popular vote in a referendum or an initiative.[1]

Limits on Supreme Court Policy Making

A closer examination, however, suggests that many Supreme Court rulings, in fact, do not prevail. The Court's rulings may fail in one of several ways. As the evidence below suggests, many Supreme Court decisions have not withstood the test of time.

In a few instances, rulings have been overturned by a constitutional amendment. Although amending the Constitution is, at the least, a lengthy and complex process, from six to nine amendments successfully reversed specific Court rulings.[2] In this sample of decisions, *Breedlove v. Suttles* (1937) and *Oregon v. Mitchell* (1970) were both so reversed — by the 24th and 26th Amendments, respectively.[3]

In many more instances Congress has reversed Supreme Court decisions by rewriting sections of law that the Court had struck down or interpreted to congressional displeasure. At times the Court even appears to invite such statutory reversal of its rulings by suggesting possible revisions or by signaling its willingness to follow the lead of Congress.[4] A 1946 ruling to permit portal-to-portal back pay for employees,[5] for example, was promptly overturned by the 1947 Congressional Portal-to-Portal Pay Act. Later, in the Tidelands Oil dispute, the Court's rulings in *U.S. v. California* (1947), *U.S. v. Texas* (1950), and *U.S. v. Louisiana* (1950) were all overridden by the 1953 Congressional Submerged Lands Act. Congress may also effectively restrict a Court ruling through routine legislation; the Hyde Amendment (limiting federally funded abortions for poor women) thereby limited the effect of *Roe v. Wade* (1973).

At other times the Court has itself reversed, distinguished, overruled, or otherwise abandoned its own rulings.[6] In some instances the Court has openly overruled its earlier decisions, but in other instances the Court has avoided expressly overruling a precedent. During the New Deal period, for example, the Supreme Court's 5–4 *West Coast Hotel Corp. v. Parrish* (1937) decision "distinguished" (and abandoned) its widely unpopular 1936 decision to strike down New York's minimum wage law (*Morehead v. New York ex rel. Tipaldo*).

At times it is difficult to determine precisely whether — and to what extent — Supreme Court decisions have prevailed. On several occasions state courts or lower federal courts appear to have evaded Supreme Court rulings.[7] Or, agencies and local officials might have ignored or reinterpreted the Court's apparent intent.[8] Still other rulings have been circumvented in some states, but not in others.[9]

Further, the Court often limits its own rulings or carves out exceptions without explicitly overruling a decision.[10] The 1966 *Miranda v. Arizona* ruling offers a striking example of such erosion. After widespread criticism of the *Miranda* ruling, the Court began to permit narrow, then even broader exceptions. In *Harris v. New York* (1971), a divided Court, 5–4, allowed statements made without a *Miranda* warning to impeach the credibility of a defendant who testified in his own defense. Later, the Court carved out another, apparently broader exception, 5–4 and 6–3, in *New York v. Quarles* (1984) — the "public safety" exception that allowed questioning without a *Miranda* warning in situations involving imminent public danger. The *Miranda* ruling presents one of the most borderline of instances, but even so, the Court has not yet specifically overruled the *Miranda* decision.[11]

Just as Court decisions may be overturned in a variety of ways, so, too, have rulings prevailed for widely varying lengths of time. In a few instances Court decisions are promptly overturned.[12] In the well-known Legal Tender Cases (1871), for example, a 5–4 decision overruled the 5–3 decision in *Hepburn v. Griswold* (1870), which had occurred barely a year earlier. In an even more extreme case, *Thibaut v. Car & General Insurance Corp.* (1947) was reversed upon rehearing within 42 days. By contrast, other decisions, such as *Hylton v. U.S.* (1796), *City of New York v. Miln* (1837), or *Low v. Austin* (1871), endured nearly a century before being overruled.

Albert Blaustein and Andrew Field reported that decisions overruled by the Supreme Court itself varied widely in their longevity, averaging a 24-year life span before being overruled.[13] The life span for rulings overturned through congressional action or by a constitutional amendment also varies widely. In one study, 21 Supreme Court decisions overturned by Congressional actions averaged 2.4 years prior to being overturned.[14] Overturnings through a constitutional amendment ranged from one year — for the 26th Amendment, overturning *Oregon v. Mitchell* (1970) — to 45 years — for the 19th Amendment in 1920, overturning *Minor v. Happersett* (1975).[15]

Clearly, Supreme Court decisions do not always prevail. Decisions may be overturned in several different ways, and Court rulings have prevailed for widely varying lengths of time. Yet the question remains: Why do some Supreme Court decisions prevail, but others do not?

This chapter examines the test-of-time linkage, to explain why some modern Supreme Court decisions prevail, but others are overturned. The key question here is whether Supreme Court rulings that reflect popular opinion prevail more frequently than rulings that disagree with the polls. The evidence below suggests that the Court's agreement with public opinion is significantly related to the Court's policy making success.

Explaining When Supreme Court Decisions Prevail

This chapter examines the test-of-time linkage by separating Court rulings into two groups: those rulings that have prevailed (through 1986), versus those that have not. Again, the sample of rulings matched with public opinion polls, described in Chapter Four, is analyzed. Then ten hypotheses are offered to explain why some Supreme Court rulings prevail, and others do not. Finally, the ten hypotheses are tested, first individually, then in combination.

Classifying the Rulings

Classifying a Supreme Court decision as either having prevailed or having been overturned is not always simple. Many borderline instances exist, and published lists of overturned decisions do not always agree. Here, the classification hinged upon two considerations: first, the specific poll item used; and second, subsequent Court rulings or other policy decisions. The list of overturned decisions in Table 7.1 differs slightly from several other widely cited listings.[16]

When a poll question named a specific person or policy the Court's decision was classified as having prevailed if the ruling prevailed in that specific instance.[17] For example, *A.L.A.*

Schencter Poultry Corp. v. U.S. (1935), striking down the NIRA, was classified as prevailing, since no version of the NIRA was later enacted. By contrast, *U.S. v. Butler* (1936), which struck down the Agricultural Adjustment Act, was classified as overturned because Congress soon reenacted very similar legislation, which the Court then sustained in *Mulford v. Smith* (1939).[18]

For most poll–decision matches, however, the poll item was worded more generally, and did not mention any specific person or piece of legislation. In these instances, a Court decision was classified as prevailing if the ruling's logic endured — even if the particular law under challenge was gradually changed over time, as circumstances changed. Thus, the Supreme Court's decisions upholding World War II wage-and-price controls,[19] an undistributed profits tax,[20] the death penalty for espionage,[21] or a ban on political pressure for relief recipients[22] were all classified as decisions that prevailed.

When a poll item referred to a more general issue (and not a specific person or law), then the Court ruling could be classified as having prevailed even if some exceptions or limitations to the original ruling later occurred. The key question is whether the original standards would continue to apply in most instances. Thus, *Miller v. California* (1973) was classified as prevailing, despite *Jenkins v. Georgia* (1974). *Miranda v. Arizona* (1966) was also classified as prevailing, notwithstanding several Court rulings that later limited *Miranda*.[23]

By contrast, a ruling was classified as overturned if later exceptions or new standards would apparently cause the original ruling to lose its force in most actual applications. This may occur when the Court overrules a decision, sub silentio, or when a later ruling virtually eliminates the vitality of an earlier one. Thus, *Dennis v. U.S.* (1951) was classified as overturned by *Yates v. U.S.* (1957), as was *Garner v. Los Angeles Board of Public Works* (1951) by *Keyishian v. Board of Regents* (1967).[24]

To avoid problems with the most recently decided cases, Court decisions since the 1980–1981 term were excluded from the analysis in this chapter. This reduces the number of Court decisions from 146 to 128. Of the 128 decisions examined here, 23 were classified as having been overturned (through 1986), and the remaining 105 were classified as having prevailed.[25]

171

Table 7.1
Supreme Court decisions classified as overturned

Decision	Overturning action
(1) Minimum wage for women — *Morehead, Warden, v. New York ex rel. Tipaldo* (1936)	*West Coast Hotel Co. v. Parrish* (1937)
(2) AAA of 1933 — *United States v. Butler* (1936)	*Mulford v. Smith* (1939)
(3) Federal taxation of state/local employee salaries — *Brush v. Commissioner of Internal Revenue* (1937)	*Helvering v. Gerhardt* (1938)
(4) Poll tax — *Breedlove v. Suttles* (1937)	24th Amendment (1964), and *Harper v. Virginia State Board of Elections* (1966)
(5) Tom Mooney — *Mooney v. Smith* (1938)	Subsequent pardon by California Governor (1939)
(6) Women on juries — *Glasser v. U.S.* (1942)	*Taylor v. Louisiana* (1975)
(7) Birth control for married persons — *Tileston v. Ullman* (1943)	*Griswold v. Connecticut* (1965)
(8) Closed shop (pre-Taft-Hartley) — *U.S. v. American Federation of Musicians* (1943)	Taft-Hartley Act (1947)
(9) Portal-to-portal back pay — *Anderson v. Mt. Clemens Pottery Co.* (1946)	Congressional Portal-to-Portal Pay Act (1947)
(10) Featherbedding — *U.S. v. Petrillo* (1947)	*American Newspaper Publishers Assn. v. NLRB* (1954); *NLRB v. Gamble Enterprises* (1953)
(11) Labor unions for foremen — *Packard Motor Co. v. NLRB* (1947)	Labor Management Relations Act (1947)
(12) Tidelands Oil Dispute — *U.S. v. California* (1947); *U.S. v. Louisiana* (1950); and *U.S. v. Texas* (1950)	Congressional Submerged Lands Act (1953)
(13) Anti-communist oath for labor union officials to use NLRB — *American Communications Assn, CIO v. Doud* (1950)	Landrum-Griffin Act (1959)
(14) Membership in the Communist Party — *Dennis v. U.S.* (1951)	*Yates v. U.S.* (1957)
(15) Right of Communists to hold civil service positions — *Garner v. Los Angeles Board of Public Works* (1951)	*Keyishian v. Board of Regents* (1967)

172

Table 7.1
Continued

Decision	Overturning action
(16) Right to a hearing before dismissal of a Civil Service employee accused of being a Communist — *Bailey v. Richardson* (1951)	*Service v. Dulles* (1957)
(17) Wiretapping evidence in a state court — *Schwartz v. State of Texas* (1952)	*Lee v. Florida* (1968)
(18) "All Deliberate Speed" Formula — *Brown v. Board of Education of Topeka, Kansas* (1955)	*Alexander v. Holmes County Board of Education* (1969)
(19) Right of policemen to join labor unions — *AFSCME v. City of Muskegon*, cert denied (1963)	*United Federation of Postal Workers v. Blount* (1971)
(20) Voting for 18–20-year-olds in state/local elections — *Oregon v. Mitchell* (1970)	26th Amendment (1971)
(21) Death penalty for murder — *Furman v. Georgia* (1972)	*Gregg v. Georgia* (1976)
(22) Warrants for newsroom searches — *Zurcher v. The Stanford Daily* (1978)	Privacy Protection Act (1980)
(23) Pen Register telephone taps without a court warrant — *Smith v. Maryland* (1979)	Electronic Communication Privacy Act (1986)

Note: A complete listing of all 146 cases is included in Appendix One.

Hypotheses

Ten hypotheses are tested to explain why some Supreme Court decisions prevailed but others did not. The hypotheses, described below, one-by-one, are tested individually in Table 7.2, then combined into a probit analysis later in this chapter.

The first three hypotheses represent the type of issue involved — in particular, a fundamental freedoms dispute, an economic dispute, or a crisis-times dispute.

(1) FUNDAMENTAL FREEDOMS DISPUTES

Attacks on the Court's fundamental freedoms decisions often involve highly symbolic, open attacks either on the Court's

173

jurisdiction or on the Court's best-known rulings. In turn, such attacks may mobilize and activate the Court's supporters in defense of the Court's rulings.[26] Here, fundamental freedoms decisions, coded (1), were predicted to prevail more often than the Court's remaining rulings, coded (0).

(2) ECONOMIC DECISIONS

Several accounts suggest that the Supreme Court's economic decisions are more often overturned than its noneconomic decisions.[27] Indeed, many of the best-known overturnings of Court rulings have occurred in economic disputes — from the "switch-in-time" reversals of the 1930s, to the labor decisions of the 1940s, to the prompt reversal of the 1984 *Bildisco* ruling. Economic rulings, coded (1), were predicted to prevail less often than noneconomic rulings, coded (0).

(3) CRISIS-TIMES CASES

As Chapter Four suggests, the Court is unusually majoritarian during crisis times. Whether crisis-times rulings persist as often as non-crisis decisions, however, is uncertain. Some evidence suggests that crisis-times decisions are overturned more often than other rulings, once public attention turns to other concerns.[28] Crisis-times decisions, coded (1), were predicted to prevail less often than non-crisis decisions, coded (0).

The next two predictors tap judicial activism and judicial restraint at the federal or state/local level. The fourth predictor represents instances in which the Court overturned or sharply limited a federal-level law or policy. The fifth predictor represents activist rulings in state/local-level controversies. For both predictors, activist rulings were coded (1), and judicial restraint decisions, (0).

(4) ACTIVISM IN FEDERAL-LEVEL CASES

Throughout its history, the Supreme Court has less often exercised judicial activism to overturn federal laws and policies than to overturn state or local laws and policies. Activist decisions in federal-level disputes were predicted to prevail less often than restraint decisions for two reasons. First, Congress can reverse a Court decision more easily than state legislatures or local councils can. Second, the Supreme Court itself is more deferential toward congressional efforts to overturn its rulings than toward similar state or local efforts.[29]

(5) ACTIVISM IN STATE-LEVEL CASES

The Supreme Court is less restrained toward state/local laws and policies, and the Court's activist rulings in state or local-level disputes are less easily reversed. Further, over time, the modern Supreme Court itself has abandoned many of its earlier, usually conservative pre-incorporation rulings.[30] In this study, the Supreme Court's activist decisions in state/local controversies were predicted to prevail more often than its judicial restraint decisions in cases from the state/local level.

The next two hypotheses test the Court's decision-making process — whether the decision involved a full, written opinion, and whether the decision was unanimous.

(6) TYPE OF DECISION

Most Court decisions here involved a full, written opinion (coded 1), while the remaining decisions involved a denial of certiorari, or summary affirmations or denials (coded 0). Full, written opinions, which carry more prestige and legal significance, were predicted to prevail more often.

(7) UNANIMITY

Since the 1930s the Supreme Court has produced a steadily dwindling number of unanimous decisions.[31] Unanimous decisions, however, may carry more prestige than nonunanimous rulings. Indeed, when the justices expect their decisions to be challenged, they may even seek unanimity to stave off anticipated attacks. Here, the unanimity hypothesis was examined in two versions: with a dichotomous variable (unanimous = 1, nonunanimous = 0), and alternately, with the actual number of dissenting opinion (ranging from 0 to 4 dissents). Unanimous decisions were predicted to prevail more often than nonunanimous decisons.

(8) DATE OF DECISION

Supreme Court decisions endure for widely varying lengths of time. Some are promptly overturned; others prevail for decades before being overturned. Here, the year of the ruling was coded to allow over-time patterns to be examined. To allow a minimum number of at least five years in which a decision could be overturned, only decisions from the 1980–1981 term or earlier were analyzed.[32] Earlier-decided cases (those from the 1930s or 1940s) were predicted to prevail less often (up to 1980) than later-decided cases.

(9) IDEOLOGY

Since the 1930s the Court appears to have abandoned its conservative rulings more often than its liberal rulings. This occurred, in part, when the Court retreated from its earlier, laissez-faire economic decisions and, in part, when the Court incorporated the Bill of Rights to strike down conservative state laws restricting civil liberties and civil rights — thereby also abandoning many of its pre-incorporation rulings.[33] Politically liberal rulings (coded 1) were predicted to prevail more often than conservative rulings (coded 0).

(10) PUBLIC OPINION

The final indicator represents the public opinion distribution at the time of the initial ruling. Unfortunately, in only a handful of instances were public opinion polls also available long after the ruling was announced. As a result, for most Court rulings it is impossible to examine public attitudes long after the initial poll sounding.

Public opinion at the time of the original Court ruling was coded in two forms. First, rulings were classified as majoritarian if they agreed with available polls (coded 1), classified as unclear (0) if polls were contradictory or evenly divided, and classified as countermajoritarian (-1), if the ruling disagreed with available polls. Alternately, the actual (ratio-level) poll margin was coded, ranging from a negative 74 percent to a positive 82 percent. Court rulings that were initially consistent with public opinion were predicted to prevail more often.[34]

DATA RESULTS

Table 7.2 reports the percentage of Supreme Court decisions that prevailed, both for the entire sample of 128 decisions, and for each of the ten hypotheses.[35] Overall, a large majority (82

176

Table 7.2
Percentage of Supreme Court decisions prevailing,
by hypothesis

Type of case	% Prevailed	Number of decisions
Overall results	82%	(128)
Bill of rights:		
Bill of rights cases	83%	(95)
Non-bill of rights cases	79%	(33)
Economic cases:		
Economics cases	75%	(36)
Non-economic cases	85%	(92)
Crisis times:		
Crisis-times cases	69%	(29)
Non-crisis-times cases	86% *	(99)
Federal-level judicial activism:		
Activist decisions	71%	(14)
Restraint decisions	87%	(54)
State-level judicial activism:		
Activist decisions	93%	(40)
Restraint decisions	67% **	(36)
Decision-making process:		
Full, written decisions	82%	(105)
Cert denials, others	83%	(23)
Unanimous decisions:		
Unanimous decisions	92%	(39)
Nonunanimous decisions	77% *	(74)
Ideology:		
Liberal decisions	96%	(68)
Unclear ideology	83%	(6)
Conservative decisions	65% ***	(54)
(reduced Ideology:)		
Liberal decisions	96%	(68)
Nonliberal decisions	67% ***	(60)
Agreement with public opinion:		
Majoritarian decisions	90%	(73)
"Unclear" decisions	92%	(14)
Countermajoritarian decisions	63% ***	(41)

Ratio-level Predictors	Point-biserial correlation	Pearson product -moment correlation
Number of dissenting votes:	−.24 **	−.23
Date (year) of decision:	.35 ***	.33
Initial poll margin:	.32 ***	.30

Note: For federal-level or state-level judicial activism, the percentages in Table 7.2 are based on subsamples. To compute the percentage of overturned decisions, subtract the percentage prevailed from 100%.
  * significant at .05
  ** significant at .01
*** significant at .001

percent) of the Court's decisions prevailed. Indeed, for each separate category listed in Table 7.2, a majority of the Court's rulings prevailed (through 1986).

Supreme Court decisions prevailed more often when they were unanimous, liberal, consistent with the polls, and occurred during non-crisis times. Earlier decisions (from the 1930s or 1940s) fared less well than later decisions. At the state or local level, activist rulings fared better than restraint rulings.

These results are not simply the consequence of the Court's realignment era decisions of the mid-1930s, many of which were later abandoned. Although earlier rulings were more often overturned than later rulings, the relationship between a decision's longevity and its (initial) agreement with the polls persisted, even when controlling for time. For the period 1934–1959, 82 percent of the Court's majoritarian rulings prevailed, but only 25 percent of its countermajoritarian decisions prevailed. For the period 1960–1980, 98 percent of the Court's majoritarian rulings prevailed — versus only 88 percent of its countermajoritarian rulings.

These results also hold when a fixed time period is applied. As an alternative test, each ruling (up to 1976) was examined to see if it had been overturned within a fixed, ten-year period. Of the initially consistent rulings, 94 percent prevailed after a fixed, ten-year lapse — versus only 71 percent of initially inconsistent rulings. The results, reported in Tables 7.2, 7.3, and 7.4 were little changed when a fixed, ten-year time lapse was examined.

Combining the Predictors

The ten hypotheses were also combined into a full prediction model. Because the dependent variable — whether the Court's decision prevailed or not — is dichotomous (1,0), a probit analysis was used.[36] As in Chapter Four, all ten predictors were first combined in a full, probit model.

The full-model probit results (see Table 7.3) correctly predicted 94 percent of the Court's decisions. However, the large number of predictors, the wide range of values that some predictors could take, and the relatively small number of rulings all suggested that a more parsimonious model should be constructed.[37]

Table 7.3
Full probit model explaining whether the Supreme Court
decisions were upheld or overturned

Variable	MLE	S.E.	MLE/S.E.
Bill of rights case?	–.91	.64	–1.41
Economics case?	.49	.68	.72
Crisis times case?	–1.31	.67	–1.94 *
Federal-level judicial activism?	.22	.80	.28
State/local-level judicial activism?	–.07	.80	–.09
Full, written decision?	–1.66	1.16	–1.43
Unanimous decision?	1.55	.60	2.58 **
Date of decision?	.07	.02	2.73 **
Liberal decision?	2.80	.71	3.94 ***
Consistent with public opinion?	.99	.28	3.56 **

% of cases correctly predicted = 94%
Constant = –.14
Mean of dependent variable = .82
Estimated R^2 = .39
–2LLR = (not significant at .05)
N of cases = 128
Percentage improvement over base rate = 67%
* significant at .05
** significant at .01
*** significant at .001

Several reduced models were tested. On the grounds of parsimony, clarity, and explanatory power, a four-predictor model stood out (see Table 7.4). This model considered only whether or not the decision was unanimous, liberal, handed down during crisis times, and whether it was initially consistent with public opinion. This four-variable model was statistically significant and had nearly as much explanatory power as the full, ten-predictor model.[38]

In the four-predictor model, Supreme Court decisions most often prevail when they are unanimous and liberal, when they occur during non-crisis times, and when the decision is initially consistent with public opinion. If all four conditions were met, a (hypothetical) Court decision would have virtually a 100

Table 7.4
Reduced probit model explaining whether Supreme Court
decisions were upheld or overturned

Variable	MLE	S.E.	MLE/S.E
Crisis times case?	–1.37	.46	–2.99 **
Unanimous decision?	1.05	.49	2.14 **
Liberal decision?	2.17	.53	4.10 ***
Consistent with public opinion?	.84	.23	3.63 ***

% of cases correctly predicted = 91%
Constant = .31
Mean of dependent variable = .82
Estimated R^2 = .50
–2LLR = (significant at .02)
N of cases = 128
Percent improvement over base rate = 50%
 * significant at .05
 ** significant at .01
 *** significant at .001

percent (predicted) probability of prevailing. By contrast, a (hypothetical) crisis-times, nonunanimous, conservative decision, inconsistent with public opinion would have only a 13 percent (predicted) chance of prevailing.

Conclusion

These results help to evaluate the test-of-time linkage, and to explain why some Supreme Court rulings prevail, but others are overturned. Unanimous rulings, liberal rulings, non-crisis times rulings, and rulings that reflect popular opinion prevail more frequently. Other predictors — which might seem equally likely to explain the Supreme Court's success as a policy maker — were not strongly related to whether Court decisions prevailed or were overturned.

Admittedly, these results should be interpreted cautiously. Classifying Court decisions as either prevailing or overturned is a somewhat arbitrary exercise. The sample of decisions here was relatively small; the rulings were entirely drawn from the modern period; and tracking polls were seldom available.

Even given these caveats, public opinion appears to affect the stability of Supreme Court decisions. To be sure, most Court rulings prevailed whether or not they (initially) agreed with the polls. However, popular decisions prevailed significantly more often. In fact, the Court's agreement with public opinion better explained a ruling's longevity than whether the decision was a full, written one; whether the decision involved fundamental freedoms or economic claims; or whether the ruling demonstrated judicial activism or judicial restraint.

The results support two of the three critical assumptions of the test-of-time linkage. First, as Chapter Six suggested, Supreme Court decisions do not themselves usually influence public opinion. Second, rulings that initially reflect the polls prevail more often than rulings that do not. Only the test-of-time model's third key assumption proved inaccurate, in that most (63 percent) of the Court's unpopular rulings prevailed, although they did so less often than rulings that reflected popular attitudes.

References

1 Throughout Chapter Seven the term "overturned" indicates any of the several ways in which a Supreme Court decision may fail — through a constitutional amendment; through congressional revision of a Court's statutory interpretation; through subsequent Court rulings that reverse, overrule, abandon sub silentio, or "distinguish" an earlier ruling; or, upon occasion, through the actions of administrative agencies or individual officeholders.
2 Henry Abraham, *The Judicial Process* (New York: Oxford University Press, 1980), 351–358, lists the 11th, 13th, 14th, 15th, 16th, 26th, and possibly the 17th, 19th, and 24th Amendments.
3 The 24th Amendment also overturned *Saunders v. Wilkins*, certiorari denied (1946), and *Butler v. Thompson*, affirmed per curiam (1951). See *The Library of Congress, The Constitution of the United States of America — Analysis and Interpretation* (Washington, D.C.: U.S. Government Printing Office, 1973, updated 1982).
4 Beth Henschen, "Statutory Interpretation of the Supreme Court — Congressional Response," *American Politics Quarterly* 11 (October 1983: 441–458; Samuel Krislov; *The Supreme Court in the Political Process* (New York: Macmillan, 1965), 143; S. Sidney Ulmer, "Judicial Review as a Political Check: A Temporary Check on Congress,"

Administrative Science Quarterly 4 (March 1960): 426–445; "Congressional Reversals of Supreme Court Decisions, 1945–1957," *Harvard Law Review* 71 (May 1958): 1324–1337; C. Herman Pritchett, *Congress Versus the Supreme Court* (Minneapolis: University of Minnesota Press, 1961); Walter Murphy, *Congress and the Court* (Chicago: University of Chicago Press, 1962); Harry Stumpf, "Congressional Response to Supreme Court Rulings: the Interaction of Law and Politics," *Journal of Public Law* 14 (1965): 377–395; Jack Peltason, *Federal Courts in the Political Process* (New York: Random House, 1955), 59–63; and John Schmidhauser, Larry Berg, and Albert Melone, "The Impact of Judicial Decisions: New Dimensions in Supreme Court–Congressional Relations," *Washington University Law Quarterly* (Spring 1971): 209–251.

5 *Anderson v. Mt. Clemens Pottery Co.* (1946).

6 For discussions of Supreme Court rulings that reversed or overruled previous rulings, see *Burnet v. Coronado Oil and Gas Co.* (1932), Justice Brandeis's dissent, at 405–407, note 2; William C. Douglas, "Stare Decisis," *Columbia Law Review* 49 (June 1949): 735–758; Albert Blaustein and Andrew Field, "Overruling Opinions in the Supreme Court," *Michigan Law Review* 57 (1958): 151–194; and *The Library of Congress, The Constitution of the United States*, 1973, 1789–1797; and 1983, S332–333.

7 "Note — Evasion of Supreme Court Mandates in Cases Related to State Courts since 1941," *Harvard Law Review* 67 (May 1954: 1251–1259; Walter Murphy, "Lower Court Checks Upon Supreme Court Power," *American Political Science Review* 53 (December 1959: 1017–1031; Charles Sheldon, *The American Judicial Process* (New York: Dodd, Mead & Co., 1974), 197.

8 For examples on school prayer, racial segregation, and other areas, see Stephen Wasby, Anthony d'Amato, and Rosemary Metrailer, *Desegregation from Brown to Alexander: An Exploration of Supreme Court Strategies* (Carbondale, Ill.: Southern Illinois Press, 1977); Sheldon Goldman and Thomas Jahnige, *The Federal Courts as a Political System*, 3rd ed., (New York: Harper and Row, 1985), 221–222; and Theodore Becker and Malcolm Feeley, *The Impact of Supreme Court Decisions*, 2nd ed., (New York: Oxford University Press, 1973); and notes 13–17 in Chapter Six.

9 After *Branzburg v. Hayes* (1972), for example, several states enacted "shield laws" for journalists, although other states and the U.S. Congress did not. See "Sixth Amendment Limitations on the Newsperson's Privilege: A Breach in the Shield," *Rutgers Law Journal* 13 (Winter 1982): 361–398; and Robert Sack, "Reflections on the Wrong Question: Special Constitutional Privilege for the Institutional Press," *Hofstra Law Review* 7 (1979): 628–654, esp. 653–654.

10 Blaustein and Field, "Overruling Opinions in the Supreme Court," 152–159; and Ulmer, "Judicial Review as a Political Check."

11 The Court also declined to apply *Miranda* retroactively to interrogations, trials, or retrials; see *Johnson v. New Jersey* (1966) and

Jenkins v. Delaware (1969). In *Lego v. Twomey* (1972) the Court held that evidence of a *Miranda* warning's voluntariness be by preponderance of the evidence. The *Miranda* decision represents one of the most borderline instances of an overturning, but was not counted as being overturned in Table 7.1 or elsewhere in this chapter. For a suggestion that *Miranda* may be overruled, see Goldman and Jahnige, *The Federal Courts as a Political System*, 234, n. 13. Another instance of loopholes in an earlier ruling is the *Reynolds v. Sims* (1964) reapportionment decision, here classified as prevailing despite the large (89 percent) population deviation permitted, 5–4, in *Brown v. Thompson* (1983).

12 Blaustein and Field, "Overruling Opinions in the Supreme Court," 159–161.

13 Blaustein and Field, "Overruling Opinions in the Supreme Court."

14 The average time until overturning was computed from the 21 instances of overturnings discussed in "Congressional Reversal of Supreme Court Decisions, 1945–1957."

15 For descriptions of Court rulings overturned through constitutional amendments, see *The Library of Congress, The Constitution of the United States*, 1275–1283, 1289–1566, 1571–1572, 1587–1588, 1593.

16 For other listings of Supreme Court decisions overturned, see notes 4 and 6, above.

17 If a poll question referred to a specific person or policy, a Court decision may be classified as prevailing even if the general logic of the decision was later overruled. For this reason, the decisions classified as overturned in Table 7.1 may differ from those reported in the citations in note 6, above.

18 For a discussion of the *Schencter* and *Butler* decisions, see Paul Murphy, *The Constitution in Crisis Times, 1918–1969* (New York: Harper & Row, 1972), 146–163.

19 *Yakus v. U.S.* (1944); *Bowles v. Willingham* (1944).

20 *Helvering v. Northwest Steel Rolling Mills* (1940).

21 *Rosenberg v. U.S.* (1953), and prior rulings. In this instance, the death penalty for espionage provision was retained by Congress in 1954, 1982, and (in a more limited form) in 1985. See also *U.S. v. Harper* (1984), and the subsequent Congressional revisions of 1985.

22 *U.S. v. Malphurs* (1942).

23 See note 11, above.

24 *Dennis* and *Yates* are often discussed as an instance of the Court's limiting an earlier ruling without expressly overruling it. For a view that *Dennis* was effectively overturned by *Yates*, see Jonathan Casper, *The Politics of Civil Liberties* (New York: Harper & Row, 1972), 66–67.

For a discussion of the *Garner* and *Keyishian* rulings, see *Keyishian v. Board of Regents* (1951), Justice Clark dissenting at 621–629; and Jonathan Casper, *The Politics of Civil Liberties*, 83.

25 Eighteen Court decisions after the 1980–1981 term were excluded from this analysis. Of these 18 decisions, 16 prevailed (through the

1985–86 term), and two were overturned. The two overturnings were *Motor Vehicle Manufacturing Assn. of the U.S. v. State Farm Mutual Automobile Co.* (1983), overturned by a June 11, 1984 Transportation Department ruling; and *NRLB v. Bildisco and Bildisco* (1984), overturned by bankruptcy law changes in PL 98-353 (1984). See also note 32, below.

26 David Adamany and Joel Grossman, "Support for the Supreme Court as a National Policymaker," *Law & Policy Quarterly* 5 (October 1983): 405–437. For a discussion of Court-curbing efforts, see notes 9–12, in Chapter Six.

27 "Congressional Reversal of Supreme Court Decisions, 1945–57,"; Samuel Krislov, *The Supreme Court in the Political Process*, 143, n. 7; Henry Abraham, *The Supreme Court in the Federal Judicial System*, 2nd ed., (New York: Holt, Rinehart and Winston, 1984), 245; and Paul Murphy, *The Constitution in Crisis Times*, 128–169.

28 Paul Murphy, *The Constitution in Crisis Times*; Jonathan Casper, *The Politics of Civil Liberties*.

29 Beth Henschen, "Statutory Interpretation of the Supreme Court — Congressional Response," 447–448; Stephen Wasby, *The Supreme Court in the Federal Judicial System*, 240–250; Casper, *The Politics of Civil Liberties*, 49–84; Philip Kurland, *Politics, the Constitution, and the Warren Court* (Chicago: University of Chicago Press, 1970), 201; Geoffrey Hazard, "The Supreme Court As A Legislature," *Cornell Law Review* 64 (November 1978): 13–17; and Wallace Mendelson, "Learned Hand: Patient Democrat," *Harvard Law Review* 76 (December 1962): 328–335.

30 Richard Cortner, *The Supreme Court and the Second Bill of Rights* (Madison, Wis.: University of Wisconsin Press, 1981); Paul Murphy, *The Constitution in Crisis Times*; and Jonathan Casper, *The Politics of Civil Liberties*.

31 David O'Brien, *Storm Center — The Supreme Court in American Politics* (New York: W. W. Norton, 1986), 262–275. See also notes 52–54 in Chapter Six.

32 Blaustein and Field reported that the average life span of cases overruled was 24 years, with a median figure of 17 years. This figure, however, includes Court decisions from the Supreme Court's earliest days. For decisions handed down since 1935 and subsequently overruled, the average life span was 1.4 years; see Albert Blaustein and Andrew Field, "Overruling Opinions in the Supreme Court," 161 and Appendix, recomputed. In another study, the average life span of a decision overturned by Congress during the period 1945–1957 was 2.4 years; see "Congressional Reversals of Supreme Court Decisions, 1945–1957." For the 128 cases here, the median life span for all overturned decisions was 7 years. The time variable also serves as a rough indicator of changes in the Court's personnel, over time. Robert Dahl estimated that a new justice is appointed, on the average, every two years; see "Decision-making in a Democracy: the Supreme Court as a National Policy-maker," *Journal of Public Law* 6 (Fall 1957): 285–286.

33 Cortner, *The Supreme Court and the Second Bill of Rights*. Both this hypothesis and the data results may well be time-bound, applying only to the modern Court period.

34 Jesse Choper, *Judicial Review and the National Political Process* (Chicago: University of Chicago Press, 1980), Chapter Three; and "The Supreme Court and the Political Branches: Democratic Theory and Practice," *University of Pennsylvania Law Review* 122 (April 1974): 857; Harry Wellington, "The Nature of Judicial Review," *Yale Law Journal* 91 (January 1982): 514–520; Alexander Bickel, *The Supreme Court and the Idea of Progress* (New Haven, Conn.: Yale University Press, 1978), 190–195; Robert McCloskey, *The American Supreme Court* (Chicago: University of Chicago Press, 1960), 23; and Kurland, *Politics, the Constitution, and the Warren Court*, 201.

35 If the full sample of 146 decisions had been used for Table 7.2, the results would have changed only slightly. For the full sample, 83 percent of the decisions prevailed, versus 82 percent cited in Table 7.2 for the subsample of 128 decisions. For the full sample of 146 decisions, the significant predictors (and their significance levels) would be: crisis-times decisions (.05); state-level activism (.01); consistent decisions (.001); unanimous decisions (.05); liberal decisions (.001); year of decision (.001); number of dissenting votes (.05); and initial poll margin (.001).

36 Probit analysis procedures are described in greater detail in Chapter Four.

37 The most problematic predictor in the full model was the date (year) of the Court ruling, which took on a large number of values. No improvement in either the full model or in the reduced model occurred when the ratio-level versions for unanimity or poll margin were used, rather than the collapsed (categoric) versions.

38 If additional predictors are added to the reduced model, some predictors change their sign directions or lose statistical significance, and the entire equation fails to achieve statistical significance (as measured by -2LLR).

CHAPTER EIGHT

Public Opinion
and the Supreme Court:
A Reassessment

Reconsidering the Twelve Linkages

Chapter Two described twelve linkages that might explain the relationship between mass public opinion and Supreme Court decision making. Each of the twelve linkages was then evaluated in Chapters Three through Seven. This chapter reconsiders the evidence for each of the 12 linkages, and proposes an empirically based linkage model.

The twelve linkages vary considerably. Four of the twelve linkages were tested by examining which Court rulings reflected the polls, and which did not. Five linkages were tested by examining the behavior of individual justices. Three linkages were tested by examining over-time changes in the polls or in the stability of Court decisions themselves. Each linkage generated a unique set of assumptions, which could, at least in part, be tested empirically.

For most of the twelve linkages, little or no empirical support could be found. The full linkage model proposed in Figure 8.1 includes parts of only five of the original twelve linkages.

(1) The State of Public Opinion

The state-of-public-opinion linkage won considerable empirical support. Where a clear poll margin existed, over three-fifths of Supreme Court rulings agreed with prevailing public opinion

— significantly more than a random-choice model would predict.[1] These results were not simply the result of biases in either the poll items or the Court rulings sampled.

When a federal law or policy is under challenge, the intervening federal policy process and the norm of judicial restraint have clearly mediated the relationship between mass public opinion and Supreme Court rulings. In disputes from the state or local level, however, a direct, unmediated linkage appears to exist between nationwide public opinion and Court decisions. The modern Court has also been significantly more majoritarian in crisis-times cases, when public attention is closely focused upon an issue. Figure 8.1 reflects the direct, unmediated linkage between mass attitudes and Court decision making.

(2) Political Socialization

Individually, the modern Court's 36 justices have differed considerably, both in their own socialization experience and in their tendency to reflect public opinion. Yet, perhaps surprisingly, very few background traits or career experiences helped to explain which of the justices would most often reflect the polls.

In the tests reported in Chapter Five, justices from top-ranking law schools, presidential confidants, and politically moderate justices were at least somewhat more likely to agree with public opinion. By comparison, many other background traits or career experiences — such as a justice's home region, race, religion, sex, officeholding experience, or past electoral success — could not explain a justice's tendency to reflect prevailing public opinion. Accordingly, only a few socialization experiences could be included in Figure 8.1.

(3) The Federal Policy Process

This linkage's critical assumptions were very strongly supported. Since the mid-1930s nearly three-quarters of challenged federal laws or policies have themselves reflected public opinion. Further, the modern Court has typically exercised judicial restraint toward disputed federal laws and policies — even when the federal law or policy itself did not reflect popular opinion. The available evidence suggests that the impact of mass public opinion is clearly mediated (or "filtered") by the federal policy process, which has been incorporated into Figure 8.1.

(4) The State/Local Policy Process

A very different pattern appeared in disputes from the state or local level. In this sample, only about half of the challenged state or local laws reflected nationwide public opinion. The Supreme Court also upheld only about half of the challenged state or local laws. Where state/local laws and nationwide polls differed, the Supreme Court more often preferred nationwide public opinion.

On balance, the evidence suggests that public opinion is not mediated or filtered" by the state or local policy-making process, at least during the post-New Deal Court.[2] Because state and local policies themselves have had no independent effect upon Supreme Court policy making, they have been omitted from the full linkage model in Figure 8.1

(5) The Appointment Process

No evidence suggested that Supreme Court nominees who showed a broad bipartisan appeal during their confirmation process were any more likely than their remaining brethren to reflect prevailing public opinion during their service on the Court. Justices who won an easy Senate confirmation, and "crossover" party nominees were neither more nor less majoritarian than other justices. The appointment process was therefore excluded from the full linkage model.

(6) Judicial Roles

As the tests in Chapter Five illustrated, chief justices more often reflected public opinion than did associate justices. However, highly regarded justices and "ambitious" justices reflected the polls no more frequently than did the remaining justices.

(7) Length of Tenure

No support at all appeared for the length-of-tenure model. The modern Court's 36 justices reflected public opinion as often during their later years on the Court as during their earlier years. Nor did any evidence appear that justices grow progressively more conservative over time, and thereby increasingly out of touch with American social values and attitudes.

(8) Realignment

Because scientific, nationwide polls did not exist before the mid-1930s, the realignment linkage could be tested only indirectly. Even so, after the mid-1930s those justices earlier appointed by pre-New Deal Republican presidents were no less majoritarian than justices chosen by later presidents. Nor did the justices' agreement with public opinion reflect periodic party turnovers at the White House after the 1930s.

Admittedly, the realignment linkage cannot now be fully or adequately tested. Until another realignment occurs, and further polling evidence becomes available, these conclusions must remain tentative. On balance, though, the largely negative evidence dictated that the realignment linkage be omitted from the full model.

(9) Short-term Manipulation

No evidence indicated that Supreme Court rulings typically influence mass public opinion over the short term. Where comparable pre- and post-decision poll items were available, the average poll shift was very nearly zero. Further, the polls as often shifted away from the Court's ruling as toward it. Along with the other research cited in Chapter Six, these results suggest that the modern Supreme Court has been neither sufficiently visible nor sufficiently popular to manipulate public opinion. The short-term manipulation linkage has been dropped from Figure 8.1.

(10) Long-term Manipulation

As with the short-term model, no evidence appeared to support the long-term manipulation model. To be sure, very few consistently worded poll items tapping Court rulings have been repeated over long periods of time. Even so, where polls are available, long-term public opinion shifts move away from the Court's position as often as toward them. By the available, albeit limited evidence, the Supreme Court cannot successfully manipulate public opinion over the long term. These results, along with those for the short-term manipulation model, just discussed, suggest that no "feedback" loop exists in the full linkage model.

(11) Interest Groups

Very little support appeared for the interest groups model. Few categories of interest groups agreed with the polls in markedly more than half of the cases in which they participated. Further, interest groups were typically much less successful when they disagreed with public opinion than when their positions reflected the polls. Finally, interest group positions were not significant predictors of Supreme Court decisions, either examined alone or when combined with other key variables.

These results do not deny that interest groups are critically important to the judicial process in many ways, such as in initiating, funding, and organizing litigation. Yet little evidence here suggests that interest groups have an independent influence on Supreme Court policy making. Accordingly, this linkage was discarded from the full model.

(12) The Test of Time

As Chapter Seven suggested, the Supreme Court's initially popular rulings are much more likely to endure than its unpopular rulings. True, the modern Court's success as a policy maker should not be underestimated, since most rulings persist over short to moderate periods of time, whether or not the rulings reflect public attitudes. Rulings that contradict the polls, however, are significantly more often overturned through legislative revision, through constitutional amendment, or by the Court's own backtracking on precedent. These results indicate that mass public opinion plays at least a limited, if imperfect role in curbing the Court over time, and that the test-of-time linkage should be included in the full linkage model.

Reformulating A Linkage Model

Figure 8.1 offers an empirically based linkage model of public opinion and Supreme Court policy making. Linkages that won no empirical support have been discarded and the remaining full model includes parts of only five individual linkages: the state-of-public-opinion linkage, the political socialization linkage, the federal policy process linkage, the judicial roles linkage, and the test-of-time linkage.

In Figure 8.1 the federal policy process mediates or "filters" the impact of mass public opinion in disputes from the federal level. In disputes from the state or local level or during crisis times, nationwide public opinion has a direct, unmediated impact on the Court's decision making. Chief justices, politically moderate justices, presidential confidants, and justices from top-ranked law schools are marginally more likely to reflect mass public opinion. Finally, rulings that agree with the polls better withstand the test of time than rulings that do not.

These results suggest that the linkage process between mass public opinion and Supreme Court policy making is a multifaceted one. No single theory could adequately explain the linkage process, and five different linkages were incorporated into the full linkage model in Figure 8.1.

At the same time, the full linkage model is considerably simpler than it is sometimes depicted. There was no evidence that interest group positions, state or local policies, political

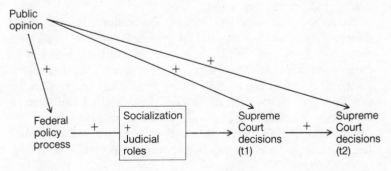

Figure 8.1 An empirically based linkage model of public opinion and the modern Supreme Court

realignments, short- and long-term feedback loops, or a justice's length of tenure affected the linkage process.

American Democracy, Public Opinion, and the Modern Supreme Court

This analysis may help to clarify the linkage process between American public opinion, on the one hand, and Supreme Court policy making, on the other. The results address two long-standing issues in democratic theory: representation and legitimation.

Overall, the evidence suggests that the modern Court has been an essentially majoritarian institution. Where clear poll margins exist, three-fifths to two-thirds of Court rulings reflect the polls. Precise comparisons with other policy makers can be offered only tentatively. However, the modern Court appears to reflect mass public opinion as often as do popularly elected officeholders. Although Alexander Hamilton may have wished the Supreme Court to be "an excellent barrier" against the "ill humors" or "dangerous innovations" of popular opinion, the modern Court has reflected mass public opinion much more frequently than it has resisted it.

The modern Court's majoritarian behavior also extends to its judicial activism. About one-half of the modern Court's activist rulings, striking down a disputed law or policy, appeared to reflect nationwide public opinion. These results challenge the commonly cited view that judicial activism is an essentially countermajoritarian practice.

To be sure, the modern Court, like other American institutions, has not represented public opinion with complete accuracy. Fully one-third of its rulings contradict the polls. In some instances — for example, the school prayer cases[3] — the Court may set out an unpopular position and persist in that position for decades. Nonetheless, these visible and extreme instances of countermajoritarian decision making should not obscure the overall pattern of the modern Court — that modern Court rulings reflect prevailing popular opinion much more often than not.

If the modern Court has been a relatively majoritarian one, the explanation has little to do with the deaths, retirements, and replacements of justices.[4] Instead, three other explanations stand out. First, the Court has been quite deferential toward federal laws and policies, which themselves typically reflect nationwide public opinion. Second, the court more closely represents public opinion during crisis times. Third, rulings that reflect the polls are more stable than rulings that do not.

The results here also address a second long-standing issue: legitimation. While Court rulings usually reflect public opinion, this is apparently not a result of the Court's own ability to "manipulate" mass public opinion. Little evidence exists to suggest that Court rulings usually greatly influence public attitudes. The Court's limited popularity and the low visibility of most of its rulings sharply limit its ability to legitimate its decisions through manipulating mass public opinion. In short, the modern Court's decisions typically represent prevailing opinion, but the Court cannot legitimate its own rulings by manipulating public opinion.

Whether these conclusions also apply to the Supreme Court before the New Deal realignment is difficult to assess. Scientific readings of mass public opinion were not available before the mid-1930s, and the early Court was much more deferential to state and local laws and policies. As a result, the linkage model outlined in Figure 8.1 cannot simply be assumed to describe accurately the first one-and-one-half centuries of Supreme Court policy making. Very little can be known of how well the Court reflected American public opinion during the 1700s, 1800s, and early 1900s.

References

1 The overall results were significantly different from a random-choice model at the .02 level.
2 Henry Abraham, *Freedom and the Court: Civil Rights and Liberties in the United States*, 4th ed., (New York: Oxford University Press, 1982); and Richard Cortner, *The Supreme Court and the Second Bill of Rights* (Madison Wisc.: University of Wisconsin Press, 1981).
3 *Engle v. Vitale* (1962); and *Abington School District v. Schempp* (1963).
4 Robert Dahl, "Decision-making in a Democracy: The Supreme Court as a National Policy-maker," *Journal of Public Law* 6 (Fall 1957): 279–295.

Appendix One

Appendix One lists the 146 matches between nationwide public opinion polls and Supreme Court rulings. The 146 matches are listed chronologically.

(1) NRA — *A.L.A. Schencter Poultry Corp. v. U.S.* (1935)
(2) Minimum Wages for Women — *Morehead, Warden, v. New York ex rel. Tipaldo* (1936)
(3) TVA — *Ashwander v. Tennessee Valley Authority* (1936)
(4) AAA of 1933 — *U.S. v. Butler* (1936)
(5) Foreign War Debts — *Cummings v. Deutsche Bank* (1937)
(6) Federal Taxation of State/local Employee Salaries — *Brush v. Commissioner of Internal Revenue* (1937)
(7) Social Security — *Helvering v. Davis* (1937)
(8) Wagner Act — *NLRB v. Jones & Laughlin Steel Corp.* (1937)
(9) Poll Tax — *Breedlove v. Suttles* (1937)
(10) Minimum Wage Legislation — *West Coast Hotel Co. v. Parrish* (1937)
(11) Tom Mooney Case — *Mooney v. Smith* (1938) and earlier decisions
(12) Federal Income Taxes on Salaries of State/local Employees — *Helvering v. Gerhardt* (1938)
(13) Sit-down Strikes — *NLRB v. Fansteel Metallurgical Corp.* (1939)
(14) Undistributed Profits Tax — *Helvering v. Northwest Steel Rolling Mills* (1940)
(15) Overtime Pay — *U.S. v. Darby Lumber Co.* (1941)
(16) Child Labor Prohibition — *U.S. v. Darby Lumber Co.* (1941)
(17) Maximum Hours Legislation — *U.S. v. Darby Lumber Co.* (1941)
(18) Influencing Votes of Relief Recipients — *U.S. v.*

194

Malphurs (1942)

(19) Women on Juries — *Glasser v. U.S.* (1942)

(20) Sterilization of Criminals — *Skinner v. Oklahoma* (1942)

(21) Closed Shop Prior to Taft–Hartley — *U.S. v. American Federation of Musicians* (1943)

(22) Birth Control for Married Persons — *Tileston v. Ullman* (1943)

(23) Death Penalty for World War II Spies — *Stephan v. U.S.*, cert denied, (1943)

(24) World War II Price Controls — *Yakus v. U.S.; Bowles v. Willingham* (1944)

(25) Federal Aid to Rental Housing — *City of Cleveland v. U.S.* (1945)

(26) Anti-monopoly Regulation of Labor Unions — *Hunt v. Crumboch* (1945); *Allen Bradley Co. v. Union* (1945)

(27) Nevada Divorces — *Williams v. North Carolina* (1945)

(28) Japanese War Criminals — *In re: Yamachita* (1946); *Homma v. Patterson* (1946)

(29) Portal-to-portal Back Pay — *Anderson v. Mt. Clemens Pottery Co.* (1946)

(30) Segregation in Interstate Commerce (Buses) — *Morgan v. Virginia* (1946)

(31) Punishment for German War Criminals — *Milch v. U.S.* (1947) and companion cases

(32) Foremen in Labor Unions — *Packard Motor Co. v. NLRB* (1947)

(33) Tidelands Oil Cases — *U.S. v. California* (1947); *U.S. v. Louisiana* (1950); *U.S. v. Texas* (1950)

(34) Coal Mine Strike — *U.S. v. John L. Lewis and United Mine Workers of America* (1947)

(35) Featherbedding — *U.S. v. Petrillo* (1947)

(36) Portal-to-portal Provisions for Back Pay — *Battaglia v. General Motors Corp.*, cert denied, (1948) and companion cases

(37) Labor Strike Cooling-off Period — *United Mine Workers v. U.S.* (1949)

(38) State Right-to-work Ban on Union or Closed Shops — *Lincoln Federal Labor Union v. Northwestern Iron & Metal Co.* (1949); *A. F. of L. v. American Sash & Door Co.* (1949)

(39) Contempt Citations for the Hollywood Ten — *Trumbo v. U.S.* and *Lawson v. U.S.*, cert denied, (1950)

(40) Anti-communist Oath for Labor Union Officials to Use NLRB — *American Communications Association, C.I.O, v. Doud* (1950)

(41) Post-Taft-Hartley Closed Shop — *National Maritime Union of America v. NLRB*, cert denied (1950)

(42) Communists to Hold Civil Service Jobs — *Garner v. Board of Public Works of Los Angeles* (1951)

(43) Right to a Hearing for a Civil Service Employee Accused of Being a Communist — *Bailey v. Richardson* (1951)

(44) Outlawing Membership in the Communist Party — *Dennis v. U.S.* (1951)

(45) Wiretapping Evidence in a Court — *Schwartz v. State of Texas* (1952)

(46) Jurisdictional Strikes — *International Longshoremen's and Warehousemen's Union v. Juneau Spruce Corp.* (1952)

(47) Anti-communist Oath Requirement for University Professors — *Wieman v. Updegraff* (1952)

(48) Featherbedding — *American Newspaper Publishers Association v. NLRB*, and *NLRB v. Gamble Enterprises* (1953)

(49) Rosenberg Treason Case — *Rosenberg v. U.S.* (1953) and prior rulings

(50) School Desegregation (First Ruling) — *Brown v. Board of Education of Topeka, Kansas* (1954), and companion cases

(51) School Desegregation (Second Ruling) — *Brown v. Board of Education of Topeka, Kansas* (1954), and companion cases

(52) Little Rock, Arkansas, School Desegregation — *Cooper v. Aaron* (1958)

(53) Segregation in Transportation Facilities — *Boynton v. Virginia* (1960)

(54) School Prayer — *Engle v. Vitale* (1962), and *Abington School District v. Schempp* (1963)

(55) Right of Government Employees (Policemen) to Join a Union — *AFSCME v. City of Muskegon*, cert denied, (1963)

(56) Combined Decision on Confessions — *Gideon v. Wainwright* (1963), *Escobedo v. Illinois* (1964), and *Miranda v. Arizona* (1966)

(57) Reapportionment of State Legislatures — *Reynolds v. Sims* (1964)

(58) Segregation in Interstate Commerce (Motels and Restaurants) — *Heart of Atlanta Motel v. U.S.*, and *Katzenbach v. McClung* (1964)

(59) Required Registration for Communist Party Members — *Albertson v. Subversive Activities Control Board* (1965)

(60) Required Blood Test for Drunk Drivers — *Schmerber v. California* (1966)

(61) Federal Voting Registrars for the South — *South Carolina v. Katzenbach* (1966)

(62) Use (Possession) of Marijuana — *Glaser v. California*, cert denied (1966), and *Aguiar v. California*, cert denied (1968)

(63) Miscegenation — *Loving v. Virginia* (1967)

(64) Federal Fund Cutoff to Segregated Schools — *Green v. New Kent Co. School Board* (1968)

(65) Racial Discrimination in Housing Sales — *Jones v. Mayer* (1968)

(66) Short Haircuts for Schoolboys — *Ferrell v. Dallas Independent School District*, cert denied (1968)

(67) Warrantless Home Searches in an Emergency — *Chimel v. California* (1969)

(68) Marijuana Sale — *Oatis v. Nelson, Warden*, cert denied (1969)

(69) Immediate School Desegregation — *Alexander v. Holmes County Board of Education* (1969)

(70) Waiting Period for Welfare — *Shapiro v. Thompson* (1969)

(71) Adam Clayton Powell's Seating in Congress — *Powell v. McCormack* (1969)

(72) State/local Voting Rights for 18-to-20-year-olds — *Oregon v. Mitchell* (1970)

(73) Federal Voting Rights for 18-to-20-year-olds — *Oregon v. Mitchell* (1970)

(74) Maximum Family Welfare Grants — *Dandridge v. Williams* (1970)

(75) Naming Father of Illegitimate Welfare Child for AFDC — *Shapiro v. Doe* (1970)

(76) Right of Government Employees to Join Labor Unions — *United Federation of Postal Workers v. Blount* (1971)

(77) Ban on Employment Discrimination by Race — *Griggs v. Duke Power Co.* (1971)

(78) Same-district School Busing for Racial Integration — *Swann v. Charlotte-Mecklenburg Board of Education* (1971)

(79) Public Employee Right-to-strike — *Rogoff v. Anderson* (1971), and *United Federation of Postal Workers v. Blount* (1971)

(80) AFDC Local Cost-of-living Adjustments — *Wyman v. Boddie* (1971)

(81) Pentagon Papers Case — *New York Times Co. v. U.S.,* and *U.S. v. Washington Post Co.* (1971)

(82) Death Penalty — *Furman v. Georgia* (1972)

(83) Warrantless Electronic Surveillance — *U.S. v. U.S. District Court* (1972)

(84) Reporters' News Source Confidentiality — *Branzburg v. Hayes* (1972)

(85) Labor Union Campaign Funds Contributed by Members — *Pipefitters Local Union, No. 562 v. U.S.* (1972)

(86) Contraceptives to Unmarried Couples — *Eisenstadt, Sheriff v. Baird* (1972)

(87) Work Rules for Welfare Recipients — *New York State Department of Social Services v. Dublino* (1973)

(88) Fiscal Disparities in Educational Spending — *San Antonio v. Rodriguez* (1973)

(89) Community Standards Test for Obscenity — *Miller v. California* (1973)

(90) First Trimester Abortions — *Roe v. Wade* (1973)

(91) Second Trimester Abortions — *Roe v. Wade* (1973)

(92) Third Trimester Abortions — *Roe v. Wade* (1973)

(93) Abortions in Clinics or Hospitals — *Doe v. Bolton* (1973)

(94) Cross-district School Busing — *Milliken v. Bradley* (1974)

(95) Federal Aid to Parochial Schools — *Wheeler v. Barrera* (1974)

(96) Voting Residence of College Students — *White v. Whatley,* cert denied (1974)

(97) Watergate Tapes — *U.S. v. Nixon* (1974)

(98) Presidential Impoundment — *Train v. City of New York* (1975)

(99) Newspaper Printing of Information Regarding Criminal Cases — *Cox Broadcasting Corp. v. Cohn* (1975), *Nebraska Press Assn. v. Stuart* (1976), and *Smith v. Daily Mail Publishing Co.* (1979)

(100) Individual Campaign Contribution Limit of $1,000 — *Buckley v. Valeo* (1976)

(101) PAC Contribution Limit of $5,000 — *Buckley v. Valeo* (1976)

(102) Public Funding for Presidential Campaigns — *Buckley v. Valeo* (1976)

(103) Limits on a Candidate's Personal Spending — *Buckley v. Valeo* (1976)

(104) Public Disclosure of Names of Campaign Donors of $100 or More — *Buckley v. Valeo* (1976)

(105) Death Penalty for First-degree Murder — *Gregg v. Georgia, Proffitt v. Florida,* and *Jurek v. Texas* (1976)

(106) Mandatory Death Penalty — *Woodson v. North Carolina* (1976)

(107) Karen Quinlan Case — *Garger v. New Jersey,* cert denied (1976)

(108) Spouse Consent Requirement for Abortion — *Planned Parenthood of Central Missouri v. Danforth* (1976)

(109) Private Homosexual Behavior — *Doe v. Commonwealth's Attorney for the City of Richmond* (1976)

(110) Pornography Distribution to Adults — *Smith v. U.S.* (1977)

(111) Concorde Landing — *Port Authority of New York and New Jersey v. British Airways Board* (1977)

(112) Corporal Punishment for Students — *Ingraham v. Wright* (1977)

(113) Mandatory Death Penalty for Killing a Policeman — *Roberts v. Louisiana* (1977)

(114) Death Penalty for Rape — *Coker v. Georgia* (1977)

(115) Contraceptives for Teenagers — *Carey v. Population Services International* (1977)

(116) Rights of Homosexual School Teachers — *Gaylord v. Tacoma School District, No. 10,* cert denied (1977)

(117) Adultery and Fornication — *Hollenbaugh v. Carnegie Free Library,* cert denied (1978)

(118) Fixed Racial Quotas in Educational Admissions — *Regents of the University of California v. Bakke* (1978)

(119) Affirmative Action without Quotas in Educational Admissions — *Regents of the University of California v. Bakke* (1978)

(120) Warrants for Newspaper Searches — *Zurcher v. The*

Stanford Daily (1978)
(121) Insanity Defense for Murder — *Moore v. Duckworth, Warden* (1979)
(122) Pen Register Telephone Taps Without a Court Warrant — *Smith v. Maryland* (1979)
(123) Random Traffic Checks by Police — *Delaware v. Prouse* (1979)
(124) Age 60 Mandatory Retirement for Diplomats — *Vance v. Bradley* (1979)
(125) Laetrile Ban for Terminally Ill Patients — *U.S. v. Rutherford* (1979)
(126) Taiwan Defense Treaty — *Goldwater v. Carter* (1979)
(127) Affirmative Action Programs in Industry — *Steelworkers v. Weber* (1979), and *Fullilove v. Klutznick* (1980)
(128) Attendance at Criminal Trials — *Richmond Newspapers, Inc., v. Virginia* (1980)
(129) Federally Funded Abortions — *Harris v. McRae* (1980)
(130) PATCO Strike — *Professional Air Traffic Controllers Organization v. U.S.*, cert denied (1981)
(131) Parent Notification of Teenage Abortions — *H.L. v. Matheson* (1981)
(132) Homosexuals in the Armed Forces — *Beller v. Lehman*, cert denied (1981)
(133) Military Registration for Men — *Rostker v. Goldberg* (1981)
(134) Military Registration for Women — *Rostker v. Goldberg* (1981)
(135) Tandem Trailers — *Kassel v. Consolidated Freightways Corp.* (1981)
(136) Censorship of School Books — *Board of Education, Island Trees Union Free School District, No. 26 v. Pico* (1982)
(137) Independent PAC Spending Limits — *Common Cause v. Schmitt*, and *Federal Election Commission v. Americans for Change* (1982)
(138) Tuition Tax Credits for Parochial Schools — *Mueller v. Allen* (1983)
(139) Tax Exemption for Segregated Schools — *Bob Jones University v. U.S.*, and *Goldsboro Christian Schools, Inc. v. U.S.* (1983)
(140) Handgun Ban — *Quilici v. Village of Morton Grove*, cert denied (1983)

(141) Airbag Requirement — *Motor Vehicle Manufacturing Assn. of the U.S. v. State Farm Mutual Automobile Co.* (1983)

(142) Bankruptcy and Labor Contracts — *NLRB v. Bildisco and Bildisco* (1984)

(143) Modifications in the Exclusionary Rule — *New York v. Quarles, Nix v. Williams,* and *U.S. v. Leon* (1984)

(144) Pornography as Sexual Violence — *American Booksellers Assn., Inc. v. Hudnut* (1986)

(145) No Pass, No Play Rules — *Stamos v. Spring Branch Independent School District* (1986)

(146) Mandatory Budget Cuts — *Bowsher v. Synar* (1986) and companion cases

Appendix Two: Table of Cases

Abington School District v. Schempp, 374 U.S. 203 (1963)
Abrams v. U.S., 250 U.S. 616 (1919)
Adamson v. California, 332 U.S. 46 (1947)
Adickes v. Kress Co., 398 U.S. 144 (1970)
Adkins v. Children's Hospital, 261 U.S. 525 (1923)
A. F. of'L. v. American Sash & Door Co., 335 U.S. 538 (1949)
A. F. of L. v. Swing, 312 U.S. 321 (1941)
AFSCME v. City of Muskegon, cert denied, 375 U.S. 833 (1963)
Aguiar v. California, cert denied, 393 U.S. 970 (1968)
A.L.A. Schencter Poultry Corp. v. U.S., 295 U.S. 495 (1935)
Albertson v. Subversive Activities Control Board, 382 U.S. 70 (1965)
Alexander v. Holmes County Board of Education, 396 U.S. 19 (1969)
Allen Bradley Co. v. Union, 325 U.S. 797 (1945)
Ambach v. Norwick, 441 U.S. 68 (1979)
American Booksellers Assn., Inc. v. Hudnut, 85-1090 (Feb. 24, 1986)
American Communications Assn, C. I. O., v. Doud, 339 U.S. 382 (1950)
American Foundries v. Tri-City Council, 257 U.S. 184 (1921)
American Newspaper Publishers Assn. v. NRLB, 345 U.S. 200 (1953)
Anderson v. Mt. Clemens Pottery Co., 328 U.S. 690 (1946)
Ashton v. Cameron Co. Water Improvement District, 298 U.S. 513
    (1936)
Ashwander v. Tennessee Valley Authority, 297 U.S. 288 (1936)
Associated Press v. U.S., 326 U.S. 1 (1945)
Bailey v. Richardson, 341 U.S. 918 (1951)
Baker v. Carr, 369 U.S. 186 (1962)
Bakery Drivers v. Wohl, 315 U.S. 769 (1942)
Bates v. Arizona State Bar, 433 U.S. 356 (1977)
Bates v. Little Rock, 361 U.S. 516 (1960)
Battaglia v. General Motors Corporation, cert denied, 335 U.S. 887
    (1948), and companion cases
Beck v. Alabama, 447 U.S. 625 (1980)
Beller v. Lehman, cert denied, 452 U.S. 905 (1981)
Berger v. New York, 388 U.S. 41 (1967)
Beuharnais v. Illinois, 343 U.S. 250 (1952)
Bigelow v. Virginia, 421 U.S. 809 (1975)
Board of Education, Island Trees Union Free School District, No. 26
    v. Pico, 457 U.S. 853 (1982)
Bob Jones University v. U.S., 461 U.S. 574 (1983)

Bowles v. Willingham, 321 U.S. 489 (1944)
Boynton v. Virginia, 364 U.S. 454 (1960)
Branzburg v. Hayes, 407 U.S. 665 (1972)
Breedlove v. Suttles, 302 U.S. 277 (1937)
Bowsher v. Synar, No. 85-1377 (July 7, 1986)
Broadrick v. Oklahoma, 413 U.S. 601 (1973)
Brotherhood of Railroad Trainmen v. Jacksonville Terminal Co., 394 U.S. 369 (1969)
Brown v. Board of Education of Topeka, Kansas, 347 U.S. 483 (1954); and 349 U.S. 294 (1955)
Brown v. Thompson, 462 U.S. 835 (1983)
Brush v. Commissioner of Internal Revenue, 300 U.S. 352 (1937)
Buckley v. Valeo, 424 U.S. 1 (1976)
Burnet v. Coronado Oil and Gas Co., 285 U.S. 393 (1932)
Bus Employees v. Wisconsin Board, 340 U.S. 383 (1951)
Butler v. Thompson, affd. per curiam, 341 U.S. 937 (1951)
Camara v. Municipal Court, 387 U.S. 523 (19667)
Cantwell v. Connecticut, 310 U.S. 296 (1940)
Carey v. Population Services International, 431 U.S. 678 (1977)
Carpenters & Joiners Union v. Ritter's Cafe, 315 U.S. 722 (1942)
Carter v. Kentucky, 450 U.S. 288 (1981)
Chambers v. Florida, 390 U.S. 227 (1940)
Chicago & Northwest Railway Co. v. United Transportation Union, 402 U.S. 570 (1971)
Chimel v. California, 395 U.S. 752 (1969)
City of Cleveland v. U.S., 323 U.S. 329 (1945)
City of New York v. Miln, 11 Pet. 102 (1837)
Cohen v. California, 403 U.S. 15 (1971)
Coker v. Georgia, 433 U.S. 584 (1977)
Colegrove v. Battin, 413 U.S. 149 (1973)
Common Cause v. Schmitt, 455 U.S. 129 (1982)
Communist Party v. Subversive Activities Control Board, 367 U.S. 1 (1961)
Cooper v. Aaron, 358 U.S. 1 (1958)
Cox Broadcasting Corp. v. Cohn, 420 U.S. 469 (1975)
Cox v. Louisiana, 379 U.S. 536 (1965)
Craig v. Harney, Sheriff, 331 U.S. 367 (1947)
Craig v. Hecht, 263 U.S. 255 (1923)
Crowley v. Christensen, 137 U.S. 86 (1890)
Curtis Publishing Co. v. Butts, 388 U.S. 130 (1964)
Dandridge v. Williams, 397 U.S. 471 (1970)
Dartmouth College Case, 4 Wheat. 518 (1819)
Davis v. Pringle, 268 U.S. 315 (1925)
DeJonge v. Oregon, 299 U.S. 353 (1937)
Delaware v. Prouse, 440 U.S. 648 (1979)
Dennis v. U.S., 341 U.S. 494 (1951)
Detroit & Toledo Shore Line Railroad Co. v. Transportation Union, 396 U.S. 142 (1969)
Deutch v. U.S., 367 U.S. 456 (1961)

Doe v. Bolton, 410 U.S. 179 (1973)
Doe v. Commonwealth's Attorney for the City of Richmond, 425 U.S. 901 (1976)
Dombrowski v. Pfister, 380 U.S. 479 (1965)
Douglas v. Kentucky, 168 U.S. 488 (1897)
Edwards v. Kearzey, 96 U.S. 595 (1877)
Edwards v. South Carolina, 372 U.S. 229 (1963)
Eisenstadt, Sheriff, v. Baird, 405 U.S. 438 (1972)
Elgin, Joliet & Eastern Railway Co. v. Burnley, 325 U.S. 711 (1945)
Engle v. Vitale, 370 U.S. 421 (1962)
Escobedo v. Illinois, 378 U.S. 478 (1964)
Estes v. Texas, 381 U.S. 532 (1965)
Ex Parte Wilson, 114 U.S. 417 (1885)
Federal Election Commission v. Americans for Change, 455 U.S. 129 (1982)
Federal Energy Regulation Commission v. Mississippi, 456 U.S. 742 (1982)
Feiner v. New York, 340 U.S. 315 (1951)
Ferrell v. Dallas Independent School District, cert denied, 393 U.S. 856 (1968)
First National Bank of Boston v. Bellotti, 435 U.S. 765 (1978)
Frank v. Magnum, 237 U.S. 309 (1915)
Frank v. Maryland, 359 U.S. 360 (1959)
Fullilove v. Klutznick, 448 U.S. 448 (1980)
Furman v. Georgia, 408 U.S. 238 (1972)
Gannett Co. v. DePasquale, 443 U.S. 368 (1979)
Garger v. New Jersey, 429 U.S. 922 (1976)
Garner v. Los Angeles Board of Public Works, 341 U.S. 716 (1951)
Gaylord v. Tacoma School District No. 10, cert denied, 434 U.S. 879 (1977)
General Committee v. Missouri-Kansas-Texas Railway Co., 320 U.S. 323 (1943)
Georgia v. Brailsford, 1 Dallas 402 (1792)
Gideon v. Wainwright, 372 U.S. 355 (1963)
Ginzburg v. U.S., 383 U.S. 463 (1966)
Gitlow v. New York, 268 U.S. 652 (1925)
Glaser v. California, cert denied, 385 U.S. 880 (1966)
Glasser v. U.S., 315 U.S. 60 (1942)
Goldwater v. Carter, 444 U.S. 996 (1979)
Gompers v. Buck Stove & Range Co., 221 U.S. 418 (1911)
Gravel v. U.S., 408 U.S. 606 (1972)
Green v. New Kent Co. School Board, 391 U.S. 430 (1968)
Greer v. Spock, 424 U.S. 828 (1976)
Gregg v. Georgia, 428 U.S. 153 (1976)
Griggs v. Duke Power Co., 401 U.S. 424 (1971)
Griswold v. Connecticut, 381 U.S. 479 (1965)
Groppi v. Wisconsin, 400 U.S. 505 (1971)
Grosjean v. American Press Company, 297 U.S. 233 (1936)
Hannegan v. Esquire, 327 U.S. 146 (1946)

Harper v. Virginia State Board of Elections, 383 U.S. 663 (1966)
Harris v. McRae, 448 U.S. 297 (1980)
Harris v. New York, 401 U.S. 222 (1971)
Hartzel v. U.S., 322 U.S. 680 (1944)
Heart of Atlanta Motel v. U.S., 379 U.S. 241 (1964)
Helvering v. Davis, 301 U.S. 619 (1937)
Helvering v. Gerhardt, 304 U.S. 405 (1938)
Helvering v. Northwest Steel Rolling Mills, 311 U.S. 46 (1940)
Hepburn v. Griswold, 8 Wall. 603 (1870)
Herbert v. Lando, 441 U.S. 153 (1979)
Hitchman Coal & Coke v. Mitchell, 245 U.S. 229 (1917)
H.L. v. Matheson, 450 U.S. 398 (1981)
Holden v. Hardy, 169 U.S. 366 (1898)
Hollenbaugh v. Carnegie Free Library, cert denied, 439 U.S. 1052 (1978)
Home Building & Loan Assn. v. Blaisdell, 290 U.S. 398 (1934)
Homma v. Patterson, 327 U.S. 759 (1946)
Houchins, Sheriff, v. KQED, 438 U.S. 1 (1978)
Hunt v. Cromboch, 325 U.S. 821 (1945)
Hurtado v. California, 110 U.S. 516 (1884)
Ingraham v. Wright, 430 U.S. 651 (1977)
In Re: Little, 404 U.S. 553 (1972)
In Re: Oliver, 333 U.S. 257 (1948)
In Re: Yamachita, 327 U.S. 1 (1946)
In the Matter of James Caplinger, 49 USLW 3863 (1981)
International Longshoremen's and Warehousemen's Union v. Juneau
    Spruce Corp., 342 U.S. 237 (1952)
Irvin v. Dowd, Warden, 366 U.S. 717 (1961)
Jacobellis v. Ohio, 378 U.S. 184 (1964)
Jenkins v. Delaware, 395 U.S. 213 (1969)
Jenkins v. Georgia, 418 U.S. 153 (1974)
Johnson v. New Jersey, 394 U.S. 719 (1966)
Joint Anti-Fascist Refugee Committee v. McGrath, 341 U.S. 123 (1951)
Jones v. Mayer, 392 U.S. 409 (1968)
Joseph Burstyn, Inc. v. Wilson, 343 U.S. 495 (1952)
Jurek v. Texas, 428 U.S. 262 (1976)
Kassel v. Consolidated Freightways Corp., 450 U.S. 662 (1981)
Katzenbach v. McClung, 379 U.S. 294 (1964)
Keegan v. U.S., 325 U.S. 478 (1945)
Keyishian v. Board of Regents, 385 U.S. 589 (1967)
Kingsley International Pictures Corp. v. Regents of the University of
    the State of New York, 360 U.S. 684 (1959)
Korematsu v. U.S., 323 U.S. 214 (1944)
Kovacs v. Cooper, 336 U.S. 77 (1949)
Kunz v. New York, 340 U.S. 290 (1951)
Lamont v. Postmaster General, 381 U.S. 301 (1965)
Landmark Communications, Inc. v. Virginia, 435 U.S. 829 (1978)
Lassiter v. Dept. of Social Services, 452 U.S. 18 (1981)
Lee v. Florida, 392 U.S. 378 (1968)
Legal Tender Cases, 12 Wall. 457 (1871)

New York State Department of Social Services v. Dublino, 413 U.S. 405 (1973)
New York v. Quarles, No. 467 U.S. 649 (1984)
New York Times Co. v. Sullivan, 376 U.S. 254 (1964)
New York Times Co. v. U.S., 403 U.S. 713 (1971)
Nix v. Williams, No. 467 U.S. 431 (1984)
Norton v. Disciplinary Committee, 399 U.S. 906 (1970)
Noto v. U.S., 367 U.S. 290 (1961)
NRLB v. Bildisco and Bildisco, 465 U.S. 513 (1984)
NRLB v. Fansteel Metallurgical Corp., 306 U.S. 240 (1939)
NRLB v. Gamble Enterprises, 345 U.S. 177 (1953)
NRLB v. Insurance Agents' International Union, 361 U.S. 477 (1960)
NRLB v. Jones & Laughlin Steel Corp., 301 U.S. 1 (1937)
O'Neil v. Vermont, 144 U.S. 323 (1892)
Oatis v. Nelson, Warden, cert denied, 393 U.S. 1108 (1969)
Oregon v. Mitchell, 400 U.S. 112 (1970)
Organization for a Better Austin v. O'Keefe, 402 U.S. 415 (1971)
Packard Motor Co. v. NRLB, 330 U.S. 485 (1947)
Palko v. Connecticut, 302 U.S. 319 (1937)
Papish v. Board of Curators of the University of Missouri, 410 U.S. 667 (1973)
Patterson v. Colorado, 205 U.S. 454 (1907)
Paul v. Davis, 424 U.S. 693 (1976)
Pell v. Procunier, Corrections Director, 417 U.S. 817 (1974)
Pennekamp v. Florida, 328 U.S. 331 (1946)
Pennsylvania v. Nelson, 350 U.S. 497 (1956)
Pennsylvania Railroad System v. Pennsylvania Railroad Company, 267 U.S. 203 (1925)
Peters v. Hobby, 349 U.S. 331 (1955)
Pinkus v. U.S., 436 U.S. 293 (1977)
Pipefitters Local Union No. 562 v. U.S., 407 U.S. 385 (1972)
Pittsburgh Press Co. v. Pittsburgh Commission on Human Relations, 413 U.S. 376 (1973)
Planned Parenthood of Central Missouri v. Danforth, 428 U.S. 52 (1976)
Poe v. Ullman, 367 U.S. 497 (1961)
Port Authority of New York and New Jersey v. British Airways Board, 434 U.S. 899 (1977)
Powell v. Alabama, 287 U.S. 45 (1932)
Powell v. McCormack, 395 U.S. 486 (1969)
Procunier v. Martinez, 416 U.S. 396 (1974)
Professional Air Traffic Controllers Organization v. U.S., cert denied, 454 U.S. 1083 (1981)
Proffitt v. Florida, 428 U.S. 242 (1976)
Public Utilities Commission v. Pollack, 34 U.S. 451 (1952)
Quilici v. Village of Morton Grove, cert denied, 464 U.S. 863 (1983)
Red Lion Broadcasting Co. v. FCC, 395 U.S. 367 (1969)
Regents of the University of California v. Bakke, 438 U.S. 265 (1978)
Reynolds v. Sims, 377 U.S. 533 (1964)
Richmond Newspapers, Inc. v. Virginia, 448 U.S. 555 (1980)

Tigner v. Texas, 310 U.S. 141 (1940)
Tileston v. Ullman, 318 U.S. 44 (1943)
Times-Mirror Co. v. Superior Court, 314 U.S. 252 (1941)
Times-Picayune Publishing Co. v. U.S., 345 U.S. 594 (1953)
Tinker v. Des Moines Independent Community School District, 393
    U.S. 503 (1969)
Toledo Newspaper Co. v. U.S., 247 U.S. 402 (1918)
Train v. City of New York, 420 U.S. 35 (1975)
Trop v. Dulles, 356 U.S. 86 (1957)
Trumbo v. U.S., cert denied, 339 U.S. 934 (1950)
Tyson and Brothers v. Banton, 273 U.S. 418 (1927)
Ullman v. U.S., 350 U.S. 422 (1956)
Union Bank v. Hyde, 19 U.S. 572 (1821)
United Federation of Postal Workers v. Blount, 404 U.S. 802 (1971)
United Mine Workers v. U.S., cert denied, 338 U.S. 871 (1949)
United Public Workers of America v. Mitchell, 330 U.S. 75 (1947)
U.S. ex rel. Toth v. Quarles, 350 U.S. 11 (1955)
U.S. v. American Federation of Musicians, 318 U.S. 741 (1943)
U.S. v. Butler, 297 U.S. 1 (1936)
U.S. v. Calandra, 414 U.S. 338 (1974)
U.S. v. California, 332 U.S. 19 (1947)
U.S. v. Carolene Products Co., 304 U.S. 144 (1938)
U.S. v. Darby Lumber Co., 312 U.S. 100 (1941)
U.S. v. Harper, 729 F. 2d. 1216 (1984)
U.S. v. Hudson and Groodwin, 7 Cranch 31 (1812)
U.S. v. Hutcheson, 312 U.S. 219 (1941)
U.S. v. Leon, 468 U.S. 897 (1984)
U.S. v. Louisiana, 339 U.S. 699 (1950)
U.S. v. Malphurs, 316 U.S. 1 (1942)
U.S. v. Nixon, 418 U.S. 683 (1974)
U.S. v. Petrillo, 332 U.S. 1 (1947)
U.S. v. Rumely, 345 U.S. 41 (1953)
U.S. v. Rutherford, 442 U.S. 544 (1979)
U.S. v. Texas, 339 U.S. 699 (1950)
U.S. v. United Mine Workers, 330 U.S. 258 (1947)
U.S. v. U.S. District Court, 407 U.S. 297 (1972)
Valentine v. Chrestensen, 316 U.S. 52 (1942)
Vance v. Bradley, 440 U.S. 93 (1979)
Virginia Railway Company v. System Federation No. 40, A. F. of L.,
    300 U.S. 515 (1937)
Virginia State Board of Pharmacy v. Virginia Citizens Consumer
    Council, 425 U.S. 748 (1976)
Walla Walla v. Walla Walla Water Co., 172 U.S. 1 (1898)
Waller v. Georgia, 467 U.S. 39 (1984)
Watkins v. U.S., 354 U.S. 178 (1957)
W.E.B. DuBois Club v. Clark, 389 U.S. 309 (1967)
Weems v. U.S., 217 U.S. 349 (1910)
Weiman v. Updegraff, 344 U.S. 183 (1952)
West Coast Hotel Corp v. Parrish, 300 U.S. 379 (1937)

Index

211

About the Author

Thomas R. Marshall is associate professor of political science at the University of Texas at Arlington. His research interests include public opinion, voting behavior, and campaigns and elections. He has also served as a polling consultant and as a statistical consultant in several lawsuits.

Dr. Marshall authored *Presidential Nominations in a Reform Age*, as well as journal articles in the *American Journal of Political Science*, *American Politics Quarterly*, *Social Science Quarterly*, *Western Political Quarterly*, and others. He holds a B.A. from Miami University, Oxford, Ohio, and a Ph.D. from the University of Minnesota.